Ezekiel

INTERPRETATION
A Bible Commentary for Teaching and Preaching

INTERPRETATION
A BIBLE COMMENTARY FOR TEACHING AND PREACHING

James Luther Mays, *Editor*
Patrick D. Miller, Jr., *Old Testament Editor*
Paul J. Achtemeier, *New Testament Editor*

JOSEPH BLENKINSOPP
Ezekiel

A Bible Commentary
for Teaching and Preaching

John Knox Press
LOUISVILLE

Library of Congress Cataloging-in-Publication Data

Blenkinsopp, Joseph, 1927–
Ezekiel / Joseph Blenkinsopp. — 1st ed.
    p.   cm. — (Interpretation, a Bible commentary for teaching and preaching)
Includes bibliographical references.
ISBN 0-8042-3118-4

1. Bible. O. T. Ezekiel—Commentaries. I. Title. II. Series.
BS1545.3.B56 1990
224'.407—dc20   89-15565
                                                            CIP

© copyright John Knox Press 1990
10 9 8 7 6 5 4 3 2 1
Printed in the United States of America
Louisville, Kentucky

SERIES PREFACE

This series of commentaries offers an interpretation of the books of the Bible. It is designed to meet the need of students, teachers, ministers, and priests for a contemporary expository commentary. These volumes will not replace the historical critical commentary or homiletical aids to preaching. The purpose of this series is rather to provide a third kind of resource, a commentary which presents the integrated result of historical and theological work with the biblical text.

An interpretation in the full sense of the term involves a text, an interpreter, and someone for whom the interpretation is made. Here, the text is what stands written in the Bible in its full identity as literature from the time of "the prophets and apostles," the literature which is read to inform, inspire, and guide the life of faith. The interpreters are scholars who seek to create an interpretation which is both faithful to the text and useful to the church. The series is written for those who teach, preach, and study the Bible in the community of faith.

The comment generally takes the form of expository essays. It is planned and written in the light of the needs and questions which arise in the use of the Bible as Holy Scripture. The insights and results of contemporary scholarly research are used for the sake of the exposition. The commentators write as exegetes and theologians. The task which they undertake is both to deal with what the texts say and to discern their meaning for faith and life. The exposition is the unified work of one interpreter.

The text on which the comment is based is the Revised Standard Version of the Bible. The general availability of this translation makes the printing of a translation unnecessary and saves the space for comment. The text is divided into sections appropriate to the particular book; comment deals with passages as a whole, rather than proceeding word by word, or verse by verse.

Writers have planned their volumes in light of the requirements set by the exposition of the book assigned to them. Biblical books differ in character, content, and arrangement. They also differ in the way they have been and are used in the liturgy, thought, and devotion of the church. The distinctiveness and use of particular books have been taken into account in decisions about the approach, emphasis, and use of space in the commentaries. The goal has been to allow writers to develop the format which provides for the best presentation of their interpretation.

The result, writers and editors hope, is a commentary which both explains and applies, an interpretation which deals with both the meaning and the significance of biblical texts. Each commentary reflects, of course, the writer's own approach and perception of the church and world. It could and should not be otherwise. Every interpretation of any kind is individual in that sense; it is one reading of the text. But all who work at the interpretation of Scripture in the church need the help and stimulation of a colleague's reading and understanding of the text. If these volumes serve and encourage interpretation in that way, their preparation and publication will realize their purpose.

The Editors

CONTENTS

INTERPRETATION

INTERPRETATION

Introduction

Reading a Prophetic Book

We speak of biblical *books,* but it would be misleading to think that the fifteen units in the Latter Prophets, ranging in length from Obadiah with 21 verses to Jeremiah with 1,364, are books in the modern sense of the word. For us a book is the product of one—less commonly, more than one—person, published on a specific date and protected by copyright from the intrusion, well-meaning or otherwise, of later hands. None of the fifteen units can be described as a book in anything like that sense. The people we call prophets were—to risk a generalization—public orators and emotional preachers rather than authors. They did not set out to write a book but to persuade by the spoken word. Sooner or later a prophet's sayings, which may have been repeated to several different audiences with appropriate modifications, were written down either by the prophet himself or, more commonly, by a disciple. Collections of such sayings would be made, arranged according to subject matter, theme, stylistic characteristics, or catchword, circulated among the prophet's adherents, and eventually incorporated into the larger prophetic collection. The titles would have been added at a very late stage, in some cases centuries after the prophet's death.

To appreciate the dynamics of this process which resulted in a prophetic book we need to bear in mind that it took place in a culture that was not dependent, as ours is, on the printed word. Memory therefore played a much greater role in the composition, rendition, and transmission of discourses, narratives, poems, and the like. Jeremiah, for example, dictated from memory sayings that he had delivered over more than two decades and was able to repeat the process, with additions, after the scroll had been destroyed (Jer. 36). This leads us to ask why prophetic sayings were written down at all. In some instances writing was an emergency measure, undertaken when the prophet had been forbidden to speak in public (e.g., Amos 7:12) or at a time of political and military crisis. Or recording a prediction may have been thought advisable in order to authenticate it upon fulfillment. With Ezekiel, the situation is rather different, since, as a priest, he belonged to a learned elite to whom writing was normal practice. As we read the Book of Ezekiel, we shall come upon many examples of his learning and literary skill.

The fact that prophecies were preserved long after the situation which they addressed had passed into history implies that they were thought to retain their validity for later generations. They were not simply scrapped and replaced by new prophecies. Some were edited and expanded to make them intelligible, serviceable, and relevant for a new generation facing a different set of circumstances. Both Amos and Hosea addressed contemporaries in the kingdom of Samaria in the decades preceding its destruction by the Assyrians, but their sayings were edited and expanded after the event to fit the quite different situation in the surviving Kingdom of Judah. This kind of updating would have been done either by the prophet himself (less commonly, herself) or, more frequently, by a disciple or other person who discovered new depths of meaning in the prophetic word for a different generation and edited or expanded the saying to bring out that meaning. So, for example, a long oracle of Isaiah directed against Moab (Isa. 15:1—16:12) is rounded off with a saying that begins, "This is the word which Yahweh spoke about Moab in the past; but now Yahweh says . . ." (Isa. 16:13–14), and a new oracle follows. Reflection on past prophecy elicits new insight into God's purposes for the present, and the new insight is embodied in a new prophetic word. In something of the same way, prophecies spoken by Ezekiel in the early phase of his career before the fall of Jerusalem have been amplified after the event to reflect the terrible experiences through which the survivors had passed. (See especially the section "A Refugee's Baggage," 12:1–16.)

Typically, then, prophetic sayings would have been orally delivered, committed to memory, and sooner or later written down either during the prophet's lifetime or after his or her death. Since the very fact of their being preserved implies their continued relevance to later ages, they would have been edited and perhaps also expanded and arranged in a meaningful pattern to bring out that relevance. The process might then be rounded off by incorporating whatever available biographical

information could contribute to understanding the message—
the confrontation between Amos and the priest of Bethel (Amos
7:10–17), for example, or the vicissitudes of Jeremiah during the
final agony of Judah (Jer. 26—29; 32; 37—44). One of several
respects in which Ezekiel diverges from this typical process is
the complete lack of biographical information. With the sole
exception of the superscription (1:2–3), the entire book is
couched in the first person. We therefore know much less about
Ezekiel than about his older contemporary Jeremiah, who was
clearly the object of considerable biographical interest.

Reading Ezekiel

It may be unnecessary to say at the outset that the important thing is to read the biblical text, that a commentary should
never become a substitute for the text itself. It may also be
suggested that the best way to begin is to read the entire book
through without interruption out loud. This will be fairly easy
with most prophetic books, and it should be possible with Ezekiel—which is no longer than a play of Shakespeare—depending on one's stamina and attention span. But even if the reading
has to be staggered, it should be done before immersing oneself
in the interpretation of the individual sections.

There is no doubt that Ezekiel is a difficult book, and not just
because of its length. The language is rich, overloaded, and
frequently hyperbolic, and the images are often strange, remote from mundane experience, and sometimes willfully repel-
lant. The vocabulary is frequently obscure and the text
imperfectly transmitted, as one may gauge by the number of
textual notes in a modern version such as the RSV. The intensity
and even ferocity of negative emotion—anger, disdain, indigna-
tion—in the first half of the book (chs. 1—24) may also be found
disturbing, though fortunately it is balanced by the prospect of
new life and hope in the second half.

On a first reading of the book, one gets an impression of
continuity, structure, and order and of its being a well thought
out whole to a much greater extent than other prophetic books.
Since the way a text is structured is an integral part of the total
meaning, it is important in the first place to understand how the
book is put together. Perhaps the most obvious structural feature is the system of dating important points in the autobiographical record. These dates are set out schematically for
convenience as follows:

3

TABLE OF DATES

1:2	June/July 593	Throne vision and call
8:1	August/Sept. 592	Vision of idolatry in the temple
20:1	July/August 591	Religious history of Israel
24:1	January 588	Beginning of the siege
26:1	January/Feb. 586	Oracle against Tyre
29:1	January 587	Oracle against Egypt
29:17	March/April 571	Conquest of Egypt predicted
30:20	March/April 587	Pharaoh's broken arm
31:1	May/June 587	Oracle against Pharaoh
32:1	Feb./March 585	Lament for Pharaoh
32:17	Feb./March 585	Pharaoh in the underworld
33:21	January 585	"The city has fallen"
40:1	March/April 573	Vision of the restored temple

Note that the month is missing in the Hebrew text of 26:1 and 32:17 and that the year 586 at 33:21 depends on a very probable emendation.

The point of departure for the dating system is the exile of King Jehoiachin in 598 B.C. (1:2), and the dates therefore (leaving aside for the moment 29:17) cover a period of twenty-five years, or half a jubilee. The vision of the restored temple is therefore the turning point, the opening up of a new future of restoration and freedom implicit in the institution of the jubilee year (see commentary on 40:1–4). Of the thirteen dates, seven are appended to oracles against foreign nations which, with one exception, are confined to the period of about twelve months following the fall of Jerusalem. The exception is the oracle occasioned by the failure of the predicted conquest of Tyre by Nebuchadnezzar, which was added at a late date—the latest in the book—to mitigate somewhat the nonfulfillment of an earlier prophecy (see commentary on 29:17–21). These oracles therefore, proclaiming judgment on foreign enemies and, by implication, salvation for Israel, function as a transitional point between the proclamation of judgment on Israel in chapters 1—24 and the prospect of a different future in chapters 34—48.

4

Since they are all concentrated at one historical moment, they also highlight the disaster of 586 B.C. as the pivotal point in the prophet's ministry. The same message is implicit in the dating of the siege of Jerusalem immediately prior to these oracles and the news of the fall of the city immediately following (24:1; 33:21); and we shall see that chapters 24 and 33 are structurally crucial in the arrangement of the material. Three of the remaining dates are appended to the visions that are at the center of the prophet's experience and message. The last date, in 20:1, introduces Ezekiel's review of Israel's history, which is of particular importance, since it explains what is happening in the present.

In all three visions Ezekiel sees the mysterious and powerful manifestation of the divine presence whose earthly location is the inner sanctuary (the "holy of holies") in the temple. We note the emphasis in the second and third of these visions that he is witnessing the same awe-inspiring and mysterious presence as in the first (10:15, 20–22; 43:3). This first vision (1:1—3:15) is the one in which he is commissioned as a prophet. The second (chs. 8—11) proclaims and explains the doom of the city and the temple, preceded by the departure of the divine effulgence by stages from the inner sanctuary to the mountain east of the city (9:3; 10:4, 18–19; 11:22–23). The narrative climax of the final vision (chs. 40—48) is the return of the divine presence to the sanctuary (43:1–5). The arrangement of the prophet's discourses in the rest of the book is consonant with this pattern of divine absence and return. The first half of the book (chs. 1—24) consists for the most part of diatribe and denunciation, designed to explain how the disaster of conquest and exile happened, while the last section (chs. 34—48) holds out the prospect of the end of exile and the return to the land, the celebration of the jubilee of freedom. Marking this transition from disaster to well-being are the pivotal chapters 24 and 33 which bracket the great turning point of the fall of Jerusalem: Chapter 24 announces the beginning of the siege and chapter 33 the news of the city's capture. Both also refer back to the prophet's call, and the loss of speech announced in 24:25–27 (cf. 3:24–27) comes to an end with the arrival of the messenger in 33:21–22. Between these two pivots the oracles against foreign nations serve both to make the transition from judgment to salvation and as a phase of dramatic stasis or rallentando as the fate of the city hangs in the balance.

5

If we accept the premise that structure is an integral part of the total meaning of a text, we must go on to ask what meaning is conferred on the prophecy as a whole by arranging the several parts in this way. The central point or fulcrum on which the prophecy turns is the fall of Jerusalem which also stands at the halfway mark between the beginning of the exile and the vision of the restored temple. It marks the death of Israel, a violent death, and the discourses, sermons, and poems of the first half explain why it came about. As we approach this central point, it is made clear that the death of Israel correlates with the absence of God. But the God of Israel is the God who can bring life out of death, the God who in ancient times created life in the dead womb of Sarah and the dead loins of Abraham. Precisely at the moment in which the news of the disaster reaches him, Ezekiel's tongue is loosened to proclaim new life and the conditions necessary for sustaining it. And since new life is made possible by the recovery of the divine presence, the resolution or denouement is reached with the return of that presence to the inner sanctuary of the temple (43:1–5).

Before we go on to read the Book of Ezekiel section by section, we should take note of other literary characteristics. The most obvious of these, already briefly noted, is that the book is basically an autobiographical narrative composed of much longer units than in most earlier prophetic collections: some in prose, others in verse. This special characteristic of the book has led several commentators to the conclusion that it originated as a written composition. While the suggestion is by no means implausible, the indications in the book of dialogue, disputation, and explanations offered to specific audiences (e.g., 24:19) suggest that the written record is based at least in part on oral communication. It is also rather gratuitous to suppose that the symbolic, mimetic acts described, however implausible some of them may seem, were pure literary creations. The exilic situation may have encouraged writing but did not exclude public speaking. Some of the longer units in Ezekiel, like those of Isaiah 40—55 and Deuteronomy from about the same time and the same situation, read like sermons intended (as sermons usually are) for oral delivery, a feature that may link up with the very probable hypothesis of an early form of synagogue service in the diaspora communities and perhaps in the homeland as well (see the targum on Ezek. 11:16).

As both prophet and priest, Ezekiel had access to a wide variety of traditional forms of speech. He makes full use of prophetic speech formulae, such as "Thus says Yahweh" and "The word of Yahweh came to me," and of such traditional genres as the judgment oracle, with its bipartite indictment-verdict form, and the vision report. His dependence on his older contemporary Jeremiah is manifest throughout and will be noted at frequent points in the commentary. He also harks back to the very early forms of ecstatic prophecy and, unlike his prophetic predecessors from Amos onward, speaks often of the spirit as the driving force of prophetic activity and the agent of human transformation. His priestly connections are equally apparent at the literary level. His use of legal formulations (e.g., 18:5–24), the case history (14:12–20), and declarative formulae of the kind found in the collections of ritual law in the Pentateuch all point in this direction. The same connection will be important for understanding the appearance and movements of the visionary throne which play such a prominent role in the book.

It remains to say a brief word about the authorial unity of the book. That we do not in every case have an exact stenographic report of a prophet's own words and that not everything in a prophetic book derives from the prophet named in the title should not perplex, much less undermine, the faith of the believer. It is difficult to see why God should not choose to communicate through many anonymous individuals—those who have annotated and expanded the prophetic sayings—rather than exclusively through the prophet whose name stands on the title page. In some instances—the last twenty-seven chapters of Isaiah, for example—the existence of later additions to the original nucleus is clear and incontrovertible. Unfortunately the situation with Ezekiel is not so clear, as a glance at any of the critical commentaries will show. The problem of the authorial unity of the Book of Ezekiel can be said to go back to Josephus, who, in the very brief mention that he makes of this prophet, reports that Ezekiel left behind two books (*Ant.* 10.79–80). We can only surmise what Josephus meant by this remark. The allusion may be to a pseudepigraphal work no longer extant or perhaps to the last section of the book, the temple vision of chapters 40—48, circulated as a separate scroll at that time. In the earlier period of critical study the structural unity of the work persuaded most scholars that, with the excep-

7

tion of minor editorial accretions, it came entirely from the prophet's own hand. Then, in the period following World War I, the perception that Ezekiel, as a poet and an ecstatic, could not have written the many prose passages in the book caused the pendulum to swing to the other extreme. The German scholar Gustav Hölscher, whose commentary appeared in 1924, carried out such drastic surgery on the book that the prophet was left with only 170 out of 1,273 verses. Writing six years later, the Harvard scholar Charles Cutler Torrey eliminated the prophet altogether by arguing that the book was a forgery perpetrated by a Jerusalem priest in the late third century B.C. Suffice it to say, nowadays these extreme positions are out of favor. Most critical scholars accept the basic authenticity of the work, while admitting significant contributions from a "school" of Ezekiel the existence of which, while not independently attested, may be deduced from the work itself. This is the view taken in the present commentary, though it is also assumed that the book may still be read as a unified and well-rounded composition independently of the question of authorial attribution.

The Prophet Himself

About Ezekiel himself we know very little and nothing apart from what we are told in the book. He was a priest or belonged to a priestly family, which amounted to the same thing, since the priesthood was hereditary. The name occurs elsewhere only in a postexilic list of priests (I Chron. 24:16), and his father's name was Buzi, which may suggest Arabian ancestry (cf. Jer. 25:23; Job 32:2, 6). If he was thirty at the time of his call (see commentary on 1:1), he would have been born about the time of King Josiah's religious reform. He was deported to Babylon after the first Babylonian conquest of Jerusalem in 598 B.C. or shortly thereafter and resided in the Jewish settlement in Tel-abib (til-abubi) on the Chebar irrigation canal near Nippur (1:1; 3:15). He was married, and his wife, the delight of his eyes, died in 588 B.C. at the beginning of the siege of Jerusalem (24:15–18). He was active over a period of more than two decades from his call in 593 to 571 B.C., the latest date in the book. About his life before and after these dates we know nothing, but it is safe to assume that his formative years were passed in the shadow of the Jerusalem temple and in the milieu of liturgy, piety, and learning of the Jerusalem priesthood.

It was inevitable that the strange and eccentric acts that he

8

is reported to have performed, the loss of speech and perhaps movement (3:25–27), the frequent experiences of bilocation, levitation, and telepathy to which he was subject, and the intemperate and sometimes uncontrolled language that he at times used should have given rise to speculation about his physical and mental condition. Explanations put forward in the modern period cover a wide range of physical and psychosomatic disorders: aphasia, catalepsy or catatonia, epilepsy, schizophrenia, to name the most common. While none of these can be categorically dismissed, especially in view of the common association between possession and sickness, and while no affliction of this kind need be incompatible with the prophetic function, they are simply too speculative to inspire confidence. If we attend to what Ezekiel says rather than to how and in what state of body and mind he says it, we will find that it is intelligible, cogent, and consonant with the sense of reality and values that we find everywhere else in the prophetic literature.

While it is possible that Ezekiel returned to Jerusalem on one or more occasions after the deportation, it is much more probable that his entire prophetic career was spent in the Babylonian diaspora. His intimate knowledge of what was happening in Judah some seven hundred miles distant does not, in any case, invalidate this conclusion. Close contacts were maintained with the homeland by exchange of correspondence (e.g., Jer. 29) and no doubt also by visits back and forth. Perhaps the only serious problem with an exclusively Babylonian location is the account of an ecstatic experience in which he was transported to the temple area and, in the course of the vision, saw the prince Pelatiah suddenly fall down dead (11:13). If we discount the possibility that this is a mere literary fiction, we would have to assume either that he was temporarily in Jerusalem or that this was a case of telepathic knowledge the accuracy of which was confirmed after the event. In any case, it does not provide adequate grounds for denying a diasporic setting for his prophetic activity.

The Historical Context of Ezekiel's Message

It is important to bear in mind that the prophet, unlike the mystic, is addressing a quite specific historical situation, generally a situation of crisis. To approach a prophetic book with the idea that it will impart "timeless truths" is to risk serious misunderstanding. The prophet's message is in time and must be

9

understood within the constraints and challenges posed by the historical situation in which it is uttered. Our task, then, is to inquire how a word spoken in that situation can apply to our quite different situation, or, to put it more theologically, what we can discern about the will and intentions of God for our situation based on an understanding of the prophet's response to that quite different set of circumstances.

During the entire lifetime of Ezekiel, Judah was a pawn in the struggle of the great powers for control of the strategic Syro-Palestinian corridor. Around the time of Ezekiel's birth Judah was still nominally an Assyrian vassal. The death of Ashurbanipal, last important king of Assyria, marked the beginning of a precipitous decline of the superpower that had terrorized the Near East for more than a century. It ended less than twenty years later with its disappearance from history, to no one's regret. (One might read the Book of Nahum for a Judean reaction to this event.) Ashurbanipal's death was also the signal for movements of national emancipation in the vassal states, including Judah. One important moment in Josiah's religious reforms, the discovery of a law book in the temple, is dated by the historian to the eighteenth year of the reign, therefore about 622 B.C., but the reform probably got under way some years earlier in connection with a bid for independence triggered by the accession of a new Assyrian king (II Chron. 34:3). After the fall of Nineveh, both Egypt and the newly founded Babylonian kingdom moved to fill the power vacuum in the Near East. Josiah seems to have decided—correctly, as it turned out—that the future lay with the Babylonians, but he lost his life attempting to oppose Egyptian passage along the coastal route (II Kings 23:29–30; II Chron. 35:20–24). His son Jehoahaz was deposed by the Egyptians after a reign of three months, after which another son, Eliakim, renamed Jehoiakim, ruled as an Egyptian puppet until the battle of Carchemish on the upper Euphrates (605 B.C.) brought the entire area under Babylonian control. The next twenty years saw Judah blundering toward total disaster as the result of weak and inefficient rule. The principal culprit was the war party at court supported by the traditionalist and nationalistic landowners ("the people of the land") who could not forget Josiah, whom they had put on the throne, and could not understand that they were now facing a completely different situation. It was their influence on Jehoiakim and Zedekiah that Jeremiah, at risk of his life, tried

10

unsuccessfully to counter. Ezekiel was deported with several thousand others shortly after the first Babylonian reduction of Jerusalem in 598 B.C. (II Kings 24:12–16). The vision of the chariot throne five years later coincided with the revolt of Zedekiah instigated by the war party and abetted by the new Egyptian ruler Psammetichus II. Its predictable outcome was the siege and destruction of Jerusalem, followed by further deportations which put an end to the nation-state and monarchy after an existence of more than four hundred years.

HISTORICAL BACKGROUND

640	Accession of Josiah
ca. 627	Death of Assyrian king Ashurbanipal
627	Call of Jeremiah (Jer. 1:2)
626	Nabopolassar, founder of Babylonian empire
ca. 623	Birth of Ezekiel
622	Religious reform in Judah (II Kings 22—23)
612	Fall of Nineveh; end of Assyrian domination
609	Death of Josiah at Megiddo (II Kings 23:29–30)
609	Jehoahaz (Shallum) deposed by Egyptians (Ezek. 19:1–4)
609	Eliakim (Jehoiakim) reigns as Egyptian puppet
605	Accession of Nebuchadnezzar; battle of Carchemish
601	Jehoiakim's rebellion against Nebuchadnezzar
598	Death of Jehoiakim; Jehoiachin exiled to Babylon
598	Mattaniah (Zedekiah) reigns as Babylonian vassal (Ezek. 12:8–13; 17:5–21; 19:11–14; 21:25–27)
ca. 595	Revolt in Babylon; Zedekiah withholds tribute
593	Psammetichus II, Egyptian Pharaoh, foments revolt
588	Jerusalem invested by Babylonians (Ezek. 24:1–2)

588	Hophra, Egyptian Pharaoh, fails to raise the siege
586	Fall of Jerusalem; second deportation
ca. 584	Assassination of Gedaliah, governor of Judah
562	Amel-marduk (Evil-merodach), king of Babylon
561	Jehoiachin set free (II Kings 25:27–30)
556	Nabonidus, last Babylonian king
ca. 548	Cyrus' conquest of Lydia; preaching of Second Isaiah
539	Fall of Babylon; beginning of Persian rule

This, then, was the situation that faced the survivors and with which Ezekiel, as one of them, was attempting to come to terms. Even those believers who have not had to live through a crisis of this kind can appreciate how it could threaten to undermine the religious assumptions on which their lives are based. Perhaps the most pressing issue for the deportees was worship. In antiquity, religion was essentially a social phenomenon dependent on communal participation in certain cultic acts. The idea of a private religion, independent of institutional allegiance and territorial location, was simply not available. With the temple destroyed, the sacrificial system brought to an end, and an entire segment of the population relocated outside the territorial jurisdiction of their God, the very possibility of worship was called into question. We may be sure that the question asked by the psalmist, how it was possible to sing hymns to Yahweh in a foreign land, arose out of a real dilemma (Ps. 137:4). The vision by the Chebar canal provided an answer in principle: Yahweh could appear and therefore be worshiped outside the land of Israel, just as, according to the Priestly author, he could appear to Moses in the land of Egypt polluted by idolatry (Exod. 6:28). It remained to work out the appropriate forms of worship in this interim period between the destruction of the old and the erection of the new temple.

The critical years leading up to and following the destruction of Jerusalem were fatal to many prophetic reputations. Optimistic prophets like Hananiah, who put their reputations on the line with short-term predictions of Babylonian defeat (Jer. 28), were obviously and quickly discredited. But even those like Jeremiah who foresaw disaster even while trying to

12

stave it off did not emerge unscathed. As we see from the rejection of Jeremiah's preaching after the event in Egypt (Jer. 44:1–19), it could be argued that they had contributed to bringing about the disaster by the very fact of predicting it or that they had advocated policies that had helped to bring it about. Conflict within prophetic circles, amply in evidence in Jeremiah and Ezekiel, and a growing public skepticism and disillusionment with respect to prophets in general, testify to the crisis that prophecy was undergoing at that time. What was worse, disillusionment with prophecy inevitably induced loss of confidence in the reality, power, and justice of the God in whose name the prophets spoke. We do not need to read between the lines to discover many indications of this theological crisis in the literature that has survived from that time. With the help of the commentary, the reader is invited to identify the points at which Ezekiel is responding to this crisis of faith and should bear in mind that this kind of situation is not confined to the sixth century B.C.

PART ONE

Ezekiel's Prophetic Call

Ezekiel 1—3

Ezekiel 1:1–3
The Title

In spite of the enormous importance of prophecy, we have very little biographical information on any of Israel's prophets, with the exception of Jeremiah, and practically none about their lives prior to their call to prophetic service. Ezekiel in particular has disappeared almost completely behind the book that bears his name. From the dates appended to various sections (see the table of dates in the Introduction), we know that he was active from 593 to 571 B.C.; that, like Jeremiah, he belonged to a family of priests; that his father's name was Buzi; and that his wife died at the beginning of the siege of Jerusalem in 588 B.C. The extraordinary symbolic acts that he was commanded to perform, some of them virtually impossible, the violence and at times crudity of the language he used, and the loss of speech with which he was afflicted (3:26; 24:27; 33:21–22) have given rise to various diagnoses of physical, psychological, or psychosomatic disorders—epilepsy, catatonia, schizophrenia—all of them speculative. The fact of the matter is that from the perspective of the biblical authors the prophet is first and foremost an instrument or agent for a particular task at a specific juncture of history. The focus, therefore, is on what he says and does rather than on matters of personal biography.

The title of this as of other prophetic books provides a minimum of chronological information. The careful reader will, however, note that we have here a combination of two different

15

introductions, one in the first person (v. 1), the other in the third person (vs. 2–3). Only the latter gives us a firm date:

> The fifth of the month: namely, in the fifth year of the exile of King Jehoiachin, the word of Yahweh did indeed come to Ezekiel, son of Buzi, the priest, in the land of the Chaldeans by the Chebar canal.

Jehoiachin was the ill-fated king of Judah who, after reigning for a mere three months, was deported by the Babylonian king Nebuchadnezzar in 598 B.C., and spent the next thirty-seven years in captivity, or at least house arrest, in Babylon (II Kings 24:8–12; 25:27–30; he is also mentioned by name in contemporary Babylonian records). The year of Ezekiel's call was therefore 593 B.C. The practice of dating from the beginning of Jehoiachin's reign is adopted throughout the Book of Ezekiel, and so this precise piece of information may have been added when the Ezekiel dossier was organized either by Ezekiel himself or by a disciple. It also serves to explain the reference to the fifth of the month in the other part of the introduction (vs. 1 + 3*b*), which, however, has "the thirtieth year." A great deal of effort has gone into the attempt to explain this "thirtieth year." The targum (Aramaic paraphrase read in synagogue worship) explained it with reference to the finding of the law book in the temple during Josiah's reign (II Kings 22)—an interesting hypothesis that is chronologically on target. Other hypotheses are listed in the commentaries (e.g., Zimmerli, *Ezekiel*, 1:113–115). The view proposed here will not end the discussion, but it is worth considering. Since it would be very confusing to date according to two quite different systems, the reference is probably to the prophet's age at the time of commissioning. Ezekiel belonged to the Zadokite priesthood, and, according to ritual law, thirty was the minimum age for assuming the office of priest (Num. 4:30). The mysterious divine effulgence (the *kabod*) which appeared to Ezekiel was also thought to appear at the climax of the ordination service (Lev. 9:6). So it is possible that Ezekiel was called to be a prophet in the same year in which he was ordained priest, perhaps during the act of worship accompanying the ordination.

16 In what follows, there is at any rate a clear connection with worship. The description of the divine throne is reminiscent of Isaiah's vision of a heavenly liturgy of which temple worship was the earthly counterpart (Isa. 6). The location is near the

Chebar canal, which, according to Babylonian sources, looped around the city of Nippur in the plains of southern Iraq. From the time of the exile it was common for diaspora communities to settle near water, since living in a land defiled by idolatry necessitated rituals of purification. It was by "the waters of Babylon" that other deportees worshiped (Ps. 137), and the practice is attested down to early Christian times (Acts 16:13).

Ezekiel is introduced as a diaspora prophet. He is among the deportees (1:1), and it is to them that his message is addressed (3:11). These communities were trying to pick up the pieces of their lives after passing through a terrible trauma. Their land had been devastated, the temple destroyed, many of their friends and relatives were dead, missing, or left behind, and they had to begin a new life from scratch. If we have not gone through something like this kind of experience, we will find it hard to imagine the impact on the tacit assumptions, religious and otherwise, that govern our lives. Survivors of the Holocaust would not have this problem. The questions are as easy to formulate as they are difficult to answer: How can one continue to believe in the reality of a God who is unable to prevent these things from happening? Or in the goodness, not to say justice, of a God who could prevent them but chose not to do so? The dilemma is stated succinctly by Archibald MacLeish in his play *J.B.,* a modern rendering of the Book of Job:

> If God is God, He is not good,
> If God is good, He is not God.

We shall encounter this problem at several points in the book and shall have occasion to note how Ezekiel's prophetic activity took up the challenge of this disorientation and loss of meaning forced on his contemporaries by the disasters through which they had passed.

Ezekiel 1:4–28
The Throne Vision

The prophet is the one who has been summoned. The summons is described as an unsolicited and unanticipated event, a personal transformation accompanied by extraordinary experiences and profoundly disturbing spiritual and psychological upheaval. It has been compared—in the shamanistic literature, for example—to the process of birth and dying. The description of Ezekiel's call begins, like that of Isaiah (Isa. 6), with a vision of God enthroned in heaven. The imagery in which the vision is described is strange, almost hallucinatory, and yet compelling. In the final summing up it is compared, in terms deliberately indirect, as "the appearance of the likeness of the effulgence of Yahweh" (v. 28). Before looking at the specific elements in the vision (living creatures, wheels, vault, etc.), we should try to determine what the term "effulgence" *(kabod)* means, especially in the context of the priestly tradition in which Ezekiel was formed.

Excursus on the Divine Effulgence

We begin with the portable shrine of the early Israelites known as the ark, later as the ark of the covenant. Like the pre-Islamic Arabic *qubba,* this object was carried into battle and used for purposes of divination. The corresponding Hebrew word *('aron)* means a chest or container. In the course of time the ark came to be thought of as containing the tablets on which the law was written, hence the title "ark of the covenant" (Deut. 10:1–5; I Kings 8:9; etc.). At an earlier stage, however, it must have served a different purpose, perhaps as a sacred relic or as a container for the oracular Urim and Thummim, a kind of sacred dice. It accompanied the Israelites on their journey through the desert and was carried into battle (Num. 10:33–36). After the settlement in the land, it served as the rallying point of the tribes in the central highlands in their life-and-death struggle with the Philistines. It was located at the tribal shrine in Shiloh (I Sam. 3:3) as the outward warranty of the presence of the invisible God, Yahweh of the hosts. After it was captured by the Philistines, the daughter-in-law of the shrine priest Eli gave birth to a son to whom she gave the name of ill omen, Ichabod. The name, which probably means "Alas, the effulgence!" is then explained: "The effulgence has gone into exile from Israel, for the ark of God is taken" (I Sam. 4:21–22). Thus the idea of the divine effulgence was associated with the ark from earliest times, an association that is richly developed in the priestly traditions with which Ezekiel was familiar. The theme of the exile of the effulgence, structurally and theologically of great importance in Ezekiel, is traceable to the same source,

18

one of many examples of Ezekiel's adaptation of traditions from the early period of Israel's history, including the early history of prophecy.

It would still be widely agreed that learned priestly circles reworked these early traditions during and after the exile in response to the needs of a new age and that the results of their labors are to be found in the first five or six books of the Hebrew Bible. According to this version, the mysterious effulgence, manifested in fire and storm cloud, appeared to Moses on Sinai (Exod. 24:15–18) and filled the mobile tent-sanctuary as the Israelites moved from one campground to the next. While its presence spelled sanctification and blessing (e.g., Exod. 29:43; Lev. 9:23), it could also be the harbinger of judgment, as in the incident of Korah's rebellion (Num. 16:19, 42) and the grumbling of the people temporarily deprived of food and water (Exod. 16:7, 10–12; Num. 20:6). It is this last aspect of priestly tradition which finds a new expression in the vision of the effulgence during which Ezekiel was commissioned to pass sentence of death on contemporary Israel.

This priestly reinterpretation of an ancient theme should be read as a theological attempt to find a way to speak about God that combines presence with transcendence. The symbolic and highly figurative language employed is not couched in our idiom, but its logic is not difficult to grasp. We might consider, for a moment, a parallel: the strange passage in which Moses asks for the assurance of seeing the divine effulgence and is permitted to glimpse not the face but the back of God (Exod. 33:18–23). The problem to be solved is, How can the transcendent God, whom to see is to die, be present to his elect and be known to be present? Different traditions in the Pentateuch express different modes of divine presence. In this instance, presence is mediated through the effulgence, the *kabod*, which is, so to speak, the recto of which the face of God is the verso. The passage therefore embodies an attempt to solve—somewhat in the manner of later midrash—a theoretical problem, that of the possibility of divine presence and the conditions under which it might be experienced. In Ezekiel, and especially in these early chapters, the answer to this question is quite literally a matter of life and death.

Prophecy and poetry have in common the extraordinary and ultimately mysterious amalgamation of traditional themes and imagery with intense personal experience, an alchemy

19

from which emerges something genuinely new which nevertheless retains its links with the past. The vision came to Ezekiel
in a state of ecstasy or trance. In an expression borrowed from
an older and more primitive type of prophecy, "the hand of
Yahweh was upon him" (cf. I Kings 18:46; II Kings 3:15). The
description of what he saw when the heavens were opened
borrows from different sources: priestly lore, ancient poetry
(e.g., Ps. 18), visions experienced by prophetic predecessors
(e.g., I Kings 22:19–22; Isa. 6:1–8). These borrowings are easily
detectable, and yet the result is quite unique and different from
anything found in the prophetic literature up to this point. It
will not be easy for the modern reader, and it probably wasn't
easy for the ancient reader either, to visualize what is being
described. There may also be a blockage for the liberal Christian who tends to undervalue the role of personal, and especially intense personal, religious experience. The logic of this
description has a dreamlike quality, and the reader's task has
not been made any easier by the frequent annotations and
expansions of those who transmitted the material. This editorial
activity, admitted by most modern commentators, marks the
beginning of the process by which this chapter was accorded a
unique position in Jewish mystical speculation. Already hinted
at by Ben Sira at the beginning of the second century B.C. (Sir.
49:8), this *merkabah* ("chariot") mysticism, as it is called, was
familiar to the Qumran sectarians and eventually was recognized as one of the two basic texts for Jewish mystical thought,
the other being the first chapter of Genesis. Originally banned
(together with ch. 16) from the synagogue lectionary as disturbing and even dangerous for the uninitiated, it was eventually
accepted as the prophetic reading, or *haftarah,* for the first day
of the Feast of Weeks.

The visual experience begins with the whirlwind, harbinger of the divine appearance, accompanied by a vast cloud
around which lightning played and, concealed by the cloud, a
brilliant source of light. Here too we see how traditional motifs
and ancient mythological themes associated with divine appearances have been fused in the moment of intense personal
experience imperfectly recollected and even less perfectly ar-
ticulated. The storm wind is the one in which Elijah was taken
up (II Kings 2:1) and in which God finally appeared to Job (Job
38:1; 40:6). It comes from the north, according to Canaanite
mythology, with which Ezekiel was familiar, the location of the

20

divine assembly (cf. Isa. 14:13). And it brought with it the storm cloud associated in Canaanite and early Israelite poetry with the appearance of the deity (e.g., Ps. 18:9–15; Hab. 3:14).

The visionary then goes on to describe the *semblance* of the four living creatures, as if to say, I will try to tell you what I saw, but it was not quite like that (vs. 5–14). From this point on, it will be helpful to bear in mind that those who have transmitted the material have filled out the description with learned elaborations of their own. So, with respect to these mysterious living creatures, bearers of the throne, we have more detailed accounts of their extremities and the direction and movement of the chariot throne. In the original version the creatures are in human form and their faces are somehow visible from all four points of the compass. In the annotated version these four facets are, respectively, human, leonine, bovine, and aquiline, thus bringing all of creation, through typical representatives, into the vision. That these representatives draw on motifs familiar in ancient Near Eastern iconography (for details, see Greenberg, *Ezekiel 1—20*, pp. 55–56) does not detract from the originality of the total image.

Only later are these living creatures identified with the cherubim (10:15, 20). According to one rabbinic tradition, God changed the ox into a cherub so as not to be reminded of the apostasy of the golden calf (tractate *Ḥagigah* 13b). Biblical cherubs have nothing to do with those naked infants with diminutive wings who fill up space in Renaissance and baroque paintings. The Hebrew *kerub* is cognate with Akkadian *karibu*, referring to one of the tutelary deities of hybrid form and massive proportions that were placed at the entrance to Mesopotamian temples. In early Israelite poetry, cherubs are associated with Yahweh, who drives his chariot across the sky (Ps. 18:10; 68:4, 17–18). More to the point, they are associated with the ark, represented as a mobile throne, bearer of "Yahweh of the hosts enthroned on the cherubim" (I Sam. 4:4). In the present context the basic idea is mobility, and it is intended to explain how Yahweh, at home in the Jerusalem temple, can now appear in the Babylonian diaspora.

A further development along the same lines follows with the description of the wheels (vs. 15–21), the most difficult and textually the most obscure part of the chapter. This entire section may well be the product of learned speculation among the prophet's disciples who were thinking in terms of surface move-

21

ment and therefore envisaged a wheeled chariot throne. The technical description of wheels inside wheels (probably to allow forward and lateral movement), hubs, rims, and bosses has its own logic which is no longer fully intelligible. The statement that the spirit of the living creatures was in the wheels (v. 21) acknowledges the need to synchronize the movements of the latter with that of the bearers of the throne through the air. The eyes, perhaps suggested by nails or ornaments with which the wheels were embossed, symbolize the all-seeing and omnipresent Enthroned One. We are here at the beginning of a process of mystical speculation which will endow the wheels with a life of their own as independent angelic beings—the *ophannim* of the mystical schools.

The seer goes on to describe the firmament which serves as a platform for the throne. It is ice-blue, lapis-blue, as in the vision granted to Moses on Sinai (Exod. 24:9–10). And then, finally, we come to the Enthroned One. Most people who were brought up in a religious environment will have asked themselves at some point, especially in childhood: "What does God look like?" "What would it be like to see God?" At this point there are no banal images. The prophet withdraws into the language of indirection and approximation. The basic image is of blinding light to which the eyes only gradually become accustomed. There is a figure the torso of which reflects the gleam of gold and silver combined. Only the upper half is at all distinct, like a figure emerging from the blinding glare of the sun, surrounded by refracted light like the rainbow after a storm. But what is, in a strange sort of way, comforting is that the profile, the outline, is like that of a human being.

At this point we might recall the creation of humanity in Gen. 1:26–27, from the same priestly tradition mentioned earlier. There humanity *('adam)* is created in the likeness *(demut)* of God. Here God appears in the likeness of humanity *(demut kemar'eh 'adam)*. Humanity is in God's image, God is in humanity's image—a mysterious connaturality, not confined to the superior faculties (as Augustine), encompassing in some mysterious way the entire person, corporeal, psychical, and spiritual. Needless to say, and sad to say, that image is not always, perhaps not often, easy to discern. It is easier to speak of it as a goal or a task rather than a present reality. Perhaps that is what Paul meant when, using the same traditional imagery, he spoke of the Christian reflecting the effulgence *(doxa)* of the Lord and being changed into his likeness from one degree to another (II Cor. 3:18).

Ezekiel 2:1—3:15
Prophetic Commissioning

Many interpreters argue that the throne vision was added as an introduction to the original commissioning only at a later editorial stage, the link being the voice the prophet hears as he lies in a trance on the ground (1:28). The point can be argued, and we shall return to it later, but for the moment we can take the narrative as it is, according to which the commission is given by the Enthroned One. In any case, visionary experiences often accompanied the call to prophesy in Israel and elsewhere in the ancient Near East. One type of prophet is regularly designated visionary (*hozeh,* e.g., Amos 7:12), several prophetic books are introduced as visions (Isaiah, Obadiah, Nahum, Habakkuk), and others are presented as the words that Amos (Micah, Habakkuk) saw in a vision. Ezekiel seems to belong to a particular type, exemplified also in the ninth-century Micaiah ben Imlah (I Kings 22:19–23) and Isaiah of Jerusalem (Isa. 6), in which the designated one is sent out from the heavenly sphere as a messenger or emissary for the performance of a particular task.

While the world, the form of society, and functions within society have changed a great deal since Ezekiel's day, the communities, Jewish and Christian, which in their very different ways claim continuity with the Israel of the Old Testament still require, by their very nature, forms of mediation and ministry that remain true to the spirit if not to the actual forms of Old Testament prophecy. In view of the endemic tendency to routinize the sense of a calling, especially in the mainline Christian churches, a reading of the present passage might lead us to ask what it would take to reproduce in our own situation something remotely comparable to the mission of an Amos, an Isaiah, or an Ezekiel.

As the next stage of the narrative opens (2:1–7), the seer is empowered to stand and receive the message by virtue of the

23

spirit which has entered into him. It has often been noted that the so-called classical prophets, from the eighth to the sixth century B.C., speak little of the activity of the spirit, perhaps in reaction to the more emotional and violent forms of ecstatic possession associated with the prophetic conventicles known in the Hebrew Bible as "the sons of the prophets." In this, as in other respects, Ezekiel draws on earlier and more "primitive" forms of prophecy illustrated, for example, in the narrative cycles about Elijah and Elisha. For Ezekiel, spirit is an energy originating in the divine sphere which manifests itself as a force that propels (1:12, 20–21), lifts up (2:2; 3:12, 14, 24), transports (8:3; 11:1, 24; 37:1), and energizes and renews both individual and community (11:19; 18:31; 36:26–27; 37:14; 39:29). The spirit works with the raw material of humanity. Here and throughout the book (ninety-three times) Ezekiel is addressed as "mortal" (literally, "son of man"), never by name. The reason may be that in his career, more than in other prophetic careers, it is the office or function rather than the person which is important. Correspondingly, the commission is not to say this or that but simply to *be a prophet*. The prospects are not alluring. There will be discomfort and danger—briers, thorns, scorpions. The prophet's public will be unresponsive, doggedly going their own way, and in so doing rounding out a history of infidelity and obtuseness which Ezekiel traces back farther than any of his prophetic colleagues (see especially ch. 20). If they will not acknowledge it at the time, they will at least be obliged to admit post factum that a prophet has been among them and that they have missed their chance. The point is that witness must be borne even if the environment is totally inhospitable, in the conviction that in some way, at some time, its value will be vindicated.

The visionary experience continues (2:8—3:3). A hand appears holding a scroll which, when unrolled, is seen to contain lamentations, woes, and dooms written on both sides—a very exceptional situation with papyrus. This the prophet is commanded to ingest. The contents of the scroll describe not what the prophet has to say but the effects of his message. They point to what is going to happen. The assumption behind the image is that these events are known to God and, so to say, written in his book, an idea reminiscent of the Tablets of Destiny of ancient Mesopotamia and hinted at elsewhere in the Hebrew Bible (Ps. 139:16; Dan. 7:10). We can trace a certain development in this kind of ritual of prophetic installation. In what is generally taken to be the call of Isaiah, one of the "fiery ones" or seraphs cauterizes his mouth with a burning coal (Isa. 6:6–7). In the commissioning of Jeremiah, Yahweh touches Jeremiah's mouth and places his words in it (Jer. 1:9). The implications of this act are explained by Jeremiah in words that bear directly on the installation of Ezekiel:

> Your words were there, and I ate them,
> Your words were to me a source of joy and happiness.
> Jeremiah 15:16

In most accounts of prophetic commissioning, especially those of Moses and Jeremiah, the designated one exhibits an initial reluctance which must be overcome by words of assurance. In the case of Ezekiel, this possibility is forestalled in the initial address to the prophet ("Be not rebellious like that rebellious house," 2:8, RSV), and he is given a direct, physical experience of the sweetness of God's word, the same kind of experience to which some of the psalms attest (e.g., Ps. 19:10; 119:103). The incident is significant in two respects. It exemplifies once again that mysterious process by which traditional materials—accounts of previous prophetic commissionings and the actual words of a prophetic predecessor (Jer. 15:16)—are appropriated and transmuted by intense personal experience. It also illustrates how, with Ezekiel, prophecy is in process of transformation into a literary activity. Julius Wellhausen, who was not fond of Ezekiel, spoke of him swallowing a book and giving it up again. The unflattering implication that Ezekiel was more of a litterateur than a prophet in the traditional sense does him much less than justice, but it at least indicates that something important was happening to prophecy and to the understanding of the prophetic office.

After this very physical symbol of the internalization of the divine word, the difficult nature of the mission is pointed out, and the prophet is equipped to perform it. This too is a regular feature of prophetic call narratives. The difficulty of communicating with people who speak a foreign language, which is a situation familiar to anyone who has traveled, is described in mythic idiom in the tower of Babel story (Gen. 11:1–9). Actually, of course, the writer is speaking symbolically of the breakdown of communication and therefore of community. At the surface level, the story reflects the multilingual population of

Babylon with its hordes of foreign workers and deportees. It was into this unfamiliar environment that the Jewish exiles addressed by Ezekiel had been thrust, and they would have been perfectly familiar with the linguistic barrier to communication. But the point being made here is that this barrier is far easier to overcome than the mental and spiritual block for which the biblical term is "hardness of heart." The prophet and his public share the same language, concepts, traditions, and history, but his words to them will be unable to surmount that barrier.

To be fair to Ezekiel's public we should have to note that prophecy was at that time as much part of the problem as it was of the solution to the problem. At the most obvious level, optimistic prophecy which apparently flourished in the Babylonian diaspora (see, e.g., Jer. 28—29) was soon to be shown up as illusory and fatally misleading. These are the prophets who proclaimed "peace, peace" when there was no peace. But even prophets of doom like Jeremiah appear to have fared little better in the popular estimation. Intercession was an essential function of prophecy, and it could be argued that their refusal or failure to intercede had left the people to their own devices or even that their predictions of doom had contributed to the situation they predicted. That this kind of prophecy was not necessarily vindicated *after fulfillment* can be seen in the failure of Jeremiah's preaching to have any effect on his audience after the fall of Jerusalem (see Jer. 44). An important corollary is that, given the nature of the prophetic claim, the collapse of confidence in prophecy at that time involved necessarily a crisis of faith in the God in whose name the prophet spoke. The implication can be seen in the statement that "the house of Israel will not listen to you; for they are not willing to listen to me" (3:7, RSV). Ezekiel himself was, as we shall see, acutely aware of the dilemma and disorientation of his contemporaries, and to meet that we shall see him coming up with original and creative, even disconcerting, forms of prophetic ministry. But at the outset the emphasis had to be on the necessity of prophetic witness even in the face of indifference and hostility. Following another Jeremian theme, he is told to make himself hard, like adamant or flint, to withstand that hostility (cf. Jer. 1:18). His determination to speak must be stronger than Israel's refusal to listen.

26

The final summons is to open his heart to communications that will be given him. At this point the order of words is interesting: "Take into your heart and with your ears hear" (3:10). It corresponds to the way in which prophetic communications were thought to be received: first, as an impulse in the heart (we would say, mind), then in a form that is intelligible and communicable in the culturally determined medium of a specific language. This at once suggests an equally specific audience for the prophet's message, namely, the Judean deportees recently settled in Babylon. Since this final charge refers to the future, encompassing messages to be received and transmitted throughout the prophet's career, these future messages are subsumed under the traditional formula of prophetic speaking, "Thus Yahweh has said." And they are to be delivered even if the public refuses to listen.

The location of Ezekiel's activity has been discussed long and inconclusively. As the text stands, the vision that is part of the commissioning took place in Babylon (1:1, 3). But some commentators suspect that the vision has been appended to a commissioning that took place in Judah before Ezekiel was deported. They point out that Ezekiel was sent *to* the deportees (3:11) and argue that the allusion to the movement of the *kabod* in 3:12*b*–13 has been spliced in, occasioning the repetition of the phrase "The Spirit lifted me up" immediately following. There are also some episodes, like the sudden death of Pelatiah in Jerusalem while a prophecy was being uttered (11:13), that are difficult to reconcile with a Babylonian location. Since the matter cannot be settled beyond reasonable doubt, perhaps all we need to say is that there are no absolutely compelling reasons to exclude a Judean location for some of the sayings in the first half of the book but that Ezekiel's ministry was essentially to the Babylonian diaspora.

The account of the commissioning ends with Ezekiel's arrival in Tel-abib, a place-name corresponding to the Akkadian *til abubi,* meaning a mound that had stood deserted (as it was thought) from the time of the great deluge. Other diaspora settlements are mentioned in Ezra (2:59; 8:17): Tel-melah, Tel-harsha, Cherub, Addan, Immer, Casiphia, all presumably in the vicinity of Nippur on the lower Euphrates. The frequency of names formed with "tel" suggests a policy of settling the deportees on previously uninhabited sites, a providential circumstance enabling them to stay together, resist assimilation, and preserve their traditional identity and way of life. It was in one of the more important of these centers that Ezekiel lived. The

27

effect of his experience is described as a state of ecstatic exalta-
tion ("in bitterness in the heat of my spirit" of RSV is misleading), a state that was succeeded, as is psychologically plausible,
by a period of a week during which he remained among his
fellow deportees in a catatonic state.

Ezekiel 3:16–21
The Prophet as Sentry

Ezekiel's appointment as sentry or lookout for the house of
Israel is repeated, with some variations, in 33:1–9, thus rounding out the prophet's career prior to the fall of Jerusalem. It
therefore serves as an inclusion, a frequent stylistic device in
ancient compositions (e.g., the epic of Gilgamesh), at the same
time providing an important clue toward understanding the
prophetic role of Ezekiel during this period. The sentry's role
was obviously a vital one at a time of crisis or war. Stationed on
a battlement or tower of the city wall (see, e.g., I Sam. 14:16 and
II Sam. 13:34), he was to warn the inhabitants of the enemy's
approach by a blast on the trumpet (cf. 33:2–6), a sound that
inspired fear (Amos 3:6) but at least allowed time either to take
up arms or to seek safety in flight. The metaphor can function
for the prophet because of the latter's ability to see farther, to
act as a sort of antenna, radar, or early warning system for the
community to which he belongs. As far as we know, Hosea was
the first to use the metaphor, about a century and a half before
Ezekiel (Hos. 9:8). As so often in the book, however, a connection can be made with Ezekiel's older contemporary Jeremiah:

> I set watchmen over you, saying,
> "Give heed to the sound of the trumpet!"
> But they said, "We will not give heed."
> Jeremiah 6:17, RSV

Later still, it was taken up by an anonymous seer who dismissed
his contemporary prophetic colleagues as blind watchmen, an
oxymoron if ever there was one (Isa. 56:10). The same metaphor
underlies the summons addressed to this same seer at a later
point:

28

Cry aloud, spare not,
　lift up your voice like a trumpet;
declare to my people their transgression,
　to the house of Jacob their sins.
　　　　　　　　　Isaiah 58:1, RSV

The sentry's task is also related to the intense concentration required of the seer preparing to receive a communication from "the other world." During the last decades of the monarchy, the prophet Habakkuk speaks of keeping vigil on his watchtower (Hab. 2:1), and an anonymous seer active toward the end of the exilic period listens intently at his station until he hears the word that Babylon has fallen (Isa. 21:6–10). This kind of language, current in prophetic-ecstatic circles, has therefore contributed to the range of this dominant metaphor for the prophetic office in Ezekiel.

Since the recapitulatory chapter 33 contains another version of this episode (33:1–9), the two passages should be read together. The passage 33:1–6 sets the scene with a city in time of war preparing for a siege. The relevance to the situation of Jerusalem is, of course, at once apparent. A sentry is appointed and his responsibilities are stated in crystal-clear terms. This passage gives us our first example of many in which Ezekiel uses legal forms of speech in his preaching. Since the earliest days of Israel the priesthood had responsibility for the formulation and transmission of laws and for handing down decisions in specific cases. This type of casuistic or common law states the facts of the case in the protasis ("if X does this or that") and the legal consequences in the apodosis. Typical examples may be found in the so-called Book of the Covenant, the earliest extant collection of Israelite laws (e.g., Exod. 21:1–6 dealing with slaves). Since Ezekiel, as a member of a priestly family, stood within that tradition, it was natural for him to make use of these formulations in his ministry. In this instance (33:1–6), it is a question whether or not the sentry performs his task and what consequences flow from the performance or nonperformance of his duty. If he warns and the hearer does not take appropriate action, the sentry is quit of responsibility for what may ensue. If he does not warn, he is accountable for the one "taken away in his iniquity." This statement of principle is then applied explicitly to the prophetic function of Ezekiel himself (33:7–9) in terms practically identical with 3:17–19. The latter passage

29

is then rounded off by contrasting the situation of the righteous with that of the wicked (3:20–21). If the righteous person sins, the prophet who has failed to warn is responsible. It would seem to follow, though it is not stated, that the prophet who has warned is quit of responsibility even if the righteous sins after having been warned.

It will be obvious by now that Ezekiel is concerned with personal responsibility, with special reference in this instance to pastoral responsibility. We do not need to be told that concern with freedom can easily serve as an alibi for avoiding responsibility for the consequences of one's acts. Concern with freedom is proper, but freedom connotes not the absence but the acceptance of limits. In the sphere of human interaction, limit and therefore responsibility are analytic to the idea of freedom. I may choose A or B, but if I choose A, I cannot at the same time choose the consequences of B. Ezekiel's views on personal responsibility will be stated at a later point (ch. 18). Here, at the beginning, he is concerned with the societal role of the prophet. There are important differences between the prophet and the mystic, for whom the discovery of God in the depths of the self is all-important. The prophet also has his (or her) inner world but is charged, against all odds, to make the vision prevail in the larger society. The metaphor of sentry highlights the critical and absolutely essential nature of this charge.

There is a final point here that is theologically perplexing, where Yahweh is said to place a stumbling block before the righteous, resulting in his (spiritual) death (v. 20). The phrase has perhaps been added in explanation of what is involved in the mysterious impulse that leads a person to embrace evil (is it heredity, environment, or a combination of both? is there a certain predestination to evil?). The time-honored translation word "stumbling block" (*mikshol* in Hebrew) means any obstacle that can lead a person to stumble or fall (e.g., Lev. 19:14; Isa. 57:14). In Ezekiel it refers to whatever constitutes an occasion of sin, whether money (7:19), alien cults (14:3–4, 7), or the company of those who practice them (44:12). Biblical statements about divine causality do not make the logical and philosophical distinctions—for example, between the absolute and the permissive will of God—which we would deem necessary. Everything that happens, whether good or ill, is directly attributed to God as agent. Sooner or later, however, the problems inherent

30

in this attribution were bound to emerge. The historian of the monarchy has Yahweh inciting David to make a census which brings disaster on the land (II Sam. 24:1), but the author of Chronicles, retelling the same event two centuries or so later, attributes the disaster not to Yahweh but to Satan (I Chron. 21:1). In the last decades of the monarchy, as total disaster became a real possibility, the problem took on particular urgency as a result of crisis and conflict within prophetic circles. One solution was to argue that false prophecy was God's way of testing his people (e.g., Deut. 13:3), but the line between testing and tempting must not always have been easy to discern. Ezekiel, one of whose principal aims was to address this crisis of faith, would go so far as to speak of God deceiving the false prophet in order to discredit him (14:9). In general, no biblical author conveys a starker and more vivid sense of the reality and ruinous consequences of sin than Ezekiel.

Ezekiel 3:22–27
Ezekiel's Loss of Speech

After the week spent immobile in Tel-abib, Ezekiel was commanded to go out of the settlement into the flat Babylonian countryside, and there he saw once again the vision of the mysterious effulgence. As on the first occasion (1:28—2:1), he was lifted up by the spirit and heard a voice addressing him. It instructed him to seclude himself in his house, where he was to be bound with cords and deprived of speech. The importance of this loss of speech is obvious: it is mentioned here at the beginning, at the conclusion of the first period (24:25–27), and in the recapitulatory chapter (33:21–22). If we take these statements as connected and at face value, we would be led to assume that Ezekiel was afflicted with aphasia seven days after his call in 593 B.C., that the end of this affliction was announced to him at the beginning of the siege of Jerusalem in 588 B.C., and that it actually came to an end when he heard the news of the fall of the city. This, however, leaves unexplained the many discourses and sayings uttered during this first period and recorded in the first twenty-four chapters. Various solutions have been proposed. Some commentators hold that the loss of

31

speech, and the binding that goes with it, are to be understood metaphorically. He was either banned by the community and its leaders, placed under house arrest, or forbidden to take part in ordinary social interaction, speaking only to deliver oracles of judgment. There are examples of private prophecies, when he was visited by the elders in his own house, but there is no support in this first section for ostracism or detention. The "dumbness" applied to nonprophetic speaking is possible, but the language used here and in the other allusions to this phenomenon suggests something rather more than this. Others have therefore been led to think of an intermittent affliction punctuated by episodes of prophetic activity. They have found confirmation for this interpretation in v. 27 read as an editorial clarification designated to make this point. But the previous verse states quite clearly that he was prevented from prophesying at all, and there are no grounds, apart from the hypothesis, for supposing that v. 27 is a subsequent addition.

Perhaps the least problematic solution is to give full weight to the loss of speech as a physical and clinical condition of aphasia but to restrict it to the end of the first period, from the beginning of the siege of Jerusalem to the fall of the city. It would not be surprising if aphasia were the result of trauma induced by the death of his wife combined with danger to the city and temple to which he was passionately attached. We would then conclude that this episode and the sign acts that follow and that certainly deal with the siege were relocated at the beginning of the book when the material was arranged in its present form. The reason would be that whoever was responsible for the arrangement saw them as having particular significance for the career of Ezekiel as a whole.

PART TWO

The Fall of the
House of Judah

Ezekiel 4—24

Ezekiel 4—5
Prophetic Theater of the Absurd

There follow three prophetic mimes introduced by one of the standard prefatory formulae in the book, "And you, mortal" (4:1, 9; 5:1). Embodying an extraordinary form of communication, one that risked bringing upon the prophet the charge of eccentricity, if not insanity, they illustrate the truth that prophetic ministry is not exhausted in the mandate to speak, especially in situations of extreme crisis.

The performance of such mimes or speech acts has been traced to the age-old practice of homeopathic or sympathetic magic, in which the acting out of the predicted or desired effect was thought to contribute to bringing it about, and no doubt it often did so. The ritual pouring out of water accompanied by appropriate words would, by striking some sympathetic chord in nature, produce rain. The depiction of the hunt on the cave wall—as at Lascaux or Altamira—would enhance the success of the hunt about to be undertaken. In the early stages of prophecy this type of symbolic act was particularly in evidence. Ahijah of Shiloh tore his garment into twelve strips and gave ten to Jeroboam to symbolize *and set in motion* the division of the kingdom (I Kings 11:29–31). Zedekiah put on an animal mask with horns and mimicked the wild ox to symbolize *and bring about* the defeat of the Syrians (I Kings 22:11–12). On his deathbed, Elisha ordered King Joash to shoot arrows out of the win-

33

dow to accomplish the same end (I Kings 13:14–19). The later prophets, generally thought to be more sober and rational, also engaged occasionally in this kind of mimetic prophecy. Isaiah walked naked in Jerusalem, a proleptic enactment of the fate of the Egyptian and Ethiopian foes of Assyria (Isa. 20). Such acts recur with remarkable frequency in Jeremiah, no doubt on account of the grave, indeed terminal, crisis through which the country was passing. They are, on the whole, hardly less bizarre than those of Ezekiel: wearing a soiled loincloth (Jer. 13:1–7), publicly smashing a clay vessel (Jer. 19), wearing a wooden and then an iron yoke on his neck (Jer. 27—28). Such sign acts should not be regarded as merely illustrative, as a kind of visual aid. Their purpose was to enhance the force of the spoken word, to make possible the more intense kind of identification with it that successful theater can achieve. We might think of these strange acts as a form of communication farther along the spectrum than simply verbalizing. And, with respect to the actor, one observable effect is their tendency toward a more complete involvement with the message. The marriage of Hosea to a sexually permissive woman (if that is what happened) presented as a sign, the celibacy of Jeremiah (Jer. 16), the refusal of Ezekiel to mourn his recently deceased wife (24:15–18)—these are sign acts that have taken over the life and personality of the actor, which are moving in the direction of a total life investment in the prophetic function.

Act I: Jerusalem Besieged (4:1–8)

In the first of the sign acts, Ezekiel is told to mimic the siege of Jerusalem by drawing the city on a clay brick complete with all the paraphernalia of a besieging army, the prophet himself acting the part of the Babylonians. The iron griddle and the hostile stare echo the language of the call ("See, I have made your face hard against their faces," 3:8). They also make the point that the besieging army is acting as agent of divine judgment. We are given to understand that this and the following acts take place in the prophet's house in Tel-abib. The use of clay bricks on which rudimentary city plans could be drawn with a stylus is attested in Mesopotamia. If, by some miracle, Ezekiel's city plan of Jerusalem ever came to light, it might help to solve the much-debated problem of the extent of the preexilic city and the location of the walls. The point has already been made that these prophetic mimes most likely come from the

34

time when Nebuchadnezzar was beginning to invest the city. The date is given at 24:1, and the bewildered response of the onlookers—"Won't you tell us what these things mean that you are doing?" (24:19)—points in the same direction.

The continuation of the account in 4:4-8 has undergone considerable editorial expansion which makes it difficult to understand. The careful reader will note several problems. Ezekiel is to be bound with cords which prevent him turning over, yet he is ordered to lie on both sides in succession. The house of Israel, which elsewhere in the book refers to Judah, here stands for the Northern Kingdom in contrast to Judah. The theme of the siege, which underlies the entire series of symbolic acts, is present only incidentally, and lying on the side seems to have nothing to do with it. All of this is quite apart from the question of whether Ezekiel remained prone on the ground for fourteen months at a stretch.

While any solution to these problems will be hypothetical, the following may at least serve as a basis for discussion. From the absence of the usual introductory formula we conclude that this passage (4:4-8) is not a separate sign act. The command to set his face toward the siege and the binding with ropes repeat what has already been mentioned (3:25; 4:3) and therefore do not constitute a new action. The lying bound on the side is a proleptic enactment of captivity and exile. By performing this act, Ezekiel both prefigures the punishment which is the result of Judah's infidelity and, at the same time, identifies himself with the suffering of his people brought on by sin. The term "to bear iniquity" belongs to the traditional vocabulary of the priest circles to which Ezekiel belonged. It can have the sense of being accountable and therefore liable for punishment (e.g., Lev. 5:1; 17:16; 19:8; Num. 5:31), and in this sense it occurs elsewhere in Ezekiel (14:10; 18:19-20; 44:10, 12). But there is also the more specialized meaning of accepting the responsibility and the consequences of the sin of others, a task that in the strictly cultic sphere fell to the priest (e.g., Exod. 28:38; Num. 18:1). This cultic idea of substitution passed over into the sphere of prophetic ministry—perhaps mediated by the distinctively prophetic idea of intercession—in the exilic poem about the Servant who silently bore the iniquities of many (Isa. 53:7, 11-12). It is entirely possible that a connection exists between Ezekiel's sign act and this justly famous poem. The resulting priestly-prophetic theme of suffering identification with a sinful

35

people provided early Christianity with a powerful means of expressing one aspect of the significance of Jesus and his mission. It also helped lay the groundwork for a distinctively Christian understanding of prophetic ministry.

Later elaboration of this mimed parable, perhaps by a disciple of Ezekiel, has transformed it into a prediction of the time assigned by God for punishment of the two kingdoms, Israel and Judah, rather comparable to the prediction in Jeremiah of seventy years of exile (Jer. 25:11; 29:10). This would therefore be only one example of a noticeable tendency toward eschatological and even apocalyptic reinterpretation throughout the prophetic corpus. Now "the house of Israel" is used in the restrictive sense of the kingdom of Samaria symbolized by the left side, that is, the north. The point of departure for the calculation of time appears to derive, once again, from priestly tradition. Pentateuchal narrative generally assigned to the Priestly source (P) assigns 430 years to the sojourn in Egypt (Exod. 12:40–41), for Ezekiel the time when Israel began to go wrong (20:5–8). The sum of 390 and 40 is 430, and according to the same priestly tradition the forty years of wandering in the wilderness was also a time of judgment and punishment. The passage in which this idea is most clearly expressed has obvious affinities with the present text in Ezekiel: "According to the number of days in which you spied out the land, forty days, for every day a year, you shall bear your iniquity, forty years" (Num. 14:34, RSV). Putting the two numbers together and assigning the shorter period of punishment to Judah, the Northern Kingdom is left to languish in exile for a period of 390 years before the eventual reunification, an event anticipated by Ezekiel (37:15–28). If these calculations are taken literally, the end of Judah's exile would be foreseen for either 558 or 546 B.C., depending on whether the point of departure is the first deportation in 598 B.C. or the destruction of Jerusalem and its temple in 596 B.C. The terminal date for the Northern Kingdom is more problematic, since we cannot be sure of the starting point. If the latter is taken to be the capture of Samaria by the Assyrians in 722 B.C., the 390 years would take us down to the time of Alexander the Great in the fourth century B.C., which may explain why the Old Greek version changed it to 190 years. If the latter is original, as some commentators hold, we arrive at a date close to that of Judah's liberation, namely, 532 B.C.

What it all amounts to is a first run at the precise calculation

36

of future events, based on prophetic texts, which we tend to associate more with Daniel and Revelation and which has lost none of its appeal for many Christians today in spite of some rather clear words of warning in the Gospels (e.g., Mark 13:22–23). In spite of all the misgivings that these attempts arouse, they can at least be appreciated as a defiance of present and overpowering evil, as an affirmation of the ultimate triumph of God's purposes in the world.

Act II: Siege Rations (4:9–17)

The silent theater continues with the command to mime the lot of the besieged by baking bread out of whatever scraps of cereal can be found. The prophet has to restrict himself to a maximum daily ration of about eight ounces of bread and one and a third pints of water, an allotment that probably corresponded to the conditions during the siege of Jerusalem which began in January 588 B.C.. After he was arrested on a charge of treason during the siege, Jeremiah received a loaf of bread a day until supplies ran out (Jer. 37:21; cf. II Kings 25:3; Jer. 52:6; Lam. 1:11; 2:12, 19). As the summer months approached, the cisterns started to run dry and could not be replenished (see, e.g., Jer. 38:6). As in other sieges, that of Leningrad during World War II, for example, there were rumors of cannibalism as the situation became more and more desperate (cf. Ezek. 5:10; Jer. 19:9; Lam. 2:20; 4:10). Here too it is important to note that Ezekiel is not just predicting disaster on others from a safe distance, like Jonah impatiently awaiting the doom of Nineveh from the safe refuge of his booth—a practice by no means unknown even today. Though he is in distant Babylon, Ezekiel fulfills the prophetic role of suffering identification and in so doing exhibits, in a form more telling than words, the meaning of solidarity and coresponsibility.

Here too the text has been expanded (in vs. 12–15) to make it refer to the condition of the deportees in Babylon. The issue is therefore no longer siege rations but the difficulty of observing the laws of ritual purity outside the land of Israel. The situation is dramatized by the command to use human excrement as fuel for cooking, provoking a protest from the priest-prophet that he had observed these laws, including the dietary laws, from his youth. (For the laws in question, see especially Deut. 14:21; Lev. 7:18; 17:15; 19:5–8). Inevitably, the reader of the New Testament will recall Simon Peter's reaction when

37

commanded to eat ritually impure food (Acts 10:9–16; 11:5–10). The fact that these laws were eventually abrogated within the mainstream of Gentile Christianity should not lead the Christian reader to misconstrue their intent. Whatever their origin, they came in the course of time to have confessional status, as one of several means of affirming the distinctive character and uniqueness of this particular community. Appreciation for these laws might even serve as a corrective to the tendency, more common among Christians than Jews, to think only of internal acts as religiously significant. There is a certain ecological concern here—for bodily states, what we ingest; in a word, for the body as that part of the world for which we are especially responsible. All of this was implicit in the priestly culture in which Ezekiel was nurtured. The preservation of that culture in the inhospitable milieu in which the deportees found themselves remained a major concern of his throughout his career.

Act III: The Results of the Siege (5:1–4)

It is now becoming clear that the three acts of the mimed drama exhibit a chronological sequence corresponding to the beginning, duration, and end of the siege of Jerusalem. In this third and last act Ezekiel has to shave off his hair and beard, divide the hair into three clumps, burn one of them, strike another with a sword, and scatter the third. In what appears to be the first of several editorial expansions, some hair from the third heap is to be set aside, one part of it to be hidden in the fold of his cloak, the other to be thrown into the fire. All of this must have seemed quite insane to any spectator who chanced to drop by, but it had its own strange logic. The shaving of the head and beard as a sign of mourning, common in the ancient Near East, is a kind of self-imposed ritual dishonoring, just as the rending of garments is a form of ritualized nudity and fasting a kind of premortem dying. In this case, however, the dishonoring is imposed by the conqueror, in the manner foretold in an earlier prophetic saying that Ezekiel may have had in mind:

> In that day Yahweh will shave with a razor which is hired beyond the River—with the king of Assyria—the head and the hair of the feet [genitals], and it will sweep away the beard also.
>
> Isaiah 7:20, RSV

38

The meaning is transparent. As the siege ends with the taking and burning of the city—as described in II Kings 25:9 and Jer.

39:8—some will perish in the flames; many of those who escape the burning city, including members of the royal family, nobility, and priesthood (II Kings 25:6–7, 18–21), will be executed; and others again will be carried into captivity (II Kings 25:11; Jer. 39:9). Among the deportees, there will be further casualties like those anti-Babylonian prophets who, as Jeremiah reports, were executed for sedition (Jer. 29:21–23). Such as these are distinguished from the true "remnant," those hidden symbolically in the prophet's cloak, those on whom the hope for a future would rest.

This Is Jerusalem! (5:5–17)

The enactment of the signs is rounded off with a short sermon that interprets them by following the prophetic pattern of construing world events in terms of divine causality. It opens with the old theme of the election of Jerusalem as the focal point of divine action in the world, the center or "navel of the earth" (cf. 38:12). This theme, which is rooted in the Davidic age and before that in Canaanite-Jebusite mythology, which received a tremendous boost with the apparently miraculous salvation of the city under Hezekiah, and which is most fully developed in Isaiah, became a central dogma of official theology during the time of the Judean monarchy. But we know how dangerously ambiguous is this idea of divine election. It can lend itself with fatal ease, now as then, to a self-serving complacency, or support an ideology of power which fails to reckon with the high cost of God's acts of grace. Misled by reliance on easy formulae based on divine election ("God is with us," "God is on our side"), Israel had neglected the heavy responsibilities, especially the responsibility of service, inherent in the idea of election. Inevitably, this misconstrual found its own expression in Israel's worship, which will help to explain why Ezekiel and so many of his prophetic predecessors condemn what they consider to be false forms of worship.

This is the point of the indictment pronounced by Ezekiel (vs. 5–6) and the verdict which follows (vs. 7–17). Here we have the traditional form of the prophetic judgment saying, related to the covenant formulation with its appended curses and, indirectly, to the form in which international treaties were cast. To grasp the point, we might compare it with the crescendo of curses in Deuteronomy 28, deriving from or based on a covenant text, which reach a climax of horror as the inhabitants of

39

the besieged city survive on human flesh (Deut. 28:52-57). These are precisely the kinds of curses appended to vassal treaties in punishment for violation of the oath of allegiance which sanctioned the treaty and gave it its force. The analogy illustrates, once again, how traditional forms of speech are taken up and transformed in the crucible of intense personal experience.

Ezekiel 6—7
The Approaching Judgment

This section consists of two sermons, each introduced by the title, frequent in Ezekiel, "The word of Yahweh came to me" (6:1; 7:1). Both are composed of two paragraphs under the rubric "Thus says Yahweh GOD" (6:1-10, 11-14; 7:1-4, 5-27), the entire section being held together by the leitmotif "You/they shall know that I am Yahweh" repeated seven times. In the context of the book as a whole, its counterbalance is the prophecy addressed to the mountains of Israel in chapter 36. Using the same form of words, it announces the reversal of the doom pronounced in the present section. It affirms, in other words, that salvation can and will follow judgment.

Death on the High Places (6:1-14)

Continuity with the sign acts is established by the hostile stare which the prophet is told to direct against the mountains of Israel (cf. 4:3), the clapping of the hands, and the stamping of the feet (6:11). All of these have their own importance as significative and, in some residual way, performative actions. Staring brings to mind the "evil eye," and eye contact, benign or, more commonly, hostile, was a significant aspect of "primitive" prophecy. Balaam had to *see* the Israelite horde in order to curse it (Num. 22:41; 23:9; etc.). On a visit to Damascus the prophet Elisha met Hazael the Syrian crown prince, future enemy of Israel, and "fixed his gaze and stared at him, until he was ashamed" (II Kings 8:11, RSV). By the same token, clapping the hands and stamping the feet are not spontaneous expressions of gloating and triumph on the part of Ezekiel himself. They are commanded and therefore relate the coming judg-

40

ment to the passionate involvement of Yahweh as a participant in Israel's history.

The reason for judgment on the mountains soon becomes apparent. The mountains of Israel can stand simply for the land of Israel, as is frequently the case in epic narrative and hymn. Here, however, the allusion is to the land desecrated by false cults. From pre-Israelite times it was customary to worship local manifestations of the fertility deities on elevated sites around the country which were thought to have a special sanctity. A raised platform, square or circular, provided the stage on which various ritual acts, including cultic prostitution, were performed before a pillar or carving or tree representing the male or female fertility deity. While these "high places" *(bamot)* were usually situated on hills, they could also be found in valleys (e.g., Jer. 7:31; 32:35) or even in towns (e.g., II Kings 17:9; 23:5, 8), a situation confirmed by excavations at such sites as Megiddo, Dan, Hazor, and Arad. The cult acts carried on at such sanctuaries included animal and occasionally human sacrifice (II Kings 23:10; Jer. 7:31), ritual copulation, and the burning of incense, generally associated with Canaanite type of cults (e.g., II Kings 23:5, 8; Jer. 1:16; 7:9; 44:17).

While worship on these "high places" was a normal feature of popular religion from the time of the settlement in the land, the inevitable accommodation to the sexually oriented cults of the native deities provoked a reaction spearheaded by Elijah and Hosea in the north and Jeremiah in Judah. In the course of time this prophetic opposition, backed by conservative and traditionalist elements among the laity, achieved official endorsement and was incorporated in reforms sponsored by the monarchy. The radical move of getting rid of these "high places" was attempted after the fall of the Northern Kingdom in 722 B.C. as part of a great religious reform set in motion by Hezekiah. The move was not an unqualified success, as is shown by the need to repeat it during the reign of Josiah, last great king of Judah, about three decades before Ezekiel began to prophesy. The account of Josiah's reforms by the historian of the monarchy (II Kings 23:4–20) parallels in some detail Ezekiel's prediction of doom on the high places: destruction of altars of sacrifice and incense altars, mass killings, desecration with human bones, and so forth. It is clear from both Jeremiah and Ezekiel that Josiah's reforms did not survive his early death at

41

Megiddo in 609 B.C. Ezekiel is saying that the high places will eventually be destroyed, but as a result not of reforming zeal but of enemy action—the sword of Yahweh (v. 3)—which will extend to the entire land.

The second part of the saying, dealing with the exiled survivors (vs. 8–10), was added after the fall of Jerusalem. We will have occasion to note at several points in the commentary that this event marked the great divide in the prophet's career, resulting in the expansion or revision of sayings from the first period (593–586 B.C.) and, more important, in a shift from unmitigated judgment to salvation following on judgment. In this respect, the last chapter of the so-called Holiness Code (Lev. 17—26), which has many points of contact with Ezekiel, provides an instructive parallel. The curse on the unfaithful land, including the destruction of the high places, incense altars, and idols, and the wasting of the entire land (Lev. 26:27–33), is followed by the disorientation of the scattered deportees who make up the remnant (Lev. 26:34–39). But then, we are told, after their heart has been humbled and they have acknowledged their sin, Yahweh will remember his covenant and reveal himself once again as their God (Lev. 26:40–45).

It is worth noting in passing how often the priestly sections of the Pentateuch, including the Holiness Code, speak of God *remembering* (e.g., Exod. 2:24; 6:5; Lev. 26:42, 45). According to this source, which bears the deep imprint of the exilic experience, the covenants that were made once and for all with humanity as a whole (Gen. 9) and with the ancestors of Israel (Gen. 17) were perpetually binding. They are therefore "everlasting" covenants (Gen. 9:16; 17:7, 13) which cannot be remade, only remembered and, by implication, reactivated. In Ezekiel, however, it is the surviving "remnant" in exile which will remember who their God is and finally acknowledge him through their sufferings. The necessary precondition is a process of reflection on the past (remembering), which will lead to self-knowledge (a loathing of the past self) and, finally, to acknowledgment of God and his purposes (knowing). Here we have a kind of prescription for surviving crisis, and we may test for ourselves whether it retains its validity for today. The breaking of the heart and (incongruously) of the eyes speaks of the need for what today we might call existential humility, an attitude that makes it possible to break with old habits and make a new beginning. The corresponding passage in Ezekiel 36 goes far-

42

ther and speaks of the need for a new heart and a new spirit (36:26). The present passage ends with the "acknowledgment formula"—"You shall know [acknowledge] that I am Yahweh"—drawn from the priestly tradition in which Ezekiel stood. It corresponds to a deep-seated conviction of Ezekiel—that in spite of the inclination of the human heart to go its own way and worship idols of its own making, the reality of God will, in the end, be vindicated and acknowledged.

As noted earlier, 6:11–14 is the continuation of the first sermon. It too begins "Thus says the Lord Yahweh"; the clapping and stamping correspond to the hostile stare and carry its implications farther. But while the first part speaks only of the sword, that is, military disaster, the second spells out the implications further by introducing the "dogs of war," adding famine and pestilence as the concomitants of military action. We are reminded of medieval representations of the "Dance of Death," of scenes depicting the horrors of the Thirty Years War on contemporary German woodcuts, and of Goya's *The Disasters of War.* The order in which the disasters are listed is somewhat confusing. Usually the juxtaposition of "those who are near" and "those who are far off" is simply a way of including everyone, so that we would not expect a third category. If this third category refers to the besieged, as seems linguistically possible, the idea would be that those who are still holding out in Jerusalem after the rest of the country had gone through the horrors of war would not escape the general devastation. We would then be brought back to the sign acts of the previous chapter.

The last part of the saying (vs. 13*b*–14) appears to be an editorial expansion using the language of 6:1–7 about the destruction of the idolatrous open-air cults and their devotees. It therefore repeats the acknowledgment formula at the end, thus forming a kind of ring composition or inclusion (see commentary on 3:16–21).

The end result of all of this is the devastation of the country from one end to the other. The wilderness is the "great and terrible wilderness" of the Sinai (Deut. 1:19, RSV), representing the extreme southern limit of the land. Riblah, a strategically important city on the Orontes in Syria, in the territory of Hamath (cf. II Kings 25:21), stands for the extreme northern limit, more usually referred to as "the entrance of Hamath" (e.g., Num. 13:21; Josh. 13:5; II Kings 14:25; Amos 6:14). The

43

choice of these places is not accidental. In ancient tradition, and very clearly in Ezekiel, the Sinai wilderness is associated with judgment on Israel. As the place that witnessed the mass execution of the royal family, the Judean nobility, and the temple priesthood by Nebuchadnezzar (II Kings 25:6–7, 18–21), Riblah must have remained in the consciousness of the deportees as a name of infamy and ill omen. It would be difficult to think of a more vivid and painful reminder of the reality of divine judgment and therefore of the need to acknowledge that "I am Yahweh."

Intimations of the End (7:1–27)

The second part of this section is addressed directly to the land of Israel and therefore forms a natural sequel to the first. Attachment to the land, to *'ereṣ yiśra'el,* became a prominent component of national consciousness only from the time of the exile, which was understandable in view of the experience of homelessness, alienation, and nostalgia which exile brought with it. The Christian might say that it has something of sacramental significance, as the outward sign and warranty of the indefectible bond that constitutes Israel as a people. It is therefore no surprise that Ezekiel speaks so often of "the land of Israel," literally, "the earth of Israel" *('admat yiśra'el).* The link between peoplehood and land has been understood in different ways throughout the history of Judaism to the present, and the relevance of biblical statements about the land has become particularly acute with the establishment of the State of Israel. The connection calls for critical appraisal, but it can be said that no Christian attempt to understand Judaism will be adequate if it neglects this spiritual and emotional link with the land.

The present chapter might be described as a sermon in verse, though this may not be apparent in the modern versions. Unfortunately the text has come down to us in an extremely confused and corrupt state, with numerous editorial annotations and expansions that make it difficult to translate and interpret. It was delivered to representatives of the exiled communities, perhaps shortly after the prophet's call (taking the dates in Ezek. 1:1–2 and 8:1 at face value), but in any case before the fall of Jerusalem. The original form of the sermon is a matter of conjecture. It will be noted, for example, that vs. 5–9 are in effect an alternative version of vs. 1–4 with 10–12, and LXX has a different version again.

44

The first section or stanza (vs. 1–4) is here translated literally to give some idea of the short, stabbing lines in which the message of doom is driven home:

> An end has come,
> The end has come on the four corners of the earth!
> Now the end is upon you;
> I will hurl my anger at you,
> I will judge you according to your ways,
> I will lay upon you all your abominations.
> My eye will not spare you,
> Nor will I have pity.

The key term is "the end" *(qeṣ)*. The picture of the final judgment, extended from the land to the four corners of the earth, draws on both prophetic and priestly tradition. If Ezekiel may be described as preaching, his principal text may have been the fourth of the five vision narratives of Amos, a vision in which he was shown a basket of summer fruit, the word for which in Hebrew is identical with the word for "end." The visual experience evoked the pronouncement that plays on this double meaning:

> The end has come upon my people Israel;
> I will never again pass by them.
> The songs of the temple shall become wailings in that day, . . .
> The dead bodies shall be many;
> in every place they shall be cast out in silence.
> Amos 8:2–3, RSV

In this context, "end" is associated quite naturally with harvesting, traditionally a time of rejoicing. As so often in Amos, however, the normal associations are turned on their head, the joy of harvest festival is turned into the grim image of Death the Reaper. Amos also introduces the traditional theme of the day on which the defeat of the enemies of Israel, who are also God's enemies, would be celebrated in a great act of joyful worship. This idea too is turned upside down:

> Woe to you who desire the Day of Yahweh!
> Why would you have the Day of Yahweh?
> It is darkness and not light.
> As if a man fled from a lion and a bear met him;
> Or went into the house, leaned on the wall, and a snake bit
>   him.
> Is not the Day of Yahweh darkness and not light,
> And gloom with no brightness in it?
> (Amos 5:18–20)

45

Or again:

> On that day, says Yahweh GOD,
> I will make the sun go down at noon,
> And darken the earth in broad daylight.
> I will turn your feasts into mourning,
> And all your songs into lamentation;
> I will bring sackcloth upon all loins,
> All heads will be shaved.
> I will make it like the mourning for an only son,
> And the end of it like a bitter day.
>
> Amos 8:9–10

Echoes of this imagery of darkness and death occur throughout Ezekiel's sermon in verse, and there can be little doubt that he had Amos in mind when he delivered it. But within Ezekiel's own priestly tradition the great paradigm of judgment is the deluge which put an end to the old world corrupted by violence and sin. The emphasis on *violence* is particularly noteworthy. A careful reading of the Priestly version of the flood story in Genesis 6—9 suggests that it was put together to reflect the historical disasters through which Ezekiel's contemporaries lived and the possibility of a new beginning. This Priestly version opens as follows:

> Now the earth was corrupt in God's sight, and the earth was filled with violence. And God saw that the earth was corrupt, for all flesh had corrupted their way upon the earth. And God said to Noah, "The end of all flesh has come before me; for the earth is filled with violence because of them; I will destroy them with the earth."
>
> Genesis 6:11–13

Ezekiel, who will have something to say about Noah later on (14:12–20), also speaks of the rise of violence in the world before the deluge (7:11). In the following stanza (vs. 10–27) the emphasis shifts to the suddenness with which the ordinary, everyday events that make up our lives and undergird our sense of reality will be brought to an end. Exactly the same aspect of judgment is expressed in a saying of Jesus that echoes Ezekiel's sermon:

> For as in those days before the flood they were eating and drinking, marrying and giving in marriage, until the day when Noah entered the ark, and they did not know until the flood came and swept them all away, so will be the coming of the Son of man. Then two men will be in the field; one is taken and one is left. Two women will be grinding at the mill; one is taken and one is left.
>
> Matthew 24:38–41, RSV

While it was certainly not intended as such, this saying may serve to interpret the basic sense of Ezek. 7:10–27. To get at that sense, we will have to pick our way among the textual obscurities and editorial debris with which the passage is littered. A close translation would run somewhat as follows:

> Behold the day!
> The doom has gone forth;
> Crookedness has flowered,
> Pride has blossomed.
> Ezekiel 7:10

As brief as it is, this opening verse poses problems. "Doom" is no more than an educated guess at the meaning of the obscure Hebrew word *ṣefirah*. "Crookedness" conceals a pun on a Hebrew word that more usually means "staff." While the context suggests an original reference to moral corruption in Judah before the catastrophe, the doom may have come to be identified with the rise of the proud tyrant Nebuchadnezzar, who was to destroy Jerusalem. It will be recalled that Isaiah referred to the Assyrians as "the staff of my fury" (Isa. 10:5, RSV)—a stick to beat Israel with—and Jeremiah uses the word "pride" as a code name for the Babylonians (Jer. 50:31–32). The meaning of the editorial comment that follows in Ezekiel (v. 11) is now impossible to unscramble. It appears to begin, "Violence has risen up in the shape of a wicked staff"; the rest cannot be made out. It may have been intended as a post factum allusion to the campaign of Nebuchadnezzar in 588–586 B.C., but that again is only an educated guess. The sermon in verse continues:

> The time has come,
> The day has arrived;
> Let not the buyer rejoice,
> Nor the seller mourn,
> For wrath is on all their throng.
> Ezekiel 7:12

Buying and selling is part of a settled order that is simply taken for granted but that is suddenly to be undermined. When there is no future, it makes no difference whether you come out of a deal at the winning or the losing end; the whole thing loses meaning. A late poem in the Isaian collection makes the same point. With the prospect of ultimate disaster, it will be "as with the people, so with the priest; . . . as with the buyer, so with the

47

seller; as with the lender, so with the borrower; as with the creditor, so with the debtor" (Isa. 24:2, RSV).

Ezekiel 7:12 has also been annotated, as is clear from the following verse which appears to be saying that the seller will not be able to go back on his deal as long as he lives. Some commentators think this refers to the jubilee, the fiftieth year, when land lost through compulsory purchase reverted to its original owner (Lev. 25:8–17, 23–55; 27:16–25; Num. 36:4). The point then would be that the present order will not survive until the upcoming jubilee. Others think that it is more likely an allusion to the situation of the deportees who were forced to sell their real estate at a loss to those who remained or, worse still, simply abandon it (cf. 11:14–15). The point then would be that the deportee can forget about returning and reclaiming his possessions. Whatever the explanation, the normal transactions of daily life lose their meaning with the prospect of imminent and catastrophic judgment.

The imagery now shifts to warfare seen from the losing side:

They blow the trumpet and prepare everything,
But no one goes into battle. . . .
The sword without, pestilence and famine within.
He who is in the field will die by the sword,
He who is in the town, famine and pestilence will consume him.
If any of them escape, they will take to the hills.
Ezekiel 7:14–16

The state of abject terror is graphically described:

All their hands hang limp,
All their knees drip urine
They gird on sackcloth,
Horror covers them.
There is shame on all their faces,
All heads are shaved.
Ezekiel 7:17–18

One has only to speak to a survivor of the Nazi concentration camps, or watch the old newsreels with their images of unspeakable degradation, or visit Yad vaShem, the memorial to the Holocaust in Jerusalem, to appreciate how quickly the veneer of civilized life and humanity can be stripped away. It is this process of the dehumanizing of the defeated which Ezekiel is here describing in terms of brutal realism. The sermon then turns to another aspect of this undermining of the reality of everyday life:

They throw their silver into the streets,
Their gold becomes an unclean thing. . . .
They cannot satisfy their appetite
Nor fill their stomach with it.

Ezekiel 7:19

After the first couplet, someone has slipped in a verse from the late preexilic prophet Zephaniah: "Their silver and gold will not be able to save them on the day of the wrath of Yahweh" (Zeph. 1:18). The point needs little elaboration. If there is anything in our everyday life that has ultimacy, that is "the bottom line," it is money. So think of a situation where the social structures essential for the functioning of a money economy have collapsed, where it is impossible to procure the basics at any price. It is not really a moralizing statement about the evil of money, the banal kind which is so familiar. It is a statement of fact; this is what is going to happen. It is also a reminder of the fragility and impermanence of an order of things which we have to take for granted in order to function.

At this point the sermon reverts to prose; why, it is difficult to say. It seems to continue—in v. 20—with a comment about gold, the finest of metals, becoming an unclean thing. This fits in very well with prophetic polemic against idols of gold and silver as, for example, in one of the great diatribes of Isaiah (Isa. 2:6–22). But it is also possible that the thing of beauty referred to here is the temple. For the preacher (in this instance speaking *after* the catastrophe) goes on to say that it has been delivered into the power of foreigners who, like robbers, have pillaged and desecrated it, reaching even into the Holy of Holies, "my secret place." The destruction will also take in the many sanctuaries up and down the land at which, in defiance of the Deuteronomic law, the people of Judah continue to worship.

As the sermon draws to an end (vs. 25–27), we see how the last defenses are broken down, and the traditional religious solutions no longer seem to apply. In their anguish the survivors seek peace, meaning some form of reconciliation with God, some way of coming to terms with the crisis that has overwhelmed them. Echoing a word of Jeremiah (Jer. 18:18), they seek a revelation from the prophet, instruction on what to think and how to act from the priest, advice from the elders, those depositories of traditional wisdom, but their questions remain unanswered. The result is paralysis on the part of both ruler and

49

people. God has dealt with them as they deserved, and this is the result. The concluding formula, "They shall know that I am Yahweh," may be taken to mean that, at this lowest and darkest point, they will come to acknowledge that God was mysteriously present in all this and that this acknowledgment may contain the seeds of a new beginning. We shall find the survivors coming to Ezekiel at a later point with the anguished question, "How, then, shall we live?" (33:10). After the predicted disasters have come about, much of Ezekiel's prophetic ministry will be concerned with answering this question.

Provisional Theological Reflections

While Ezekiel was not proclaiming the end of the world, he was proclaiming to his contemporaries that *their* world was coming to an end. How we today, who are, on the whole, comfortably at home in our own world, react to these grim scenarios and predictions might reflect in interesting ways on our own theological thinking. Prophetic predictions of the end of human history, or at least of our phase of that history, would not be problematic for many contemporary Christians. They affirm it as an essential ingredient of their faith and even proclaim it on bumper stickers attached to their automobiles. It could easily be affirmed that the Parousia, the coming of Christ in glory to fold up the historical record, should not be problematic, since it appears to be an essential feature of early Christian faith and has been incorporated into the creeds. Yet it is probably correct to say that it does not make a significant impact on the thinking and the lives of what are sometimes still called mainstream Christians, and it certainly does not impact significantly on mainstream Christian theology. At the most obvious level, predictions of an *imminent* end are fatally subject to falsification, leading to assorted rationalizations for nonfulfillment, rescheduling of the eschatological event (as already in Dan. 12:11–13), and the like. In the lifetime of Ezekiel himself there were those who either doubted ("The days grow long, and every vision comes to nought") or found a way to reinterpret ("The vision that he sees is for many days hence, and he prophesies of times far off") (12:21–28, RSV). Likewise in early Christianity, there were those who were hinting broadly that there wasn't going to be a Second Coming (e.g., II Peter 3:3–4).

Another problem is that to accord prominence to this form of eschatological belief seems to be inconsistent with a theology and ethic that take life in the world seriously, including genuine ecological concern for the world in which we live and for which we are responsible to those who come after us. We are all the more ready, therefore, to appreciate the various forms of "realized eschatology" which emerged out of early Christian experience and to accept without demur the spiritualization of the biblical eschatological drama, restating it in terms of the postmortem destiny of the individual.

A reading of Ezekiel 6—7, and similar passages in the first half of the book, will not solve this theological problem, but it might provide clues to at least an interim coming to terms with it. By means of vivid imagery, Ezekiel shows up the fragility and impermanence of those realia which make up the fabric of our taken-for-granted existence and contribute to our sense of personal and social identity. History, to which in however limited measure we contribute, and over which we have so little control, produces events that can, with unanticipated suddenness, reveal the insubstantial nature of what passes for solid reality. Such an event was the fall of Jerusalem in 586 B.C. experienced by Ezekiel and his contemporaries. We today have less reason to ignore the point, since we can now foresee the possibility of different apocalyptic scenarios which we ourselves can contribute to bringing about. The question, which a reading of Ezekiel might help to pose, is whether we can summon the moral resources to live responsibly in a world that can no longer be taken for granted.

Ezekiel 8—11
The Temple Vision

The visionary experience that follows occurred in the prophet's house in Tel-abib during a consultation session with the elders of the diaspora communities (see also 14:1; 20:1). The date, in the month Ab (late July–early August) of 592 B.C., or about a year after the inaugural vision, is carefully noted. It seems that the state of trance ("the hand of Yahweh") came over Ezekiel suddenly, without preparation or solicitation. His care to describe precisely what he recollected seeing and hear-

51

ing is noticeable here, as it is elsewhere in the book. He sees again the fiery figure emerging from a brilliant source of light (cf. 1:27) and feels what he takes to be a hand grasping him by the hair and transporting him to Jerusalem, depositing him at a point north of the temple. As the vision ends, the spirit takes him up and brings him back to Babylon, where he recounts what he has seen and heard to the representatives of the community who presumably remained with him while the trance lasted (11:24–25).

Before coming to the narrative content of the vision, we need to make a few observations by way of clarification.

First, there is no reason to doubt that what is being described is a visionary experience that came to Ezekiel in the Babylonian diaspora. Nothing in this description obliges us to conclude either that he was then still resident in Jerusalem or that he is using this means to record his impressions of a visit to the city. As elsewhere in the book, however, there are clear indications of editorial activity. Prophetic sayings were not covered by copyright. The great esteem in which they were held did not prevent the persons who transmitted them from annotating, expanding, and making them more readily available to a new generation. In this instance, the oracular saying directed against the twenty-five royal counselors ending with the sudden death of one of their number (11:1–13) and the vindication of the diaspora community's land claims (11:14–21) were probably added at a later point in time. That the former (11:1–13) originally stood on its own is apparent from the command to prophesy and the description of the onset of ecstasy occurring *within* the vision (11:4–5); and that it originated in Jerusalem is strongly suggested by the fact that the death of Pelatiah occurred while the prophecy was actually being delivered (11:13). The following passage (11:14–21), which speaks of a return to the land and a new lease of life, belongs by rights to a later part of the book (see 36:22–31) and is out of place in this scenario of doom and destruction. It may have been added here as a response to the agonizing cry of Ezekiel, "Are you about to destroy completely the remnant of Israel?" (11:13). Whoever arranged and transmitted the words of the master felt that this terrible possibility should not be left hanging in the air, without an immediate answer.

52

We also note the concern to relate the experience to the initial vision of the throne and its occupant during which Ezekiel was called to prophesy. This is apparent at the outset in the description of the mysterious being who transports him and conducts the guided tour of the temple area (8:2), whose function precludes identification with Yahweh himself and yet who speaks in the name of Yahweh as the narrative progresses (8:17–18). We may also note how the effulgence *(kabod)* distances itself by stages from the temple as preparations for the destruction are completed: first, from the Holy of Holies to the threshold (9:3; 10:4), then to the east gate of the temple, where the cherubim are waiting (10:18–19), and finally to the Mount of Olives east of the city (11:22–23). This movement to the east is in counterpoint with the prophet's movement by stages into the doomed building from the north, the cardinal point from which, according to ancient representations, danger and disaster are to be expected. It also signifies that the divine presence is henceforth to be sought among the deportees until the time of the return, at which time its reentry into the city will be explicitly noted (43:1–5).

The temple vision is unique in the annals of "classical" prophecy in assuming the form, well attested in shamanistic cultures, of soul travel. The term denotes the sensation of the soul or conscious self leaving the body behind and being transported to another place, in this instance some five hundred and fifty air miles. Here too the closest parallels are to be found among those great "primitives," Elijah, Elisha, and their associates, the "sons of the prophets." Elijah was renowned for his ability to levitate (I Kings 18:12; II Kings 2:1–12, 16–18), while for Elisha the psychic powers of precognition, extrasensory perception, and bilocation seemed almost to come naturally (II Kings 5:26; 6:17, 32–33). It is also worth noting that both Elisha and Ezekiel have these extraordinary experiences while at home in the presence of elders, who are therefore able to authenticate them in the name of the community they represent (cf. II Kings 6:32–33).

Scene I (8:1–6)

Ezekiel, then, was transported in vision to the temple mount in Jerusalem with which, of course, he was thoroughly familiar. While the topographical details are not always clear, he approached from the northern perimeter of the temple area, through an outer into an inner courtyard, in the direction of the eastern entrance leading into the atrium. At each of four stages

53

in this progress he is invited to observe idolatrous cults being carried out. Attempts have been made to integrate these into one cultic act with successive phases, but without success. It is therefore better to take them separately, as examples of the disintegration of the cultic and religious life of Judah during the last quarter of a century of its independent existence. The first was on the northern side of the inner court gate where Ezekiel was asked to observe an "image of jealousy, which provokes to jealousy" (v. 3, RSV) standing on its pedestal. The allusion is certainly to the representation of a human figure in defiance of the prohibition against images (Exod. 20:4–6; Deut. 5:8–10), but we are not told of what deity. While the prohibition of images is associated with Yahweh's jealousy, that is, his exclusive claim on Israel, it is also possible to translate, "the lustful image which incites to lust." If this is correct, what Ezekiel was seeing was the image of the fertility goddess Asherah, queen of heaven, who seems to have had a particularly strong appeal during the last decades of the Kingdom of Judah. Her cult was introduced into both kingdoms at an early stage (I Kings 15:13; 18:19) and was officially sponsored under Manasseh, who set up her statue in the temple precincts (II Kings 21:7). Though removed during Josiah's reform (II Kings 23:6), it found its way back after the death of that king at Megiddo in 609 B.C. While their interpretation is still being disputed, inscriptions recently discovered at Kuntillet 'Ajrud on the northern border of the Sinai, dated to the ninth or the eighth century B.C., associate Yahweh with "his Asherah" and confirm the impression gained from certain passages in the Hebrew Bible that in the popular religion she was understood to be Yahweh's consort. It was perhaps in this capacity that her cult was established in the temple alongside that of Yahweh himself and was still being advocated by survivors of the disaster in the Egyptian diaspora, according to Jer. 44:17–19 (an interesting text, since, for once, women have their say on the subject of religion).

Scene II (8:7–13)

The second tableau takes place at the entrance to the courtyard, in a large room—large enough for seventy people—entered through a recess in the wall. The details are not entirely clear, and the command to dig through the wall is puzzling, since there was a hole there already. It may have been suggested by the sign act in Ezek. 12:5. As he entered, Ezekiel saw

54

that the walls were covered in paintings of all sorts of fauna, including animals considered ritually unclean according to priestly law (Lev. 7:21). The seventy elders, who were taking part in a liturgy with incense thuribles, were the official representatives of the tribes that, according to one tradition, accompanied Moses and Aaron at the ratification of the Sinai covenant (Exod. 24:1, 9). The scene is reminiscent of Egyptian burial chambers, the walls of which were covered with brilliantly painted images of deities in animal form, including Anubis, the jackal-headed god who weighed the souls of the dead. Egyptian influence was pervasive in Judah from the death of Josiah, beginning with the first four years of his successor Jehoiakim, who ruled as an Egyptian puppet. But even after the crushing defeat of the Egyptians at Carchemish in 605 B.C., there was a strong pro-Egyptian party at court which looked in that direction for backing against the new Babylonian overlord. And, in fact, an Egyptian army succeeded in temporarily raising the siege of Jerusalem, thus giving rise to hopes of deliverance which proved to be short-lived (see Jer. 34:21; 37:5–10). Thus, the ceremonies being conducted by these official representatives of Judean society were probably aimed at enlisting the support of Egyptian deities, which of course also implied a loss of confidence in the God of Israel and his power to act: "Yahweh does not see us, Yahweh has abandoned the land" (8:12).

Scene III (8:14–15)

At the entrance of the north gate of the temple, women were engaged in ritual lamentation for the dead vegetation deity Tammuz. The cult of this god, identical with the Sumerian Dumuzi known from the third millennium B.C., may have been introduced into the country by the Assyrians. As with his counterpart Baal-hadad among the Canaanites (cf. Zech. 12:11) and Adonis among the Greeks, the life cycle of Tammuz corresponded to the unchanging round of the agrarian calendar in the Middle East. With the onset of the dry season he disappeared into the underworld, was sought for and lamented by his lover and consort Ishtar (Inanna, Anath, Aphrodite), and in the course of time rose from the realm of the dead to new life with the rebirth of the vegetation. That this ritual was being carried out in the temple precincts suggests that it too was part of an officially sponsored syncretism involving the monarchy, the ruling class, and the priesthood.

55

Scene IV (8:16)

The last scene takes place in front of the temple, between the atrium, which ran the width of the temple on the east, and the altar, which stood in the open space a little to the north of the main entrance. This was the area in which the sacrificial cult took place, an area therefore of special sanctity corresponding to the court of the priests in Herod's temple. Here Ezekiel was invited to witness about twenty-five men (twenty in LXX) facing east, with their backs to the temple, worshiping the rising sun. Who these men were we are not told. It has been suggested that the group was composed of representatives of the twenty-four priestly courses led by the high priest, but it seems that this institution (the courses) came into existence at a later time. That they conducted their ritual in this place of special sanctity at least suggests a body with official standing. The worship of the sun (*shemesh* in Hebrew) as a powerful deity dispensing life, health, and justice was age-old in Israel, as it was elsewhere in the ancient world. Suffice it to recall place-names like Beth-shemesh (temple of the sun) and personal names like that of Samson, who was named for the sun-god. The Deuteronomic author warns against the temptation of worshiping the heavenly bodies (Deut. 4:19). How necessary the warning was is shown by the setting up of altars to them in the temple courts by Manasseh (II Kings 21:5) and the chariot and horses of the sun removed from the same location by Josiah (II Kings 23:11–12).

The turning of their backs on the temple and the Presence within has a symbolic as well as a literal meaning. A prose passage in Jeremiah might have been written as a commentary on these *tableaux vivants* in Ezekiel: "They have turned to me their back and not their face; and though I have taught them persistently they have not listened to receive instruction. They set up their abominations in the house which is called by my name, to defile it" (Jer. 32:33–34, RSV). In Ezekiel the mysterious guide, speaking now for the first time in the name of Yahweh, links these cultic abuses with violence, disorder, and lawlessness of the kind that brought the old world to an end in the deluge. The final insult—"They put the branch to their nose" (RSV)—is obscure, deliberately so, since it alludes to an obscene gesture. The result is total alienation expressed in the same language as the preceding sermon: "My eye will not spare, nor will I have pity; they will cry out loud to me and I will not listen" (cf. 7:4, 9, 25). As the truth finally dawns on them, their prayers will bring back to them nothing but the echo of their own voices.

The Seven Agents of Destruction (9:1–11)

In its own way Ezekiel 8—11 conforms to the classic pattern of the prophetic judgment saying: the inspection of the temple area corresponds to the indictment, following which the verdict is pronounced and immediately carried out. The description of this second stage opens with an ironic contrast:

> They will cry out loud in my hearing, but I will not listen to them.
> Ezekiel 8:18

> He cried out loud in my hearing, "The executioners of the city are at hand."
> Ezekiel 9:1

And indeed, no sooner is the announcement made than seven "men" appear at the gate of the outer court facing north—known as the Benjamin Gate (Jer. 20:2)—each with a club or ax in his hand. These executioners (the Hebrew word means "overseers," but the use is ironic) are the destroying angels familiar to readers of the Book of Revelation (especially Rev. 15—16). The idea of a supernatural agent of destruction is an ancient one. It makes its first and most memorable appearance in the Passover story, destroying all those not marked with a distinctive sign (Exod. 12:23). Once again, on the occasion of David's census referred to earlier, the destroying angel appeared and was restrained at the last moment from falling on the city (II Sam. 24:15–17). Ezekiel may have had both these occasions in mind as he described the scene unfolding. This representation of the Destroyer *(mashhit),* like that of the Satan who features in the other version of the census taking (I Chron. 21:1), might be thought of as a projection of the negative energy of the deity, the anger, grief, and frustration generated by unreciprocated love. The Hebrew Bible never hesitates to speak of God in terms of human emotion, and Ezekiel expresses more of this than almost any other biblical author. The truth, discovered experientially by Pascal, that the God of Abraham, Isaac, and Jacob is not the god of the philosophers, is nowhere more clearly exhibited than in Ezekiel.

57

One of the seven approaching was a scribe clothed in white

linen, with the tools of his trade attached to his belt. On the foreheads of those to be spared he was to put a mark in the form of a *tav*, the last letter of the Hebrew alphabet, shaped like an X, with two crossed strokes. (Thus, incidentally, the sign of the cross did not originate with Christianity.) Its function was the same as the "mark of Cain" (Gen. 4:15)—a notoriously misinterpreted text—which served to protect him from the consequences of blood guilt. The seven took their station by Solomon's bronze altar, which had been moved to the northeast corner of the temple court to make way for the stone altar set up by King Ahaz in the eighth century (II Kings 16:14). They were therefore in close proximity to the twenty-five sun worshipers. The movement of the effulgence from the inner sanctum, under the outstretched wings of the cherubim (cf. I Kings 8:6–7), to the threshold at the east end of the building is parenthetical—a deliberate anticipation of the first stage of its departure (Ezek. 10:4–5). The intent is to state clearly the source of the commands that follow. The first is addressed to the scribe, to mark with a cross those to be spared. The mark, a kind of tattoo or brand indicating ownership, set aside those who belonged to Yahweh, those who, in the words of the Gospel, hunger and thirst after justice. Christian writers, beginning with Origen and Jerome, not unexpectedly read this as a prefiguring of the cross of Jesus, and their interpretations contributed to the salvific significance of the sign of the cross. According to a Jewish tradition (*b. Shabbat* 55a), the *tav* written on the foreheads of the faithful stood for *tiḥyeh*, you shall live, while the *tav* written in blood on the foreheads of the unrighteous stood for *tamut*, you shall die. After the faithful were thus singled out, the other six were to proceed to destroy the remaining ones without exception, beginning in the temple area itself, without regard for the ancient right of sanctuary. The first to die were the sun worshipers (here called elders) whose corpses rendered the entire sacred area ritually impure and thus unfit for worship.

In the midst of this scene of carnage Ezekiel found the courage to speak, discharging the traditional prophetic role of intercession. He will do it once more, and in much the same words, after the sudden death of Pelatiah (11:13). Intercessory prayer is one of the most overlooked aspects of prophetic ministry, for the prophet is, above all, an intermediary between God and the community, and the mediation moves in both directions. In interceding for the doomed city of Sodom, also unsuccessfully, Abraham was fulfilling this prophetic role (Gen. 18). Amos, who saw in a series of visions the disasters awaiting Israel, also interceded in moving language that by some means they might be averted (Amos 7:1–6). The experience of failed intercession, which Ezekiel shared with Jeremiah (Jer. 14:11–12; 15:1), produced in him, as it did in Jeremiah, a profound sense of the reality of sin, of the desperate sickness of the human heart (see, e.g., Jer. 13:23; 17:9). This is something which is very difficult for us to share today. We are more comfortable with the categories of psychological illness and therapy than with those of sin and salvation, and for us it is never too late. And, correspondingly, it is much easier to think of ministry as a form of social service rather than as prophetic in the sense just indicated. So Ezekiel prays, but the answer is, in effect: Too late! Sin has reached its full measure, the land is full of bloodshed, the city is filled with impurity. As the scribe reports on the completion of his mission, the familiar theme is repeated: My eye will not spare, nor will I have pity.

Departure of the *kabod* and Burning of the City (10:1–22)

According to our sources, Jerusalem was put to the torch subsequently to its capture in a distinct and deliberate act of the occupying army. The distinct phases in the catastrophe were well remembered and commemorated in liturgies of fasting in the corresponding months (Zech. 8:18–19), as indeed they still are in the one festival of Tishe b'Ab. They are also presented as distinct phases in Ezekiel's vision. The scribe is commanded to take some of the live coals in the midst of the living creatures (cf. 1:13), now identified with the cherubim (10:15, 20), and scatter them over the city like incendiary bombs. At this point the account is interrupted by editorial comment on the location of this act which leaves us somewhat confused (10:3–5). The cherubim are said to be south of the temple, no doubt in contrast to the abominations going on to the north. But then we are told that the effulgence rose up from the cherubim on which it rested in the inner sanctum, or Holy of Holies, as described in I Kings 6:23–28; 8:6–7. It then proceeded to the entrance on the east side. We can only suppose that these are distinct editorial amplifications that have not been harmonized. Then the command is repeated, to signify the resumption of the narrative line after the insertion (v. 6). The scribe approached, one of the mysterious hybrid creatures reached in and handed him burn-

59

ing coals from the fiery center of the chariot throne, and he took them and left (vs. 7–8). There may have existed an account of the actual conflagration which has been omitted—as was the account of the slaughter preceding it—but more probably it was simply left to the reader's imagination.

We now hear of the departure of the divine effulgence. The personal experience of the reality and presence of God, which is an essential ingredient of the religious phenomenon, can come about in different ways and be expressed in many forms, most of which are represented in the religious literature of Israel. For some, the events of everyday life may manifest that presence; others may experience it through personal relations—friend, spouse, lover; others again may feel themselves summoned by God to give themselves to a mission or cause. In the tradition that formed Ezekiel, that of the Zadokite priesthood, the paradigmatic mode of divine presence is liturgical; that is, God chooses to be present to his people through the social institution of worship. Correspondingly, one experiences the presence in the act of worship, as many of the psalms attest:

> Thou hast said, "Seek ye my face."
> My heart says to thee,
> "Thy face, LORD, do I seek."
> Hide not thy face from me.
> Psalm 27:8–9, RSV

The faithful person baffled by the problem of undeserved suffering and triumphant evil in the world sees it in a different light after entering the sanctuary and experiencing in some degree the divine presence:

> Nevertheless I am continually with thee;
> thou dost hold my right hand.
> Psalm 73:23, RSV

At times, we hear in the psalms an intense, almost mystical longing for this experience (read, e.g., Ps. 42:1–2; 63:1; 84:1–2). But there is also, equally intense, the experience of divine absence, expressed in the metaphors of concealment (Ps. 10:1; 89:46), hiding the face (Ps. 10:11; 13:1), and silence (Ps. 22:1–2; 83:1). We can hardly doubt that this is the more common experience today.

60

The Pot and the Meat (11:1–13)

The first of the two expansions of the temple vision also deals with the situation immediately preceding the fall of Jerusalem, though there are indications that it was written up after the disaster had happened. It shares the dramatic character of the vision, beginning with a gathering of royal counselors near the temple entrance and ending with the sudden death of one of them and the agonizing cry of the prophet. This narrative context brackets a type of prophetic saying common in Ezekiel, one in which the words of the "opposition" are quoted verbatim and then refuted (see also 8:12; 9:9; 12:22, 27; 18:2, 19, 25, 29). The scene is a special session or caucus of royal advisers or cabinet ministers, among whom the prophet recognized two high officials. The historical context is the political life of the capital during the reign of its last king, Zedekiah (598–586 B.C.). The situation can be reconstructed from the biblical sources, principally II Kings 24–25 and Jeremiah (chs. 21; 24:8–10; 27— 29; 32; 34; 37—39; 52). Zedekiah, a weak individual, was torn between the faction that advocated submission to the Babylonians and the war party, which looked to Egypt for support. In spite of his own misgivings, and the pleadings of Jeremiah, he was persuaded by the warmongers to rebel, the anticipated assistance from Egypt was not forthcoming, and the city was taken and burned.

The policy advocated by the twenty-five is couched in parabolic and enigmatic terms. Some commentators have taken the first part of the quotation as a question: "Is not the time at hand to build houses?" which would imply confidence in a settled and peaceful future. The following statement, "This [city] is the pot and we are the meat," would then have a positive sense, as if to say that the city will protect us as a pot protects what is inside it. But once stated, it will be seen that the metaphor is quite inappropriate. Things are put in a pot to be cooked, not to be protected, as in the more extended use of the metaphor in 24:1–14. It is therefore much more likely that the paired statements allude to jeopardy and crisis: this is no time to build houses; we are shut up in the city and are lost unless we do something soon. As to what they proposed to do, what their plotting was about, we can only speculate. In the historical context as described above, the most likely suggestion would be alliance with Egypt which had not yet abandoned the struggle for supremacy in Palestine and Syria. Like Jeremiah, and indeed all his prophetic predecessors, Ezekiel was not prepared to leave politics to the politicians. His ministry was not confined to "the care of souls," the spiritual needs of the individual. It was also, and essentially, concerned with the commonwealth, the

61

political community. In this as in other instances, therefore, we find the prophets striving to make their vision prevail in the larger society, the political community, which necessarily involved embracing particular solutions to social and political problems. It was a dangerous business, but an inevitable consequence of the public and social character of the prophetic function.

In this instance the prophetic response has been elaborated and expanded after the event, as can be seen in the many repetitions. What does emerge clearly is a reinterpretation of the saying about the pot and the meat in the light of what actually happened after the city was taken. Now the meat is identified with the victims of internal strife, principally the opponents of the war party. The plotters and those of their faction will, however, be taken out of the city, judgment will be passed on them, and they will be executed on the border of Israel, which is to say at the army headquarters at Riblah on the Orontes (see commentary on 6:14). This is what actually happened (see II Kings 25:18–21), and as a premonitory sign of the future, Ezekiel records the sudden death of one of the twenty-five before the prophecy had come to an end.

Vindication of the Deported and End of the Vision (11:14–25)

We have seen that this saying was also originally quite independent of the temple vision. It has its own introduction, one of the most frequently encountered in the book ("The word of Yahweh came to me") and it is quite out of character with the message of the vision as a whole. Why, then, was it included? It may have been seen to provide an answer to the question put by Ezekiel in the previous verse—whether this was really the end, whether there was to be any future at all. This would hardly be surprising, since much of the preexilic doom prophecy was later recast to convey a message of salvation through judgment. It may also have been suggested by the movement of the divine effulgence from the inner sanctuary, understood as the first stage in its own exile. The essential part of Ezekiel's answer derives, in fact, from the assurance of divine presence with the deportees provided by the vision of the chariot throne.

62

The form in which the present passage is cast is that of a dispute saying, of frequent occurrence in Ezekiel (see also 12:11–25, 26–28; 18:1–29; 33:23–29) and occasionally in later prophetic books, conspicuously in Malachi. The layout is quite simple: an accusation, charge, or allegation is quoted verbatim and the refutation follows, generally in the form of an oracular saying. The allegation advanced by those who remained in Judah is that the deportees have, in effect, been expelled from the cult community (on account of sin, understood), and that they have therefore forfeited title to real estate. To understand the force of this allegation we must recall the intimate association between deity, cult, and land in antiquity. Deities had their own jurisdictions coterminous with the territory of their devotees. When David had to flee for his life to Philistine territory, he cursed those who had driven him out "to serve other gods" (I Sam. 26:19). When the Syrian general Naaman, obliged to return to Damascus after being cured by Elisha, wished to worship Yahweh there, he took with him a cartload of Israelite earth on which to build a shrine (II Kings 5:17–19). These old ideas of territoriality died hard; and we may be sure that the deportees really meant it when they asked how it was possible to sing the hymns of Yahweh in a foreign land (Ps. 137:4). So we have here what is, in effect, a theological explanation of exile from the side of the nonexiled, an explanation that had the additional advantage of justifying the expropriation of the property abandoned by the deportees.

Ezekiel's refutation of these rationalizations contains the obscure statement that Yahweh has been for the expatriates "a sanctuary for a little while" or perhaps "a sanctuary in some degree," depending on how one understands the Hebrew phrase *miqdash me'at*. The Aramaic targum paraphrases: "Therefore I have given them synagogues second only to my holy temple, because they are few in number." In other words, it reflects a tradition that the origin of the synagogue is to be sought in Babylon during the exile and the belief that this institution permitted the continuance of a full religious life even in the absence of the temple. This corresponds to the situation after the second destruction of the temple in A.D. 70 when, as many rabbinic statements attest, Torah study, prayer, and acts of charity took the place of animal sacrifice. We may add that the same idea lies behind the use of cultic terminology in the New Testament to describe the Christian life in its different aspects. The targum may well point us in the right direction, but in view of the promise of return to the land which follows, the reply probably implies a *temporary* substitute for temple

63

fellowship. Yahweh is himself present among the deportees, proof of which is his appearance there; hence it is possible to continue worshiping even though the sacrificial liturgy of the temple is in temporary abeyance. Paradoxically, it was the priestly tradition inherited by Ezekiel, a tradition firmly attached to the idea of a sacred center, which broke decisively with the old idea of territoriality. We saw at an earlier point that this tradition broke with its predecessors in locating the revelation to Moses in Egypt (Exod. 6:28). While we can hardly exaggerate the importance of this breakthrough, the tension between territorial particularity and universalism continued long after the time of Ezekiel. We see it, for example, in the story of Jonah, who flees from the presence of Yahweh (Jonah 1:3, 10), indeed is cast out from his presence (Jonah 2:4), yet encounters him on the high seas and in the heathen city of Nineveh.

The vision account ends with a broad perspective of hope for the future (vs. 17–21). Very likely, this was a deliberate editorial move which draws on the word of assurance in 36:24–28 and gives the temple vision the same shape as the book in general: judgment on Israel, judgment on the nations (here, those left behind in Judah), salvation for Israel. Return to the land will be made possible by an inner transformation—a new heart and spirit—by virtue of an unanticipated and unmerited act of grace. (See further 36:24–28.) The vision narrative is then rounded off by doubling back to, and repeating, the earlier allusion to the throne propelled by the cherubim and the wheels (10:19). The divine effulgence, which was stationed at the east gate of the temple, now moved over the Kidron ravine to the Mount of Olives. This is the last we hear of its movement until its return to the city as reported in another temple vision dated nineteen years later (43:1–5). For the doomed land and city, the intervening period is marked by the absence of God.

Ezekiel 12—14
True and False Prophecy

Though this section appears to deal with a wide variety of subjects, they are all related in one way or another to the defense of Ezekiel's prophetic credentials against current misunderstandings and misrepresentations. Following his older contemporary Jeremiah (see especially Jer. 14:1—15:4 and 23:9–40), Ezekiel exposes the failure of professional prophecy to meet the crisis of the age, to provide guidance and leadership at a time of political and religious disorientation. In this kind of situation, which has a tendency to recur, it is fatally easy to speak peace where there is no peace, to tell people what they want to hear, to play on the hopes and fears generated by insecurity. It will also be well to bear in mind that the kinds of prophecy under attack were the culturally and religiously sanctioned forms of mediation and that the assault on them came from one who stood outside the consensus. As we read on, we can hardly avoid raising questions about our own culturally and religiously sanctioned forms of ministry, in what sense they can be said to be prophetic at all, and to what extent they satisfy the criteria for authenticity enunciated by men like Jeremiah and Ezekiel.

A Refugee's Baggage (12:1-16)

The connection with the temple vision suggests that Ezekiel barely had time to recover from it before being commanded to resume the mime acting already described (in chs. 4 and 5). The two scenes that follow (vs. 1–16 and 17–20) certainly belong to the same category of word signs. They are undated, but there can be little doubt that they were written down before the fall of the city and expanded afterward, as is particularly clear in the allusion to the terrible fate of Zedekiah, the last of the Judean kings to occupy the throne. In much the same way, sayings of Jesus came to be written up to reflect events that took place years after his death, such as the fall of Jerusalem.

Ezekiel is told to bundle up his belongings, leave them outside his house as if preparing to depart, and then dig his way through the adobe wall of the house—an odd feature the meaning of which remains to be clarified. All of this is meant as a kind of sign language for the house of Israel no longer receptive to ordinary speech. The dominant motif is *looking and not seeing*. Seven times he is told to do these things "in their sight," so that perhaps they will see and get the point. The idea of people who have eyes in their heads but cannot see is a familiar theme of prophetic preaching:

65

> Hear and hear, but do not understand;
> see and see, but do not perceive.
>
> Isaiah 6:9, RSV

> A foolish and senseless people.
> They have eyes but do not see, ears but do not hear.
>
> Jeremiah 5:21

> Bring forth the people who, having eyes, are blind,
> Who, having ears, are deaf.
>
> Isaiah 43:8

It is taken up by Jesus, who taught in parables "so that they may indeed see but not perceive, and may indeed hear but not understand; lest they should turn again, and be forgiven" (Mark 4:12, RSV). In reality, of course, both parables and sign acts, which are parables acted out, are intended to create awareness, to coax or shock the audience out of its self-induced anesthesia to see what is really there. This is what Ezekiel set out, once again, to do.

The pattern of this kind of saying, which occurs frequently in the book, includes command (vs. 1–6), execution (v. 7), and explanation (vs. 8–16). As suggested a moment ago, this last has been expanded to refer explicitly to the fate of Zedekiah as described in II Kings 25:4–7 (see also Jer. 39:4–7 and 52:7–11). When it became apparent that the situation in Jerusalem was hopeless, a breach was made in the wall and Zedekiah and a military escort left under cover of darkness on the south side but were overtaken by the Babylonians in the vicinity of Jericho. Brought before Nebuchadnezzar at Riblah (cf. 6:14; 11:10), Zedekiah's sons were slaughtered in his presence and Zedekiah himself was blinded and led off in shackles to Babylon. Ezekiel himself is therefore a sign in the first place for the house of Israel, then more specifically for its ruler, in his own person and by virtue of his own suffering identification with their imminent fate. Here too, however, there is a glimmer of hope. Some few will survive, like the remnant hidden in the fold of the prophet's robe (cf. 5:3; 6:8–10).

Fear and Trembling (12:17–20)

The second symbolic act has a similar format, though the execution of the command is not explicitly noted. It parallels rather closely the eating of siege rations (4:9–17), but its location at this point suggests allusion to conditions in Judah after

66

the destruction of Jerusalem and subsequent deportations. In this respect, it anticipates the final scene in this section (14:12–23). Ezekiel is told to simulate the condition of the half-starved population left in the devastated land. Uncontrollable trembling is a well-attested concomitant of intense religious experience; one thinks of the Quakers, the New England Shakers, and the ultra-orthodox Haredim (Tremblers). It also frequently accompanies the onset of ecstasy in the experience of prophets like Habakkuk (Hab. 3:16), Jeremiah (Jer. 4:19), and no doubt Ezekiel himself. In this instance, typically, the trembling arises not from self-absorption but from intense identification with the suffering of the prophet's fellow Judeans who were to be overwhelmed by the disaster which could no longer be averted.

Popular Reaction to Ezekiel's Prophesying (12:21–28)

There follow two more or less parallel passages (vs. 21–25 and 26–28) that illustrate different facets of the crisis through which prophecy was passing at that time. The quotation-rejoinder format in which they are cast is a special feature of Ezekiel's preaching of which we have seen several examples (8:12; 9:9; 11:3–12, 15–16). It no doubt arose out of a real situation of confrontation between the prophet and his audience. As a rhetorical device, it marks an interesting development in prophetic discourse, preparing the way for the fully evolved kind of disputation that we find in Malachi about two centuries later. These two examples also serve as a reminder that prediction is an important aspect of prophetic activity—one that is often underestimated in modern scholarship but certainly not by Ezekiel's contemporaries.

The first passage cites a saying that was going the rounds, to the effect that time passes and predictions of doom remain unfulfilled. Obviously this comes from a time prior to the Babylonian invasion and siege of Jerusalem. With unfulfilled prophecy there was always the danger of passing from the failure of predictive prophecy to the failure of the God in whose name the prophet spoke. By providing this means of mediation and communication, and then failing to validate the credentials of the chosen mediator, he has left the way open to doubts about the possibility of any reliable knowledge of his character and intentions. The crisis of confidence in prophecy tended, therefore, to generate a deeper malaise about the reality and inten-

67

tions of the God of traditional religion. We hear it often in Jeremiah and Ezekiel: God will do nothing (Jer. 5:12), perhaps he does not see what is going on (Ezek. 8:12; 9:9), perhaps he is absent.

It has just been noted that these exchanges between the prophet and his public convey the assumption that prophecy is in the first place predictive and that this conclusion goes against the grain of critical scholarship on prophecy in the modern period. Perhaps we should reaffirm the predictive element as the starting point for understanding Israelite prophecy, with the proviso that the difficulty between prophet and public lay in the latter's failure to grasp the connection between present attitudes and conduct and the course of future events. It is the insistence on this connection, very clearly formulated in Ezekiel, which distinguishes this kind of prophecy from divination and soothsaying. This latter kind, incidentally, has lost little of its popularity for our contemporaries today.

The reaction to Ezekiel's prophecy was then, in effect, a shrug of the shoulders: life goes on in disregard of your rantings; or, if there is anything more to it, it deals with the distant future and is therefore no concern of ours. The rejoinder is a simple reaffirmation: the time draws near and every vision will come to fulfillment (emended text); there will be no more empty visions and self-deceptive (literally, "slippery") divination. In both exchanges we hear a distant echo of the words from the burning bush (Exod. 3:14): I will be what I will be; I will speak what I will speak. An affirmation, therefore, of the reality of God and his freedom of action over against what are, after all, quite plausible alternative explanations.

Empty Words, Empty Visions (13:1–9)

The rejoinder to popular misconceptions of his activity leads Ezekiel to an assault on current deformations of the prophetic role in which he takes over, expands, and intensifies Jeremiah's critique of contemporary prophets (Jer. 14:1—15:4; 23:9–40). Both should therefore be read together. Ezekiel's diatribe is more closely structured than might appear at first sight. The traditional pattern of indictment followed by verdict is repeated for both male (13:1–9, 10–16) and female prophets (13:17–21, 22–23), and each of these sections is marked by the characteristic finale "You shall know that I am Yahweh" (vs. 9, 14, 21, 23). The following chapter, which deals with disingenu-

68

ous consultation of prophets and the impossibility of intercession, also borrows from Jeremiah, as we shall see. The novel element here is the singling out of female prophets engaged in divination and witchcraft, which suggests that traditionally Israelite forms of prophetic activity were losing out to contemporary Babylonian practices.

It will be obvious that many of the charges that Jeremiah and Ezekiel leveled against contemporary prophets are incapable of verification: that the prophets have not been commissioned by God to speak; that God does not stand behind their words even though they mouth the time-honored formulae; that their dreams, visions, and revelations are empty and meaningless; and that they are engaged in a self-serving and accommodating collusion with their public to tell them what they want to hear. The charge of immorality, a routine way of discrediting the opposition (see Jer. 23:11, 14), is not repeated by Ezekiel, but that may be due to an oversight. It will be obvious in all of this that we are hearing only one side of the case. This is, in a real sense, the weakness of prophecy: that, in the last resort, it depends on the ability of the prophet's public to discern in the absence of objective criteria. The final appeal is therefore to a certain self-authenticating quality which distinguishes the genuine from the fake:

> What has straw in common with wheat? Is not my word like fire, and like a hammer that breaks the rocks in pieces?
> Jeremiah 23:28–29

One charge that really sticks and can most readily be substantiated is that of social irresponsibility in a time of crisis. The basic metaphor, carried over into the following section, is that of building and manning a wall capable of defending the community when the time of testing comes. In this one vital respect the socially sanctioned forms of prophecy prove to be inadequate. There are, to be sure, times when morale needs to be reinforced and optimism encouraged. But there are also times when people need to be told unpalatable truths about themselves and the state of their society to which they themselves have contributed, at least by self-serving inaction and acquiescence. Experience shows that the prophet who is committed to the status quo, who is part of the political or religious establishment and dependent on it for his livelihood, cannot easily discharge this task.

69

INTERPRETATION

The Whitewashed Wall (13:10–16)

The image is that of a shoddily built wall daubed with white-wash (crushed limestone mixed with water) to give it an appearance of solidity. The biblical terminology of "daubing" and "whitewashing" implies the creation of an illusory and specious appearance of truth designed to conceal a fundamental inauthenticity. In this sense, for example, Job's "friends" are described as "daubers of falsehood" (Job 13:4). In this instance, the prophet-dauber not only acquiesces but actively cooperates in a collective exercise in self-deception. The situation is familiar. We know that appearance is not reality, but we hope that if enough people accept the appearance, it will somehow become reality; and, indeed, it does become reality for us. Unfortunately for us, however, reality does not always cooperate; there are circumstances beyond our control. The storm clouds are already gathering, the deluge strikes, and the wall is washed away, together with its veneer of plaster. The prophetic specialist in self-deception is revealed for what he is.

Witchcraft, Sorcery, and the Occult (13:17–23)

Recourse to the occult is particularly likely to happen in times of crisis, for example, in Germany after World War I. It probably happened more often in the history of Israel than appears from the record. We may be sure that Saul's visit to the witch of Endor (I Sam. 28) was not an isolated occurrence. In the ancient Near East, prophecy appears to have been an equal opportunity profession. Prophets of both sexes are attested in the kingdom of Mari in northern Mesopotamia and in Assyria, and several are known by name in Israel: Miriam (Exod. 15:20), Deborah (Judg. 4:4), Huldah (II Kings 22:14), Noadiah (Neh. 6:14), and Anna (Luke 2:36). Women also functioned as prophets in early Christian communities (e.g., Acts 21:9), as they did in other ministries, a situation that unfortunately was not maintained as Christianity developed into a male-dominated religion. The women condemned here were not really prophets but witches masquerading as prophets. We know too little about this shadowy underworld of Israelite popular religion to understand precisely what they were up to. Tying bands around wrists and covering the head of the client with a shawl were no doubt magical actions accompanied by spells that were believed to have either beneficial or maleficent consequences,

70

depending on the situation. Binding and loosing are part of the vocabulary of magic and exorcism which, given the disposition to believe in their efficacy, may well have produced the effects predicted by the sorceress. Such recourse is condemned in the laws (e.g., Deut. 18:10–14), as it is here, because it perverts the genuine means of revelation which God has provided for Israel through prophetic intermediaries.

Consulting the Prophet (14:1–11)

Here and elsewhere in the book (8:1; 20:1) we find the elders of the diaspora communities gathering in Ezekiel's house, which may have served as a kind of embryonic synagogue. We are not told the purpose of the consultation. They may have inquired about the length of their exile and the time of deliverance. If the passage that follows (14:12–23) is thematically linked, there may have been a request to intercede with God for the land of Judah threatened with destruction. In view of the denunciation of idolatry which follows, some scholars have even wondered whether the elders may have been seeking Ezekiel's support for setting up a separate sanctuary in exile, one that would have accommodated local cults in addition to that of Yahweh (see further the comment on Ezek. 20). What is at issue, in any case, is not so much the subject of the inquiry as the conditions under which any prophetic communication can take place. While there is no suggestion that the approach of the elders was disingenuous, it was vitiated by their covert attachment to idolatrous, that is, non-Yahwistic, cults—a kind of religious hedging of bets that must have been fairly common in the post-catastrophe years (compare the situation in the early years of the Egyptian diaspora, Jer. 44). We are reminded of the severe injunctions against covert idolatry in Deuteronomy 13, a passage that also deals with prophetic intermediaries. In reacting to their inquiries, Ezekiel manifests the essential prophetic quality of spiritual discernment. He sees through to their divided loyalty and addresses not the inquiry itself but the religious attitude that underlies it.

In keeping with prophetic usage, the verdict opens with the customary "Thus says the Lord Yahweh" (v. 6) and, following a pattern frequently found in Ezekiel, ends with "You shall know that I am Yahweh" (v. 8). It is rounded out with an additional verdict on the prophet who compromises his mission by cooperating in this kind of transaction (v. 9–11). A peculiar

71

feature of this verdict is the format of sacred law in which it is couched and which reminds us that Ezekiel is priest as well as prophet. The casuistic formulation ("If a person does X, then Y follows"), the terminology of excommunication (v. 8–9), and the phrase "to bear one's guilt," that is, to bring guilt upon oneself, of frequent occurrence in ritual legislation (e.g., Lev. 20:20; 24:15; Num. 5:31), all point unmistakably in this direction. Correspondingly, the scope of the judgment is broadened to take in the entire house of Israel inclusive of resident aliens and of prophets whose responsibility to the community is thereby emphasized. We note that to be cut off from the community is a kind of death, an exclusion from that space in which alone it is possible to experience the divine presence. Even here, however, judgment is not the last word; otherwise stated, judgment is a function of the divine will to save and confer life. For the verdict is preceded by an invitation to repentance or, to use the more literal and telling rendering of Martin Buber, that "turning" which implies a basic reorientation of one's life and reordering of one's priorities. The passage then concludes with the prospect that, against all the odds heaped up by obduracy and self-deception, the covenant relationship will again become a reality.

Noah, Daniel, and Job (14:12–23)

One of the functions of the prophet is intercessory prayer. Moses, the protoprophet, interceded for the Israel of the wilderness years (Exod. 32:11–14; Num. 14:13–19; Deut. 9:25–29). Amos interceded for the Northern Kingdom during the last years of its history, until the point was reached beyond which prayer no longer availed (Amos 7:1–9). In the last period of the Kingdom of Judah a similar point was reached when Jeremiah was forbidden to intercede (Jer. 14:11–12). At that point not even the presence of Moses and Samuel, the great models of intercessory prayer, could make a difference (Jer. 15:1). But prayer is only one aspect of a life ordered to God and based on the quality known in Hebrew as ṣedaqah, a term only imperfectly captured in the usual translation word "righteousness." Whether the righteous can influence the fate of an evil city or country, not by their actions but by virtue of their ṣedaqah, is the question at issue in Abraham's conversation with God over the fate of Sodom and Gomorrah, a remarkable passage that may have been written up to reflect the situation at the time

72

of the destruction of Jerusalem (Gen. 18:22–33). This passage should be read in conjunction with the text of Ezekiel under discussion. We will note, however, that the solution to the problem is different. For, unlike Ezekiel, the Genesis passage implies that the possibility exists, though in the case of Sodom, failure to reach a minimum or critical mass doomed the attempt to failure.

The same issue, incidentally, underlies the rabbinic tradition about the thirty-six righteous, the *lamed vavniks*, whose presence, unknown to themselves, preserves the world from destruction and dissolution. The same theme, in a somewhat different form, is the basis of André Schwarz-Bart's well-known novel *The Last of the Just.*

Using the casuistic form noted earlier, Ezekiel takes the case of a sinful land (Judah, e.g.) which is afflicted successively by famine, wild animals, military invasion, and epidemic. Unlike Jeremiah, who uses figures from Israel's early history, namely, Moses and Samuel, Ezekiel takes his paradigms of righteousness from ancient myth and legend. (It will be evident as we proceed how wide his acquaintance is with the literature of Semitic antiquity.) From biblical tradition we learn that Noah was "a righteous man, blameless in his generation" (Gen. 6:9, RSV). But the biblical Noah is borrowed from ancient Mesopotamian myth and folklore. He is the same wise and righteous hero as the Utnapishtim who tells the story of the flood on the eleventh tablet of the Gilgamesh epic or the Atrahasis of the poem, only imperfectly preserved, which is known by that name. Daniel is known from the Late Bronze Age poems discovered at Ugarit on the Syrian coast as a wise and good Phoenician king. He has no connection with the Daniel of the biblical book of that name but is mentioned again by Ezekiel in a poem about the prince of Tyre (Ezek. 28:3). Job, described in the biblical book as blameless and upright, is also a legendary figure, perhaps of Edomite origin. It is interesting to note how, by taking models of great antiquity from outside and before the appearance of Israel, Ezekiel, in contrast to Jeremiah, universalizes the situation he is addressing.

His solution to the problem, which is basically a problem of theodicy posed by the disasters listed in his case history, is consistent with his teaching on personal accountability which will be set out schematically in chapter 18. No one, not even those closely related by family ties (one thinks of the sons and

73

daughters of Job), can depend for salvation on the virtue or merit of another. There is no salvation by proxy. Having said this, however, we recall what was said earlier about the prophet's suffering identification with his people, his "bearing their punishment" in performing the sign acts, which brings with it a reminiscence of the Servant who "bore the sins of many" (Ezek. 4:4; Isa. 53:12). There is tension rather than contradiction here, one that carries over into Christian theology and generates its own energy. The situation addressed by Ezekiel called for emphasis on personal accountability and the acceptance of responsibility, and this is the main point of the case history presented here.

The concluding section (vs. 21–23) applies the case history, not quite consistently, to the actual disasters attendant on the Babylonian occupation of Judah. While the situation is not entirely clear, this is probably one of several instances in chapters 1—23 of postbellum comment on sayings that circulated before 586 B.C. As the final statement makes clear, the purpose is to exonerate Yahweh of responsibility for the massive disasters that had overtaken his people. As the new deportees begin to arrive among those already settled in the diaspora, the latter will begin to understand why it happened as it did, and this understanding will help to assuage their grief and bewilderment.

Ezekiel 15—19
Images of Israel

The long section, chapters 15—23, shows little evidence of careful structuring, and we should resist the temptation to impose on it a structure of our own devising. The dominant note of censure and condemnation continues throughout, though there are occasional words of consolation, some but not necessarily all of which have been added after the fall of Jerusalem. The most obvious reason for bringing together such relatively heterogeneous material may be simply chronological: they are all dated between the sixth and the ninth year of Jehoiachin, that is, between 592 and 589 B.C. (see 8:1; 24:1). Some sayings have been grouped together on the catchword principle—the sword sayings in chapter 21, for example. There is no obvious uniformity of genre. Ezekiel was known to his contemporaries as a composer of parabolic or allegorical utterances *(meshalim)* and songs (see the remarks quoted at 20:49 and 33:32). In agreement with this is the designation of the eagle narrative as an allegory and a riddle *(mashal, ḥidah,* 17:2) and the poem about the lioness and her cubs as a lament *(qinah,* 19:1, 14). There are correspondences within this collection—the vine image occurs at the beginning and at 19:10–14, and the story of the nymphomaniac bride in chapter 16 is taken further in that of the two sisters in chapter 23–but they do not seem to add up to a well thought out structure. With few exceptions the language is figurative, taking up in succession a series of clearly etched images: the vine, the dissolute woman, the eagle, the lioness and her cubs, the forest fire, and the sword. Even in the theoretical and scholastic treatment of individual responsibility in chapter 18, the use of the case history maintains the impression of concrete narrativity. The historical review of Israel's history in chapter 20, in more or less the central position, draws together these different cameos in one comprehensive statement that is of basic importance for understanding the theology of the prophet and his book.

The Useless Vine (15:1–8)

The figurative chain begins with the seminal image of the vine, associated with Judah in ancient oracular poetry (the oracle of Judah in Gen. 49:11–12) and carried over into the stock of prophetic imagery by Isaiah (Isa. 5:1–7) and Jeremiah (Jer. 2:21). In so much of the poetry of the Mediterranean world, as well as in the New Testament (see especially John 15:1–5), the vine is the symbol of plenitude of life and organic growth. Here, though, it is dead, and the only question is whether the wood can be put to any use. The section follows the now familiar pattern of statement (vs. 1–5) followed by explanation or application (vs. 6–8). The former, couched in rhythmic prose, is in the form of a series of rhetorical questions. Once the plant is dead (its natural life is about forty years), the wood cannot be used to make even the simplest artifact, such as a peg on which to hang a kitchen utensil. All it is good for is burning. The application that follows was hardly necessary. Israel, a strong, healthy stock brought from Egypt (Ps. 80:8–13) and planted in a vineyard on a fertile hill (Isa. 5:1–7), is now no more than dead

75

wood. All that remains is for it to be burned as fuel. There we have a history of Israel from the beginnings to the destruction of Jerusalem presented in the most succinct form possible, and it is a history of radical failure. This history will be spelled out in different ways, and under different images, in the chapters that follow.

The Nymphomaniac Bride (16:1–63)

The need to relate present disaster to a sinful past led Ezekiel to a radical rewriting of Israel's history, most clearly stated in the survey of chapter 20. Accompanying and filling out this more explicitly theological interpretation are several essays in figurative narrative, some restricted to the last few decades of Judah's existence (chs. 17 and 19), others going back to the beginning of the monarchy or even earlier (chs. 16 and 23). The use of familial imagery to express the God-people relationship was certainly not restricted to Israel. The gods were often represented as parents in Mesopotamia, for example. It seems to have entered the tradition of prophetic discourse with Hosea's metaphor of the divine marriage with the land of Israel and the birth of three children (Hos. 1:2–9). There is already a rudimentary historical dimension here, for the names suggest a progressive alienation from the parent-god, ending with the annulment of the relationship: "You are not my people, and I am not your I AM" (Hos. 1:9, referring back to the revelation in the burning bush, Exod. 3:14). The father-son relationship became, not unexpectedly, the dominant metaphor in Judaism and Christianity. But in view of the contractual nature of marriage, the spousal relationship lent itself to expressing the centrality, permanence, and emotive content of the covenant bond between God and people. Under whatever form it appears, familial relationship is deeply embedded in the tradition and provides an inexhaustible source of theological reflection.

Whereas the history of a faithless partner and broken marriage is only touched on lightly in Hosea, it is spelled out in crude, almost pornographic detail by Ezekiel, so much so that the modern versions have felt it necessary at some points to fall back on paraphrase and circumlocution. One of the early rabbis, Eliezer disciple of Johanan ben Zakkai, forbade its liturgical use, and though, notwithstanding, it was retained in the lectionary, it was stipulated that it must always be followed by its targum (*m. Megillah* 4.10). This targum substantially rewrites

76

the passage, reducing the sexual element to an absolute minimum, beginning the story with Abraham and the "covenant of the pieces" (Gen. 22) and introducing Sarah as the Hittite mother alluded to in v. 45. Later commentary—for example, that of Rashi—interpreted it in allegorical terms, as we would expect.

It has been suggested that the story of the foundling who is rescued from death, eventually weds her rescuer, and comes to queenly estate has drawn on a romantic folktale with a distinctly erotic component. The suggestion is plausible, if unprovable, but the narrative as it stands is satire, the savage kind which we associate with moralists like Dean Jonathan Swift; hence the element of unrelenting hyperbole and caricature that prevails. In this respect it moves far beyond other parabolic narratives in the Hebrew Bible that have the purpose of involving the hearer and compelling a reaction, stories such as the one told by Nathan to David to bring home to him the consciousness of guilt (II Sam. 12:1-6).

Ezekiel, then, is told to make known—we should say rather, bring home—to Jerusalem her vileness and to do so by telling her the story of her life (vs. 1-5). Unflattering allusion to ancestors is a regular feature of vituperative satire. Take, for example, the story of Lot and his daughters which is, in effect, a political satire or spoof directed against Moabites and Ammonites (Gen. 19:30-38). The allusion here is to the ethnic origins of Jerusalem, in the period before David made it his capital. The pre-Israelite Jebusites were probably in part at least of Hurrian ("Hittite") extraction; the city ruler who appears in the Amarna letters from the early fourteenth century has a name formed with that of the Hurrian goddess Hepat. "Amorite" is a more generic term for the early inhabitants of the land. The implications are not meant to be complimentary. Exposure of unwanted children, especially female children, was the alternative to birth control or abortion in several ancient societies. The obstetric procedures alluded to—such as the severing of the umbilical cord from the placenta, washing, rubbing with salt to promote circulation, and wrapping tightly in swaddling clothes—are all well attested down to modern times.

Yahweh's first "passing by" and his decision to save the child wriggling in its birth blood by the roadside (vs. 6-14) corresponds to the time of the ancestors. A remote parallel might be the story of the endangered ancestress (Gen. 12:10-20

77

and parallels) or the Aramean ancestor doomed to perish memorialized in Israelite worship (Deut. 26:5). The narrative then passes at once to puberty: physical growth, sexual development, periods; but unaccountably the girl is still stark naked. This, then, was the stage reached when Yahweh passed by a second time. The "time of love," when he decided to marry the wild girl, alludes to covenant making, probably the covenant with the ancestors (Gen. 17), though we should not look for exact correspondences in this kind of symbolic narrative. Spreading the hem (literally, "wing") of the garment over the girl signified a commitment to marry her (cf. Ruth 3:9). The solicitude of the claimant is described in painful and embarrassing detail, the unrelenting attention to often disgusting physical detail being a mark of this Swiftian kind of satire. Eventually the bride-to-be is clothed and adorned in splendid array. The queenly estate to which she attained may allude to the time of the monarchy, but more likely it simply reflects the common description of the bride as queen, in which respect the lovesick girl in the Song of Songs may serve as a parallel (see especially Cant. 1:9–11; 7:1).

The turning point, the *peripateia,* of the narrative occurs, as often, at the apogee of success. Ezekiel does not pause to reflect on this mysterious turning to evil, except to note that it grows out of the young woman's confidence in her beauty and fame and forgetfulness that everything is the result of an unsolicited and unanticipated benefaction. The catalog of evil includes the construction of "high places," the setting up of ithyphallic images and ritual prostitution—all well-attested features of Israelite popular religion. Marked out for special reprobation is the obscenity of child sacrifice to Molek, a ritual borrowed from the Phoenicians and practiced at least sporadically during the time of the monarchy (e.g., II Kings 16:3; 21:6; 23:10). Ezekiel spares his readers no detail in cataloging the woman's nymphomaniac excesses in consorting with foreigners. In all of this, he concludes, she is worse than the prostitute who, more often than not, is driven to it by economic privation. The historical allusion is, of course, to foreign alliances, opposition to which is a constant feature of prophetic diatribe on account of the introduction of foreign cults which more often than not they brought with them.

78

The indictment, one of the longest in the prophetic literature, is followed by the verdict (vs. 35–43) threatening the prescribed punishment for an adulterous and murderous wife, including exposure (cf. Hos. 2:10; Isa. 3:17) and stoning (Gen. 38:24; Deut. 22:21–24). The violence of the language is so deliberately offensive that we can well understand why it would be considered unsuitable for liturgical reading. We shall have to make of it what we may, but it may at least serve as a reminder that the kind of pain and anger from which the language springs is, more often than we care to think, integral to the act of loving.

The sudden focusing of attention on the hitherto unnamed mother and equally sudden appearance of two other daughters (vs. 44–52), not to mention granddaughters, is generally explained as a later addition. If it is a later addition (which is not particularly important), it follows as a fairly natural narrative development. The point is, quite simply, that the conduct of Jerusalem was so execrable that she made both Samaria and Sodom, notorious for immorality, look good by comparison. The hyperbole is understandable as a requirement of the literary genre. It is interesting to observe that Sodom is castigated not for sexual deviance but for arrogance induced by affluence, resulting in indifference to the needs of the poor and disadvantaged—a point that has lost none of its relevance in our contemporary society. The same indictment is leveled against Sodom in the Jewish exegetical tradition on Genesis 18–19, beginning with the targums. According to one midrash, the people of Sodom even covered the trees to prevent the birds from eating the berries.

The concluding promise of restoration (vs. 53–63) was added after the catastrophe. Jerusalem has already become an object of reproach for her neighbors (vs. 57–58; cf. 5:14–15), there is a hint of return from exile in the opening promise of the rehabilitation of the three sisters, and the language about God remembering his covenant, the indefectible covenant made with the ancestors, is elsewhere associated with the exilic situation (Exod. 6:5; Lev. 26:42).

Ezekiel would have agreed with Jeremiah that "the heart is deceitful above all things, and desperately corrupt" (Jer. 17:9, RSV). If anything, Ezekiel describes the corruption of the human will in even darker colors than his older contemporary. The story of the nymphomaniac bride expresses this conviction in violent language, at the risk of sickening the reader, in order to set over against it the saving will of God and the possibility of renewal.

79

The Great Eagles (17:1–24)

The dramatic depiction of the two eagles is presented as a riddle and a parable. The purpose of these literary forms was to tease the mind into activity and open up fresh perspectives on reality. In this case, the symbolization of history is limited to the immediate past, from the first deportation in 598 B.C. to the time of writing (or speaking) shortly before the fall of Jerusalem. As occasionally is the case with the parables of Jesus, an explanation is added (vs. 11–21) and the saying is rounded out—as in the preceding narrative—with a word of hope and promise, probably added after the predicted disasters had taken place (vs. 22–24).

Ezekiel's use of zoomorphic imagery anticipates a common feature of apocalyptic writing in the Greco-Roman period as, for example, in Enoch and Daniel. The eagle, lord of the sky, has already made its debut in the book (1:10; 10:14). It stands for swiftness and strength (cf. II Sam. 1:23; Jer. 4:13; Hab. 1:8) but also for sinister and destructive power (Lam. 4:19; Job 9:26). The first great eagle, of wide wingspan and splendid coloring (perhaps the prophet had in mind a pictorial representation), stands for Nebuchadnezzar II, who campaigned in Judah (Lebanon) in 598 B.C. and carried away King Jehoiachin ("the top of the cedar") into exile in Babylon, the land of trade and city of merchants. From II Kings 25:27, supported by a fragmentary list of rations for deportees discovered in Babylon (the so-called Weidner Tablets), we know that Jehoiachin and his family were detained in that city for thirty-seven years. His place on the throne was taken by his uncle Mattaniah, who, as the puppet of Pharaoh Neco, was renamed Zedekiah (II Kings 24:17). He is here referred to as "the seed of the land" and as "a low spreading vine," recalling the parabolic saying of chapter 15.

The dramatic turning point of this brief symbolic narrative is the arrival of a second eagle to which the vine turns—incongruously—in the hope of bettering its condition. As the explanation makes clear, the allusion is to Zedekiah's rebellion against the Babylonian overlord (II Kings 24:20) inspired by the invasion of Palestine by Psammeticus II in 591 B.C. Negotiations between Zedekiah and Psammeticus may be referred to on one of the Lachish ostraca which tells of the visit to Egypt by a Judean general, and the situation in Jerusalem subsequent to these overtures may be reflected in Ezek. 8:7–12, where Ezekiel discovers high Judean officials engaged in worshiping theriomorphic deities, probably of the Egyptian kind. The parabolic narrative ends with a saying threatening the total failure of this misplaced diplomatic maneuver.

The historical detail provided here, including the death of Zedekiah in Babylon, suggests that this is another instance of the amplification of a predisaster saying, originating within a year or so of the Egyptian alliance, after the destruction of Jerusalem and subsequent deportations (cf. 12:10–16). We note how important it is for Ezekiel that solemn political commitments be honored. Zedekiah's rebellion was not just politically suicidal. It was an irreligious act, a violation of commitments supported by religious sanctions, for the treaty into which he entered with the Babylonian king was guaranteed by an oath in the name of Israel's God. It is therefore *my* oath, *my* treaty (v. 19). As we had occasion to note earlier, there is no question for the prophets of regarding the political sphere as the exclusive preserve of the politicians.

Moral Accountability (18:1–32)

There follows a well-constructed disputation that illustrates the rhetorical skills for which Ezekiel was well known even during his lifetime (see, e.g., 33:32). Its principal feature is the quotation of the opponent's words (vs. 2, 19, 25, 29) followed by detailed refutation. The main point is stated at the beginning and at the end—"The soul that sins shall die" (vs. 4, 20, RSV)— and is explicated by the case history of a family traced through three generations. A further stage provides a more direct answer. In it the accusation implicit in the opening proverbial saying ("The fathers have eaten sour grapes, and the children's teeth are set on edge," v. 2, RSV) is stated explicitly, again at the beginning and at the end ("The way of Yahweh is not right," vs. 25, 29). An important consequence, the possibility and necessity of moral choice, is located between these two phases of the disputation (vs. 21–24) which concludes with an appeal to choose life rather than death (vs. 30–32). The entire section should therefore be read as a well-rounded statement of a crucial aspect of Ezekiel's teaching. It has been located at this point in the book in order to forestall a theological objection arising out of the presentation of the national history as a story of moral failure leading to disaster. There seems to be no need to suppose that it has undergone any significant editing. Commenta-

81

tors tend to date it after the fall of Jerusalem. This may be the case, though the problem of divine justice and governance of the world—the problem of theodicy—would have been unavoidable during the decades preceding the disaster.

The saying that was going the rounds—it is also quoted by Jeremiah (Jer. 31:29–30)—is not concerned with the influence of heredity on moral behavior, about which Ezekiel's contemporaries were not well informed. It deals with the way justice was perceived to operate in a world believed to be under divine governance. This is unmistakably clear in the follow-up quotation, "The way of Yahweh is not right," which states clearly what the first only hints at. Ezekiel is therefore taking issue with the old adage according to which the sins of the fathers are visited on the children to the third and the fourth generation (Exod. 34:7; Num. 14:18). It is interesting to note how the meaning of this formulation is subtly but decisively altered in the Decalogue by the addition of the phrase "of those who hate me" (Exod. 20:5; Deut. 5:9). For now the implication is that, if the descendants are punished, it is not because of the family connection but because they reproduce and perpetuate *freely* the conduct of the parent. It seems that this important shift was connected with changes in the actual administration of justice in Israel. The Deuteronomic law stipulates that "the fathers shall not be put to death for the children, nor shall the children be put to death for the fathers" (Deut. 24:16, RSV), and the historian of the monarchy provides an example of the implementation of this principle of law (II Kings 14:6). While the denial of legal and moral imputability in these terms by no means voided the old idea of solidarity and coresponsibility (nor should it for us), it is interesting to note that, by the time of Deuteronomy, the principle of corporate liability was restricted in law to cases of apostasy and homicide that remained undetected (Deut. 13:12–18; 21:1–9).

The general principle—the soul (i.e., the person) that sins shall die—is illustrated by a case history the formulation of which is drawn from the traditional legal repertoire of the priests. The choice of a three-member genealogical sequence, generally the maximum number simultaneously alive and active as moral agents, was no doubt suggested by the old adage about the sins of the fathers being visited on the children to the third and the fourth generation. There is no reason to believe that it contains a cryptic reference to Judean kings (e.g., Hezekiah, Manasseh, or Josiah).

82

The list of attributes of the righteous person is given in full only for the first generation. In putting together this list, Ezekiel could have drawn on several sources. There are psalms that specify ritual and ethical qualifications for participating in public worship and that have sometimes been described as Torah liturgies (Ps. 15 and 24). These provide an important clue for understanding ethics in Israel by associating moral performance with the holiness of the God who is approached in the act of worship. The point may, incidentally, be somewhat opaque for many Christians today for whom periodic worship is a fairly routine activity with no obvious connection with the moral life. In other psalms (e.g., Ps. 50:16–21), judgment is passed on the wicked in terms similar to Ezekiel's list. Here too we note the insistence on the correlation between ethics and worship. The prophets do not hesitate to condemn the kind of religious observance that manages to coexist with active or even passive collusion with injustice. Indeed, one of the most disturbing aspects of prophetic teaching for the Christian reader should be their attack on contemporary worship (e.g., Amos 5:21–24; Isa. 1:12–17; Micah 6:6–8). Ezekiel's own denunciations may well have been influenced by Jeremiah's one-man picket of the temple (Jer. 7:1—8:3), an action that led to his arrest and almost to his death. For a country like the United States, which has the highest statistics for church attendance in the world, the relevance of these prophetic texts should be obvious.

Ezekiel's catalog may also be compared with what is sometimes called "the oath of clearance," in which an accused party dissociates himself under oath from a list of criminal or immoral acts. Perhaps the best example is Job 31, which ends with the protagonist, who has desperately proclaimed his innocence, issuing a kind of subpoena on God to appear and state his case—which in due course he does, but not in the way Job expected. The most obvious parallel is, of course, with the laws in the Pentateuch. While not all the stipulations in the Decalogue are represented in Ezekiel's list, the decalogic sequence, with offenses against God preceding those against the neighbor, is preserved. Ezekiel's "mirror of virtue" ends with a declarative formula of priestly vintage: he is righteous, he will surely live. This assurance of life, in the context, means rather more than a promise of survival in the coming holocaust (which would then demand a date before the fall of Jerusalem). It also implies rather less than eternal life in the usual sense of postmortem existence—though that dimension cannot be absolutely ex-

83

cluded at least at the implicit level. Life here has the broader and less precise connotation of association with God, some sense and intimation of which is available for the person who desires it in the act of worship. Here too a reading of those psalms which speak of the divine presence as life-giving and joy-conferring would be appropriate. The death which is the absence of that association is the lot of the son who chooses evil (vs. 10–13). *His* son sees all of this and yet determines not to follow his father's example. There is therefore no predetermined carryover from one generation to the next. Ezekiel does not, of course, bring up the matter of nurture and environment as bearing on the development of the individual. We may, and must, do this, but not at the cost of forgetting that the individual is a moral agent who makes decisions and bears responsibility for the conduct of his or her life.

The point about freedom of the will is further emphasized in the middle section (vs. 21–24), which defines the situation of the individual moral agent, whatever his genealogical anteced-ents, and affirms the possibility of change. The English word "repent" is perhaps a less than adequate rendering of the original, since it connotes overmuch a psychological process and looks to the past. The corresponding Hebrew word *shub* ("return, turn"), on the contrary, draws attention to the importance of action and an orientation to a possible different future. The term "conversion" would be etymologically closer, but its connotations in English are too specifically religious. Perhaps Martin Buber's literal rendering of the Hebrew substantive *teshubah* as "turning" best captures the sense of what is implied in the prophet's concluding appeal (vs. 30–32). What God offers is the possibility of life, and that possibility is available to all in spite of human misery and sin.

The Lioness and Her Cubs; the Vine (19:1–14)

The literary skill of Ezekiel is further illustrated by the lament that follows and that, so the concluding statement affirms, actually passed into use (v. 14*b;* cf. also 32:16). Despite the quite different images in the first and second parts, it is presented as one composition in two stanzas, both dealing with the "mother" of the princes, namely, Judah. The form of the lament *(qinah)*, attested and unchanged from the earliest period, has an irregular 3 + 2 beat which may have originally corresponded to a limping dance associated with seasonal ritu-

84

als, of the kind performed by the prophets of Baal on Mt. Carmel (I Kings 18:26). Ezekiel was not the first prophet to make use of this genre, as we may see from the proleptic lament for the Northern Kingdom composed by Amos:

> Fállen, no móre to rise,
>   is the virgin Ísrael!
>   Amos 5:2, RSV

The first stanza speaks of a lioness and her two cubs. The lion, whose habitat still included the wooded parts of Palestine in biblical times, symbolized Judah in ancient tribal poetry:

> Judah is a lion's whelp;
>   from the prey, my son, you have gone up.
> He stooped down, he couched as a lion,
>   and as a lioness; who dares rouse him up?
>   Genesis 49:9, RSV

The two cubs are Jehoahaz and Jehoiachin, among the most tragic and least reprehensible of the kings of Judah in the last period of its existence. Both reigned for only three months. Jehoahaz, son of Josiah, came to the throne after the tragic death of his father at Megiddo in 609 B.C. but was deported by Pharaoh Neco and died in Egypt (II Kings 23:30–34). Jehoiachin, son of Jehoiakim, was taken into exile in Babylon by Nebuchadnezzar in 598 B.C., remaining a virtual prisoner there for thirty-seven years (II Kings 24:8–16; 25:27–30). The second stanza may also have been inspired by the Judah oracle in Genesis which combines the images of lion, scepter, and vine (Gen. 49:8–12). The vine is, in any case, a favorite image of Ezekiel, as we have seen in chapters 15 and 17. The strongest shoot of the vine is the ruler, and the ruler in question here is undoubtedly Zedekiah, last king of Judah, who reigned from 598 to 586 B.C. It was his rebellion against the Babylonians that led to the end of independence and the exile.

Ezekiel is therefore here in line with that earlier prophetic theme, whose clearest expression is in Hosea, which sees the monarchy as the cause of Israel's ruin. The condemnation is not absolute, however, since Ezekiel has a place for the Davidic dynasty in his projection of the future commonwealth (see 34:23–24; 37:24–25). Its role is, however, severely circumscribed, as it is in Deuteronomy (17:14–20), one indication of which is Ezekiel's preference for the term "prince" *(naśi')* rather than "king" *(melek:* see 12:10; 21:25; 34:24; 37:25; and

85

often in chs. 40—48). The lament conveys a genuine sadness and pathos, especially in the first stanza, but it also communicates a political message. The political realm does not exist as an independent and autonomous entity; it therefore cannot claim absolute status. No human institution, however well established and powerful, is exempt from divine judgment.

Ezekiel 20—23
The Last Phase of the History

As we move chronologically from Ezekiel's call in 593 to the final act of the history when the Babylonians laid siege to Jerusalem in 588 B.C., we detect an increasing need to seek explanations of the current crisis in the past. Ezekiel's survey of Israel's history from its beginnings in Egypt occurs in the middle of this period (see the date at Ezek. 20:1) and is followed by a group of mostly short discourses that sharpen the "sense of an ending." Viewed in this context, one of the principal objects of the survey is to make the point that the contemporary crisis is explicable in the context of that history, that it was in fact preordained by God, and that, in spite of everything, there will be a future.

A Revisionist History of Israel (20:1–44)

The setting, once again, is a consultation by a delegation of elders. The date is the tenth of Ab, 591 B.C., less than a year after the temple vision. As on the previous occasion, we are not told the specific purpose of the visit. One ingenious suggestion (A. Malamat, *Supplements to Vetus Testamentum* 28:130 [1975]) links it with the prophet Hananiah's prediction of a return from exile within two years (Jer. 28:1–4). If, however, the prophecy was uttered in 594 B.C., the deadline for its fulfillment would have already passed. The allusion at the end of the survey (v. 32) to what was in their minds—namely, emulation of forms of worship practiced by other nations—allows the alternative suggestion that the elders were proposing to set up their own center of worship in Babylon which would incorporate the cult of deities other than Yahweh, as the Jews of Elephantine in Upper Egypt were to do some years later. The suggestion finds

86

some support in Ezekiel's direct address to them toward the end (v. 39), where he tells them, in effect, to make up their minds whether to serve Yahweh alone or engage in idolatry. The request was not, in any case, answered, or perhaps we should say that the answer was concealed in the apparent non sequitur of the historical survey. This would then be another example of the enigmatic, parabolic, and riddling element in Ezekiel's discourse; and in that case we would have an interesting parallel to the survey in Psalm 78 which presents the history of Israel's endemic infidelity as a riddle (Ps. 78:2).

The survey is tripartite: Egypt (vs. 5–9), the wilderness (vs. 10–26), and entry into the land (vs. 27–31). Unlike other historical surveys, such as those in certain psalms, in the prophetic books, and in Deuteronomy, Ezekiel traces the history of infidelity back to the very beginnings in Egypt. The story of the ancestors, corresponding to Genesis 12—50, is omitted, since for Ezekiel, following priestly tradition, their history is subsumed in the indefectible promise of peoplehood, land, and divine presence made to Israel through them (Gen. 17). The recurring pattern is clearly presented: beneficent divine action, ungrateful human reaction, and judgment decreed but then postponed. The effect, and no doubt also the intent of this pattern, is to draw attention to the present impasse as the result of these accumulated overdue judgments which have now caught up with them. We now see more clearly that Ezekiel's teaching on moral accountability in chapter 18 served to forestall an objection arising out of his theology of history. By choosing freely to replicate the conduct of their forebears, they, unlike the son who sees the sins of his father yet does not do likewise (18:14), place themselves within that historical pattern and so perpetuate it.

If we compare the pattern in this chapter with the rather different Deuteronomic cycle of infidelity, punishment, prayer, and divine response followed by relapse, the entire cycle repeated indefinitely (e.g., Judg. 2:11–23), we see that Ezekiel is presenting present and future disasters as the climax of a history of estrangement but a climax that also entails an unanticipated new beginning (vs. 33–44). And this remains true even if, as seems plausible, much of this last section was added after the judgment had become unmistakably clear with the Babylonian conquest and ensuing exile.

For Ezekiel, the history of Israel begins with their election

87

in Egypt, an event that determines everything that follows. In outlining this phase (vs. 5–9), Ezekiel follows priestly tradition according to which the divine name is first revealed in Egypt (Exod. 6:2–3, 28–29). This is quite different not only from other traditions about the origin of the divine name (see Gen. 4:26; Exod. 3:13–15) but from the alternative account according to which Moses had to retreat into the wilderness of Midian to encounter Yahweh. It is also in Egypt that, according to priestly tradition followed by Ezekiel, Yahweh swears the oath to give Israel "the most glorious of all lands" (20:15, RSV; cf. Exod. 6:4–8). But Ezekiel differs from priestly or any other tradition in one important respect. While there are occasional allusions to the pagan origins of Israel (Josh. 24:2, 14), nowhere else is the history of apostasy traced back to these Egyptian beginnings. Worship of Egyptian gods may have been suggested by the—for Ezekiel—baleful influence of Egypt on Judah during the last decades of its independent existence (see 8:7–13; 16:26 and the anti-Egyptian diatribe in chs. 29—32). It is, nevertheless, a bold move which goes significantly beyond previous historical reinterpretations, as, for example, that of Hosea, for whom Israel's deviation began with settlement in the land and the establishment of the monarchy. It would be comparable to a leading churchman arguing that Christianity had taken a wrong direction from apostolic times.

The forbearance of Yahweh on account of his name, that is, his reputation among the nations, is reminiscent of the theologically naive appeal to self-interest which we find in some of the older traditions (e.g., Exod. 32:12; Num. 14:13–16). It is rather more than that here. For Ezekiel, it is one way of expressing the intense reciprocal involvement of Israel and its God. To speak of the name in this context is to say that Israel exists not for itself but to fulfill the divine purpose in history. That is why Israel must on all occasions sanctify the name, a profound conviction expressed by Jesus in the first petition of the Lord's Prayer. For Ezekiel, the history of Israel is a long and ultimately unsuccessful attempt to evade the consequences of this commitment.

It appears from the reference to "the wilderness of the peoples" and "the wilderness of Egypt" (vs. 35–36) that the term is being used metaphorically of exile understood as a condition of estrangement. As he goes on to speak of the first wilderness generation (vs. 10–17), Ezekiel gives the impression that the exodus was more a forcible break with Egyptian idola-

88

try than a seizing of the initiative by Israel to secure its liberation. Unlike Hosea, who speaks of the wilderness as the idyllic epoch of Israel's existence, Ezekiel views it as a time of infidelity and judgment. The distinction between the two wilderness generations, based on ancient tradition (e.g., Num. 14:20–38), permitted a further illustration of the principles respecting imputability and moral responsibility. The first generation received the life-bestowing commandments only to transgress them and thus choose death instead of life. The prime examples were the worship of the golden calf (Exod. 32) and violation of the Sabbath ordinance while harvesting the manna (Exod. 16). Ezekiel views Sabbath as the visible sign of the life-enhancing relationship made possible by the law. This too is in keeping with priestly tradition which concludes the giving of the law with an injunction to observe Sabbath:

> You shall keep my sabbaths, for this is a sign between me and you throughout your generations, that you may know that I, Yahweh, sanctify you.
>
> Exodus 31:13, RSV

Emphasis on the Sabbath, both in the priestly traditions and in Ezekiel, no doubt reflects the increasing importance of this observance during the late monarchy and the exilic period as a distinguishing mark of the true devotee of Yahweh.

The second generation (vs. 18–26) perpetuated, by its own free choice, the sins of the first. Its situation was, in that respect, worse, and we even have Yahweh swearing an oath to exile the Israelites before they entered the land (v. 23). At this point we come upon what is perhaps theologically the most problematic statement in the book: "I gave them statutes that were not good and ordinances by which they could not have life" (v. 25, RSV).

What were these no-good and death-dealing laws? Did Ezekiel know of customs or laws from that time that were seen, with the benefit of hindsight, to be wrong and misguided? The following verse (v. 26) may provide a clue. It speaks of the horrible practice of "passing the firstborn through the fire," a crematory sacrifice which we know to have been practiced in several parts of the ancient world, conspicuously in Phoenicia and its colonies. While the evidence for Israelite practice is concentrated in the later period of the monarchy (II Kings 16:3; 17:17; 21:6; 23:10, 13), the story of the "binding of Isaac" in Genesis 22 could be read as recommending the substitution of

89

an animal, and this could be taken to imply that the practice was not unknown in early Israel. Ritual substitution is incorporated in the laws (Exod. 13:13; 34:20; Num. 18:15), but there are also laws without it (e.g., Exod. 22:29b).

The targum on this passage sets an example, followed by many commentators Jewish and Christian, of mitigating the language in order to remove the theological scandal:

> They followed their stupid inclination and they obeyed religious decrees which were not proper and laws by which they could not survive.

Perhaps that is what it comes down to, that God left the Israelites to their own misguided devices. Our liberal theological way of thinking finds it difficult to assimilate these darker and more destructive aspects of divine activity of which the Hebrew Bible occasionally speaks—the hardening of Pharaoh's heart, the deception of Ahab through his prophets, and, here, the giving of death-dealing laws. It may, nevertheless, be a valuable corrective to complacent views of the divine reality aligned with our own assumptions.

The review closes with the briefest summary of the entire period from the settlement in the land to the time of Ezekiel, a period of more than six centuries (vs. 27–31). The condemnation of the high places assumes that the Deuteronomic law of cult centralization was in force from the beginning, which in fact was not the case. An aside, probably added by a glossator, explains the word *bamah* ("high place") by assonance with *ba* ("going") and *mah* ("what"); the punning wordplay is aptly translated by Moffatt, "What is the *high place* to which you *hie?*" This third and last phase is rounded out with the repetition of the refusal to be consulted—another example of the stylistic device of inclusion (v. 31). But the sequel is not, as in the first two sections, a postponement of judgment, for we have come to the end of the line. There will be another exodus accomplished, as of old, by the mighty hand and outstretched arm of God, in which the Israelites will be brought, in spite of themselves, from the land of exile into the "wilderness of the peoples"—the desert between Mesopotamia and Israel—and thence to the land of Israel, where they will at last acknowledge Yahweh's kingship.

90

It is interesting to note that this statement of God's plan, countering *their* plan to be like the other nations, corresponds structurally to the historical survey, as if to say that God is to make a fresh start with Israel, that the Israelites have to go through the whole process again. This will happen in spite of anything Israel will do because of the indefectible nature of the covenant. It was not Israel's doing, and it is not within Israel's power to annul it. The metaphor of passing under the rod alludes to the practice of counting sheep and selecting those to be set aside for tithing or slaughter. There is therefore to be a sifting, a weeding out of the dispersed. Not all will take part in the new exodus and "enter the kingdom."

The injunction to go, worship idols rather than continue with the contaminated cult that Israel had been offering to Yahweh, including infant sacrifice, is perhaps the closest approach to a direct reply to the elders' request (v. 39). The final passage (vs. 40–44) opens up the prospect of eventual reconciliation, when a purified people will worship in the land to which they have returned. It therefore anticipates the program that will be set out in detail in chapters 40—48.

Fire and Sword (20:45—21:7)

That a separate section begins here is clearer in the Hebrew Bible, which opens a new chapter at this point. The sayings that follow are clearly indicated by the heading "The word of Yahweh came to me" (20:45; 21:1, 8, 18; 22:1, 17, 23; 23:1). The first two are equally clearly connected by matching terminology and are therefore intended as a kind of diptych: the south and the forest of the south corresponding to Jerusalem, the sanctuaries (or sanctuary), and the land of Israel; the fire to the sword; the green and the dry to the righteous and the wicked; and so on. In the first panel Ezekiel is told to gaze toward the south, this point of the compass being indicated by three different words in Hebrew. This is the fixed and hostile stare, accompanied by an oracular saying, which we encountered earlier (4:3, 7; 6:2). "The forest of the south" *(negeb)* does not refer to the desert region in southern Judah known as the Negeb, which we have no reason to believe was covered with vegetation at that time. The use of this term may, nevertheless, have brought to the mind of a later reader the Edomite-Arab occupation of that area after the Babylonian conquest. The metaphor was probably suggested by "the house of the forest of Lebanon" (I Kings 5:6; cf. Jer. 21:14), a figurative designation of the royal palace, and the correspondence is strengthened by the parallel

91

mention of Jerusalem in the second saying (21:2). Perhaps Ezekiel is represented here as a fire raiser, one of those dangerously endowed individuals thought to be capable of causing spontaneous combustion by concentrated mental energy. The result, at any rate, is a forest fire that spreads from south to north, consuming both the green wood and the dry, interpreted in the corresponding panel as the righteous and the wicked. (We recall an echo of this saying in the words of Jesus to the women of Jerusalem on his way to execution, Luke 23:31). The destruction of the righteous may seem inconsistent with Ezekiel's teaching on divine justice (14:12–20). His concern in that passage, however, was not to deny that the righteous also suffer from circumstances that they have done nothing to bring about but to reject the possibility of vicarious salvation for the wicked. That the righteous are swept away with the wicked in the destructive flow of historical events is only too true to our experience.

Both panels conclude with an exchange between the prophet and his audience whose words are quoted—a common feature of the book (see also 12:22, 27; 18:19, 25, 29). In the first, they complain, not without reason, that Ezekiel speaks in figurative and enigmatic language; he is a parablemonger (20:49). In the second, the sighing with breaking heart (literally, "loins") and bitter grief is intended to provoke a response, like the trembling that accompanied his eating and drinking at an earlier point (12:17–20). In this it succeeded, and the explanation that follows takes up again the doom-laden language of the sermon on imminent judgment in chapter 7. It reminds us, once again, that the prophetic role thrust upon Ezekiel called forth intense emotional identification with the fate of his people.

His Terrible, Swift Sword (21:8–32)

The next two sayings are linked with the preceding and with each other by the catchword "sword." The common association between fire and sword (as earlier in 5:1–4) is also in evidence, the four sayings in 20:45—21:32 beginning and ending with the image of fire. The depiction of Yahweh as a warrior god, lord of the hosts, is frequent in ancient Israelite poetry and epic narrative, which is understandable, since, in Wellhausen's phrase, war was the cradle of the nation. The so-called classical prophets continued to use imagery associated with warfare for obvious historical reasons; hence the frequent occurrence of the sword as instrument of judgment in the hands either of Yahweh himself or of an agent acting in his stead (e.g., Isa. 31:8; 34:5–7; Jer. 50:35–38; Zeph. 2:12).

The first of the two sayings (vs. 8–17) begins with a poem in two stanzas, apparently in lament form, though extensive textual corruption makes it difficult to detect the meter, and the sense is, in places, beyond recovery. (The RSV makes a brave if overoptimistic attempt but falls back on prose.) The first couplet is tolerably clear:

> A sword, a sharpened sword / polished as well
> Sharpened to slay and slaughter / polished to be like lightning

All we can deduce from what follows is a visionary glimpse into an armorer's workshop where a sword is being whetted and polished for an executioner. We must imagine the poem to have been recited in a state of great agitation. There is talk of crying and wailing, of slapping the thigh, which is a gesture of grief and frustration, and then of clapping the hands to simulate and anticipate the triumphant swordsman as he goes about his work. Perhaps the prophet mimed what was to happen by brandishing a sword, as he is reported to have done on a previous occasion (5:1–2). Identification of the victims as the princes of Israel suggests a specific allusion to the mass executions at Riblah on the Orontes which followed the capture of the city (II Kings 25:18–21).

The second of the two discourses (21:18–32) opens with another of the mimetic actions for which Ezekiel must have been well known. He draws a road junction with a stick on the ground—or perhaps with a stylus on a tablet—and attaches a signpost pointing in two directions: to Rabbah the Ammonite capital (now Amman in Jordan) and to Jerusalem. The location may have been at Riblah, Nebuchadnezzar's headquarters during the campaigns of 589–586 B.C. (see 6:14), or in Babylon itself. A decision is about to be made that will have ominous consequences. Since, as the Old Testament attests at numerous points (e.g., I Sam. 23:2–4; I Kings 22:5–12), it was considered *de rigueur* to seek divine guidance before embarking on a military campaign, Nebuchadnezzar has recourse to divination by several different means. The first involved shaking up inscribed arrows in a quiver and pulling one out—rather like drawing straws. The second called for consultation by means of figurines of deities, known as teraphim; exactly how is not clear. The third was the well-known practice of hepatoscopy, that is, divining by means of the model of an animal liver with the different sections carefully marked. Several such models have been recovered from excavations in Mesopotamia and even in Israel. Though people in Jerusalem make light of these procedures (how the people knew of them, we are not told), they are to have fateful consequences. They will lead to the devastation of Judah and to the siege and eventually the destruction of Jerusalem. The God of Israel will have made use of these divinatory techniques, forbidden in Israel (see Deut. 18:9–14), to achieve his purpose.

Nebuchadnezzar's fateful decision at the road junction is therefore, in reality, dictated by Yahweh. The reason is stated, once again, in the ensuing verdict (vs. 24–27). Nebuchadnezzar, here represented by his sword, acts as the agent of Yahweh in executing judgment on Zedekiah for the violation of his oath of allegiance, sworn in the name of Yahweh (see ch. 17). The result will be "chaos come again," the overthrow of the political and social order described earlier by Jeremiah as a reversal of creation (Jer. 4:23–26). The verdict ends with a cryptic allusion, again, to the Judah oracle in Genesis 49: "until he comes whose right it is." It is tempting to think that this is an ironic reference to Nebuchadnezzar as agent of divine justice. But since we have already heard echoes of this tribal oracle with the expected allusion to the Davidic dynast (ch. 19), it more probably refers to the future restoration of the disturbed order by one of David's line who will undo the damage caused by Zedekiah. The most likely candidate would therefore be the exiled Jehoiachin or one of his descendants.

The final section (vs. 28–32), which reverts to the language of the sword song and was suggested by the alternative route that Nebuchadnezzar might have taken but did not, was added after the fall of Jerusalem, probably at the same time as the anti-Ammonite saying to follow (25:1–7). Ammon, corresponding to the central part of the Hashemite kingdom of Jordan, conspired with Judah against Babylonian rule (Jer. 27:1–3), and the Ammonite king was behind the assassination of Gedaliah, who was appointed governor of Judah by the Babylonians after the conquest (Jer. 40:13—41:18). The Ammonite kingdom was eventually to be absorbed by the expansion of the Kedarite Arab tribes, precursors of the Nabateans. Unlike Judah, it disap-

94

peared from the historical arena, thus fulfilling the prediction with which this saying ends.

Fire and sword, images of destruction and death, underline the basic prophetic conviction that, in spite of appearances to the contrary, historical events fall within the sphere of divine judgment and are explicable in terms of moral causality. However irrelevant and unrealistic it may appear to the proponents of *Realpolitik*, those Christians and Jews who take the Scriptures seriously cannot in good conscience opt out of the political community.

The Unholy City (22:1–31)

In chapter 22, three prophetic discourses have been combined into a Savonarola-like sermon denouncing the corruption of the city and its inhabitants. All have the same heading—"The word of Yahweh came to me" (vs. 1, 17, 23)—probably added when the Ezekiel material was collected and arranged in its present form. As we have come to expect, additions were made subsequent to the fall of the city. The summary statement at the end (v. 31) refers to this event in the past, and, in addition, there are clear connections between the third discourse and Zeph. 3:1–4, though the uncertain date of the latter makes it impossible to be sure which has priority. It is distinctly possible that three utterances of Ezekiel, perhaps delivered at different times, were combined into a sermon aimed at drawing the appropriate lessons from the destruction of the city.

In the first of the three discourses (vs. 1–16), Ezekiel is again commanded to indict the city in order to make its inhabitants aware of their atrocious conduct. To create a state of awareness is one of the primary functions of the authentic prophet even when, as generally with Ezekiel, there is little expectation of success. The conduct of the city's inhabitants has created a state of defilement and has hastened the day of reckoning. Their failure to respond by acknowledging the situation in no way will affect the outcome.

In keeping with the forensic model, which is of frequent occurrence in the prophetic literature, indictment is followed by verdict. The first indictment is addressed to the city which is accused, in general terms, of bloodshed and idolatry, as a result of which it has become an object of reproach and mockery to the nations. It may not be coincidence that this accusation corresponds to the Noachic laws which, according to Jewish

95

tradition based on Gen. 9:4–7, are binding on all humanity. Ezekiel simply juxtaposes the two accusations, but the juxtaposition invites reflection on a possible connection between acknowledgment of God and ethical conduct. For Paul, such a connection was not in doubt. Exchanging the glory of the immortal God for idolatrous images leads inevitably to moral degeneration, including envy, murder, and strife (Rom. 1:18–32). This may be far from obvious in the contemporary world where both religious belief and what is known as life-style are commonly thought to be a matter of individual choice, but for the Christian it ought to provoke reflection.

After this prefatory address, the prophet singles out the princes of Israel, though it is fairly clear that the entire population is involved in what follows. The list of charges in this indictment (vs. 6–12) is not the random outcome of prophetic diatribe. It is based on the general principles and the specifics of a legal tradition the function of which, as opposed to the general prohibitions noted above, is to preserve this community with its own distinctive identity and ethos. In the first place, all the charges here itemized can be related to the Decalogue understood as a kind of distillation of that tradition, a statement about the level of moral performance compatible with being *this* community. That practically all of them occur in one section of what is sometimes called the Holiness Code, namely, in Leviticus 18—20, indicates more specifically the source on which Ezekiel has drawn. It should be noted that no distinction is made between ethical and ritual precepts either here or in "the law of the priests" (Leviticus), and there is no reason whatever to believe that the ritual transgressions have been added to the list by "the school of Ezekiel." This distinction, which occurs routinely in discussions of the teaching of Jesus vis-à-vis contemporary Jewish halakah, is in any case very misleading. There is, of course, a difference between Sabbath violation and murder, but it is begging the question to restrict the scope of ethics to the latter to the exclusion of the former. Neither Ezekiel nor Paul was a philosophical ethicist. The concern of both was the conduct of the individual as regulated in every respect by membership in a particular religious and moral community. In combining social injustice with cultic and sexual aberrations, therefore, Ezekiel was condemning the Jerusalemites as members of a community with its own unique identity and self-understanding.

On the individual charges only the briefest comment need be made. Dishonoring of parents, prohibited in the Decalogue (Exod. 20:12; Deut. 5:16) and in Leviticus (Lev. 19:3; 20:9), is addressed not to small children but to the younger members of the extended family of the sept or tribe. Care for the resident alien *(ger)*, the fatherless, and the widow, representing the disadvantaged classes in society in general, is inculcated everywhere in the laws, including Leviticus (Lev. 19:3, 10, 33; 20:9). Observance of Sabbath is a decalogic precept (Exod. 20:8–11; Deut. 5:12–15) and is also linked with respect for *the* "holy thing," namely, the sanctuary, in Lev. 19:30. Slandering that results in bloodshed probably refers to giving false witness in a capital case (Exod. 20:16; Deut. 5:20; Lev. 19:16). The charge of taking part in cultic meals on hilltops is probably connected with that of "lewdness" immediately following, referring to well-attested orgiastic rites associated with fertility cults (cf. Lev. 18:17; 20:14). It recalls the worship of the golden calf during which the apostate Israelites sat down to eat and drink and rose up to play (Exod. 32:6), the play being of the sexual sort. As is clearer in the Levitical list of prohibitions of sexual connections (Lev. 18:7; 20:11), "uncovering the father's nakedness" meant violating the marital rights of the father. The prohibition of sexual relations with a woman in her menses, not unconnected with atavistic fear of and revulsion for bodily emissions in general, is stipulated in Leviticus (Lev. 18:19) and merits an entire tractate in the Mishnah. Adultery is prohibited in the Decalogue (Exod. 20:14; Deut. 5:18) and also in Leviticus (Lev. 18:20; 20:10). Of the forbidden degrees of sexual relations in Leviticus (Lev. 18:7–8, 15; 20:11–12, 17) only two are mentioned here. Bribery, profiting on loans, and extortion, the only ones not in Leviticus 18—20, close the list. The verdict is announced with a clapping of the hands, which is a gesture of scorn as is the snapping of the fingers (cf. 21:14). The threat of exile highlights once again the intimate connection between land, law, and cult, which is a major theme of the book.

In the second discourse (vs. 17–22), Ezekiel takes over a familiar prophetic metaphor, that of smelting metal in a furnace. The process of separating the metal from the alloy or slag could serve as an apt figure of purification and refinement, as it does in Isaiah (Isa. 1:22; 48:10). Both Jeremiah (Jer. 6:27–30) and Ezekiel, however, speak of a process from which nothing survives except the slag which serves no useful purpose. The

97

metals, in descending order of value, are probably intended to represent the orders or classes in society, thus anticipating the specific accusations leveled against these classes—also five in number—in the final discourse. This may be seen as a variation on the metallurgic metaphor applied to historical epochs, kingdoms, or rulers as, for example, in Nebuchadnezzar's dream of the statue in Daniel 3.

In the final section (vs. 23–31), which may be a postbellum addition, the metaphor changes to a land on which no cleansing rain or shower has fallen, thus echoing the ancient idea that moral disorder pollutes the natural environment. The cause of this situation emerges from the indictment of the civil and religious leadership: members of the royal family (the "princes" of v. 25), priests, tribal leaders, prophets, and landowners ("the people of the land"). Throughout the history of Israel, priests were the repositories of the legal tradition, charged with responsibility for teaching and interpreting the laws (e.g., Jer. 18:18; Mal. 2:7), including laws governing temple worship, essential for the well-being of the community. Doing violence to the law refers either to deliberate misinterpretation and misrepresentation or to exacting payment for instruction or to both. To neglect the distinction between secular and sacred, between clean and unclean, meant surrendering what signified and, by signifying, constituted the unique character of Israel. A passage in the aforementioned Holiness Code states clearly this connection between the distinctiveness of Israel and this basic requirement of ritual law:

> I am Yahweh your God, who have separated you from the peoples. You shall therefore make a distinction between the clean beast and the unclean, and between the unclean bird and the clean.
>
> Leviticus 20:24–25, RSV

Prophets also had an essential role, neglect of which put the entire community at risk (cf. ch. 13). There could be no clearer statement on the social responsibility of religious leaders, not just for their own limited constituency but for the society as a whole.

The Two Sisters (23:1–49)

98

Taking up from the story of the nymphomaniac bride in chapter 16, and more particularly the story of the three sisters with which it concludes (16:44–52), Ezekiel now relates the misadventures of Oholah and Oholibah, identified as Samaria and Jerusalem respectively. They are not described as brides of Yahweh, but this would seem to be implied in the statement that "they became mine" (v. 4, RSV). The motif of the divine marriage, familiar in the mythology and cult of the entire region, was first exploited in prophetic preaching by Hosea, who, as Yahweh's proxy, marries Gomer and has three children by her. (For our present purpose it will be unnecessary to decide whether this reflects Hosea's marital experience or is purely fictional.) In this instance, however, as in many others, Ezekiel seems to be more directly indebted to Jeremiah, who gave the Hosean motif a broader and more contemporary application. A prose commentary to one of Jeremiah's early sayings speaks of the adulterous Meshuvah (= Faithless) whose sister Bagodah (= False) followed her on the path to ruin, a small-scale allegory of the John Bunyan kind with obvious application to the situation of the two kingdoms (Jer. 3:6–10). Ezekiel simply develops this further with the same Swiftian violence and crudity noted in chapter 16. We cannot, and should not, ignore the current of antifeminism in the prophetic literature and indeed in much of the literature of antiquity. A later commentator on the story of the two sisters has even departed from the main drift of the narrative to add a moralizing admonition to women in general to learn from it (v. 48). With few exceptions, the literature of antiquity was written by men for men. The ambiguity, suspicion, and fear aroused by female allure, and even more by the biological processes connected with birth and menstruation (one thinks of Baudelaire's *la femme est naturelle, donc abominable),* may help to explain but do nothing to render these attitudes less distasteful to the enlightened modern reader. In reading the story, all we can do is concentrate on the point of the allegory, which is Israel's history of infidelity and failure.

The story begins abruptly, without the usual introduction. The names of the sisters are obviously allegorical but conform to an attested type, for example, Oholibamah, the Hivite wife of Esau (Gen. 36:2, 5). Oholah ("her tent") and Oholibah ("my tent is in her") recall the sojourn in the wilderness when the ark was housed in a tent *('ohel),* but the similar Oholibamah ("tent of the high place") suggests even more strongly a pagan shrine, which would certainly be consistent with the life histories of the two women. Their promiscuity in Egypt is in line with Ezekiel's

99

radical view of Israel's history as having gone wrong from the beginning. Israel's "original sin" in Egypt returns to haunt her throughout the history. Passing over the intervening years, the narrative moves to the history of Israel, the Northern Kingdom, in its relations with the Assyrian empire. The metaphor of an illicit liaison for foreign alliance had been pioneered by Hosea (e.g., Hos. 8:9). Ezekiel was also an isolationist, opposed to foreign alliances which often entailed acceptance of foreign cults. The allusion here is to the acceptance of vassalage to Assyria by several of the Northern kings: Jehu, depicted on his knees before the Assyrian king on the Black Obelisk of Shalmaneser III; Menahem, who also paid tribute (II Kings 15:19); and Hoshea, last of the line (II Kings 17:3). Oholah's sexual submission does not pay off, however; for, as often happens, lust turns to disgust, and she is finally abused and killed, together with her children, by her former lovers.

Far from learning from the disastrous experience of her older sister, Oholibah outdid her in unbridled lust, beginning where her sister left off with the Assyrians. The historical reference would be either to the overtures of Ahaz to the Assyrians during the Syro-Ephraimite war or, since this took place before the fall of Samaria, more probably to the submission of Manasseh, successor to Hezekiah. After the Assyrians had passed from the scene, she was then tempted by the painted reliefs of Babylonian gallants and sent messengers inviting them to her bed. But the time came when she tired of them and turned back to her earlier partners, the Egyptians notorious for their insatiable sexual appetite. The allusion here is transparently to the Egyptian alliances of the last decades of Judah's existence (II Kings 24:1; Jer. 27:3–7), the predictable outcome of which was destruction at the hands of the Babylonians and their allies.

The sentence on Oholibah is made up of four oracles introduced by the formula "Thus says Yahweh" (vs. 22, 28, 32, 35). In the first of these the carrying out of the sentence is entrusted to her former lovers, namely, peoples with whom she had entered into compromising alliances. Of these, the Assyrians and the Babylonians are well known. The latter are distinguished from the Chaldeans *(kasdim)* mentioned earlier (v. 14), perhaps reflecting awareness of the Aramean origins of these people. The three names following, chosen perhaps for the sound of the names, correspond to tribes at the eastern end of the Babylonian empire (Puqudu, Sutu, Qutu?). The sentence, unsparingly

100

spelled out as usual, includes disfigurement, attested in Assyrian and Egyptian annals as punishment for rebellion, loss of children, and being stripped naked. The second pronouncement (vs. 28–31) is couched in more general terms and adds nothing to the first.

At this point the sentence on Oholibah has been filled out with a poem or song suggested by the catchword "cup" immediately preceding. Like "the song of the sword" (21:8–17), this "song of the cup" is in such a condition of textual disorder that it is difficult to detect the meter and even at times the meaning. One is tempted to think of an adaptation of a drinking song poking fun at a particularly severe hangover, in which case we might compare it with another remarkably vivid description of the effects of imbibing (Prov. 23:29–35). The song may be translated literally, if tentatively, as follows:

> You shall drink your sister's cup
> Deep and wide;
> You shall be laughed at and derided
> Because of the amount it contains;
> You shall be dead drunk and sad—
> Cup of horror and desolation,
> Cup of your sister Samaria.
> You shall drink and drain it,
> You shall gnaw its sherds (?)
> Tear your breasts.

The cup motif, like that of the sword, is well represented in the prophetic books, and Ezekiel's use of it may be another example of dependence on Jeremiah (see Jer. 25:15–29; 49:12–13; 51:7). Its adaptation here subverts the normal associations of hospitality and conviviality, functioning instead as a symbol of anger, pain, and death. We recall the question put to Jesus' disciples, whether they could drink the cup he was to drink, and the prayer in Gethsemane that the cup might pass from him. Inclusion of the song—whether by Ezekiel himself or by an editor, we do not know—necessitated a recapitulation of both the indictment and the verdict (v. 35).

At this point, when the story and its commentary appear to have reached their natural terminus, it is somewhat surprisingly followed by further articles of indictment followed by a final verdict which add little to what has gone before. Perhaps the idea was to recapitulate by bringing together the two sisters. The charge opens with the same rhetorical question as in

101

the previous chapter (22:2). It includes adultery, bloodshed, and infant sacrifice as an act deemed compatible with the usual round of temple worship. The frequency of this particular accusation in Ezekiel (see also 16:20–21, 36; 20:25–26) may reflect actual usage as the nation passed through the most critical period in its history. That both kingdoms are accused of profaning the sanctuary reminds us that Ezekiel never lost sight of their fundamental unity and the hope of eventual reunification. There is also a suggestion of participation in orgiastic rites, degenerating into drunken revelry with foreign riffraff (vs. 40–42). The final verdict on the adulterous women is meant to conjure up the image of a besieged city. The suggestion that the story can serve as a cautionary tale for women tempted to infidelity or promiscuity (v. 48), whatever its origin, was no part of the original purpose of the narrative.

Ezekiel 24
Jerusalem Besieged:
The Beginning of the End

We now come to a major turning point in Ezekiel's career to which everything since the call has been leading. The arrangement of the actions and sayings is clearly intended to emphasize the beginning of the siege and the announcement of the fall of the city as the decisive events in his career. Both, therefore, are carefully dated (24:1; 33:21). In one way or another, all of the prophetic activity recorded in the previous chapters leads up to this moment of judgment, objections had been answered, wishful thinking had been brushed aside. The correspondence between the loss of speech recorded at the beginning (3:26–27), the anticipation of its end at this point (24:25–27), and the opening of his mouth on the arrival of the fugitive after the fall of the city (33:22) points in the same direction. For the same reason, the miming of the siege occurs at the beginning of his prophetic career (ch. 4), corresponding to the historical actuality five years later. The description of the fate of the two sisters in terms reminiscent of a siege (23:46–47) facilitates the transition to this event which brings to an end the first phase of Ezekiel's activity.

The date at the head of this chapter, corresponding to January 588 B.C., marks therefore the beginning of the siege of Jerusalem. It raises at once the question of how Ezekiel, living hundreds of miles away in Babylon, could have known this. For those who locate part or all of his early activity in Judah, the problem would not arise, but we have seen that this is unlikely. The more popular alternative, therefore, is to assume that the date has been added following that given in II Kings 25:1 (see also Jer. 39:1; 52:4), and the assumption is supported by the fast that commemorates this event in Judah after the return from exile (Zech. 8:19). While this possibility cannot be eliminated, we must not overlook that Ezekiel was commanded to write down this precise date, the purpose of which was, most plausibly, to verify his statement at the time when the news arrived through normal channels. However we care to explain them, such feats of extrasensory perception are well attested, and many in the diaspora communities must have been aware, in any case, that the siege of Jerusalem was inevitable and indeed imminent.

To mark the occasion, Ezekiel composed a song that, like the song of the cup (23:32–34), is full of bitter irony. This Cooking Pot Song, celebrating the preparation of a festive meal, is an example of those occupational ditties which are common to all peoples. It might be compared to the song of the well diggers in Num. 21:17–18. A more or less literal translation would run as follows:

> Put on the pot, put it on,
> Pour water in it;
> Bring the joints together,
> All the good cuts, thigh and shoulder.
> Fill it with the choicest bones,
> Take the best of the flock.
> Pile the logs under it.
> Boil the joints, parboil the bones in it!

This distinctly unpolished composition is presented as a *mashal*, a parable, since its point remains opaque without interpretation. It soon becomes apparent that here too Ezekiel is taking his cue from the preaching of Jeremiah inaugurated with the ominous vision of a pot boiling over (Jer. 1:13–14). At the same time, he is responding to the misplaced confidence and elitism of those in Judah who had survived the first deportation, for whom Jerusalem was a secure refuge—"this city is the pot and

103

we are the meat" (11:3)—an interesting variation on the theme of the inviolability of Zion which informs several of the psalms.

There follow two variations on the theme of the song, each beginning "Woe to the bloody city!" (vs. 6–8, 9–14, RSV). The first plays on the idea of the pot as rusty or blood-encrusted (the meaning of the word *hel'ah* in v. 6, translated "rust" in RSV, is uncertain). Perhaps we are meant to think of a bloody scum which overflows on to the bare rock, which remains uncovered by the earth and therefore cries to heaven for vengeance (cf. Gen. 4:10; Job 16:18). The second stays closer to the language of the song. Logs are heaped up under the copper pot, but the purpose now is to burn away the scum and remove the rust with which the pot is encrusted. This difficult process will continue until the dirt is scoured away, but in the meantime nothing inside the pot will survive. Judgment on the bloody city (cf. 22:1–5) will then be complete.

The death of Ezekiel's wife coincided with the beginning of the siege. It occasions one of the very few glimpses into the inner, emotional life of the prophet who is otherwise totally sacrificed to his calling. His account of how it happened *could* be explained as the outcome of reflection on the symbolic meaning of the death and the subsequent absence of mourning. The intent, however, is to present it as symbolic *and* as an act of precognition: he announced it in the morning, and in the evening she died. Addition of the phrase "at a stroke" is, moreover, meant to exclude the possibility that it could have been easily foreseen. It happened suddenly, like the death of Pelatiah recorded earlier (11:13). Ezekiel's refusal to mourn must have been as disconcerting as David's similar behavior following the death of his son by Bathsheba (II Sam. 12:20–23). He is not to mourn; there are to be no tears, no audible sighing and moaning of the kind still in evidence at funerals in the Middle East, no covering the head with dust and ashes, no veiling the lower part of the face, no going barefoot. He must also abstain from taking part in the funeral meal, the *marzeah*, of which we hear in Amos (Amos 6:7) and in Jeremiah (Jer. 16:5–8). All of this *could*, again, be explained as the result of trauma, especially in view of a previous record of catatonia (3:15, 25–27; 4:4–8); there is no reason to believe that psychological and specifically religious explanations need be mutually exclusive. Whatever the case, it is presented with symbolic reference to the temple, the imminent loss of which would go unmourned, since none of the usual mourning rites would be adequate.

104

This refusal to mourn the death of his wife, "the delight" of his eyes, is not just another of those strange and disconcerting sign acts which Ezekiel performed from time to time. Ezekiel is himself to be a sign. The prophetic calling takes over his life and invades his innermost being. This situation is anticipated by Hosea's marriage in the last days of the Kingdom of Israel, and especially by the denial of wife, family, and everyday social contact to Jeremiah at the time of Judah's death agony (Jer. 16:1–9). We are reminded of Dietrich Bonhoeffer's remark that when God calls someone, he calls that person to die.

As usual, the remarkable conduct of the prophet elicits, and was meant to elicit, a request for an explanation (v. 19). The temple, your proud boast, the delight of your eyes, the desire of your soul, will be destroyed, and, with it, your own children whom you have left behind. You will refrain from mourning, as I have done, since the customary rites of mourning will be totally inadequate, faced with such an unparalleled disaster. But in your grief and bewilderment you will be led to acknowledge the mysterious purpose of the God who is now speaking through his prophet.

The section ends with the prediction that Ezekiel's temporary loss of speech will end when he and his fellow expatriates hear the news of the fall of Jerusalem and destruction of the temple (vs. 24–27). The date of this event, which is given later as the tenth month of the eleventh year (33:21, emended text), that is, January 585 B.C., followed the destruction of the temple by some four or five months (cf. II Kings 25:8). We have seen that this speechlessness of the prophet, however it is explained, cannot have lasted from the year of his call in 593 B.C. until several months after the fall of Jerusalem. If we are to be guided by the dates given in the two linkage chapters, 24 and 33, reading the eleventh for the twelfth year at Ezek. 33:21, we would have to conclude that he remained silent for about nineteen months during the siege, and then only sporadically, since several other sayings are dated within this period (26:1; 29:1; 31:1). This final passage, at any rate, is intended to serve as a link with the recapitulatory chapter 33, now separated from it by a collection of sayings directed against foreign nations.

PART THREE

Judgment on the Nations
EZEKIEL 25—32

The Book of Ezekiel seems to be constructed deliberately on the pattern of judgment on Israel, judgment on the nations, and salvation for Israel—a pattern also detectable in Isaiah and in the Old Greek version of Jeremiah where the oracles against foreign nations are located in the middle of the book. Since the nations are the agents of divine punishment, this type of saying stands in a kind of dialectical tension with the pronouncement of judgment on Israel by reaffirming Yahweh's purpose in the arena of international affairs and the centrality of Israel in the working out of that purpose. We note too that this collection has been spliced in between the beginning of the siege of Jerusalem (ch. 24) and the fall of the city (ch. 33). It therefore introduces an element of dramatic tension and highlights the fall of the city as the turning point, the *peripateia,* of the book. The dates, more numerous in this section than elsewhere, fit into this scheme. The dates in chapters 1—24 cover the period from 593 to 589 B.C.; in the foreign nations section, 588 to 586 B.C. (with one exception, 571); and in the last part of the book, they correspond to the period from the fall of the city to 573 B.C.

This collection of sayings has been put together out of diverse material according to a definite pattern arranged in groups of seven. There are, to begin with, seven nations, as there are in Amos (Amos 1—2) and in the lists of indigenous peoples encountered by the Israelites after the settlement in the land (e.g., Deut. 7:1). An originally separate collection of seven anti-Egyptian sayings has been introduced by a brief word of promise addressed to Israel (28:24–26), and the other major collection, directed against Tyre, is also sevenfold, the

107

individual units distinguished by their headings (26:1, 7, 15, 19; 27:1; 28:1, 11). There may not be any particular significance in this, except to indicate the care with which the material in the book has been arranged.

One of the main functions of the professional prophet, in Israel as elsewhere in the ancient Near East, was to provide assurance of success before a military campaign or, less frequently, to warn against undertaking it. A good example of the former is the assurance of success, accompanied by mimetic gesture, which the prophet Zedekiah and his colleagues gave Ahab before his campaign against the Syrians (I Kings 22). To this we may add the solemn pronouncement of a curse on the enemy, admirably illustrated by the story of Balaam hired by the Moabite king to curse the Israelites (Num. 22—24). Though grounded in these traditional practices, the sayings preserved here are literary products which in some cases (e.g., the lament over the king of Tyre) reach a high level of sophistication.

This type of prophetic saying reflects the reality of international relations seen from the Israelite perspective, especially relations with immediate neighbors, which is to say enemies. While affirming the universal sovereignty of the God of Israel, it does not begin to offer a solution to the problem of international conflict, and certainly cannot be appealed to as providing biblical support for political ideology in the modern context. The choice of targets was dictated by the political situation of that time, the decades immediately preceding and following the fall of Jerusalem. Five of the seven peoples indicted here were coconspirators with Judah against the Babylonian overlord; they managed, for a time at least, to extricate themselves from serious trouble (Jer. 27:3), a situation that goes far to explain the bitter resentment of the indictments. It may also be worth noting that four of these seven appear, in the same order, in the list of those disqualified, in different degrees, from membership in the Yahwist cult community, according to Deut. 23:1–8 (Ammonites and Moabites in perpetuity, first and second generation Edomites and Egyptians). This is one text that has contributed to the general impression of early Judaism as exclusivist and xenophobic, one of the stock charges of anti-Jewish polemic in antiquity and, of course, also in modern times. Since the oracles against the nations tend to convey the same impression, it would be important to recall that out of this defeated and despised nation developed a confessional community open in principle to all peoples. Nationalism and exclusivism continued to have their supporters without ever dictating the course of the future. Isaiah 56, from the early Persian period, assures the foreigner of his good standing in the community, and both Ruth from Moab and Achior from Ammon (Judith 14:10) were accepted into it without demur. It is therefore both historically and theologically misleading to contrast Christian universalism with Jewish exclusivism, a practice that has contributed significantly to the centuries-long mutual alienation of the two faiths.

A Historical Survey, 598–570 B.C.

Before we turn to the sayings themselves, it may be helpful to survey briefly the course of international affairs as they affected Judah during the period of Ezekiel's activity. Max Weber remarked long ago that the Israelite prophets were concerned above all with international politics, since for them that was the sphere of divine action. Their words have presumably survived because the solutions they offered to contemporary issues were seen to contain elements of permanent value. Acquaintance with the historical situation being addressed is, nevertheless, the first and indispensable stage for understanding a prophetic book.

Most of the sources on which we must draw for our knowledge of those critical decades are easily available. The biblical sources are II Kings 23—25, composed most probably around 560 B.C.; the alternative version in II Chronicles 34—36 from about two centuries later; several passages in Jeremiah; some duplicating material in II Kings; and allusions here and there in Ezekiel. The Babylonian Chronicle covers the years 616–594 B.C., including a brief account of the capture of Jerusalem in the seventh year of Nebuchadnezzar. Some gaps can be filled with the help of Josephus' *Antiquities of the Jews* (bk. 10), the *History* of Herodotus, and sporadic references in other Greek historians. Archaeological data, while not particularly abundant, provide a valuable supplement and often corrective to the strictly literary sources—for example, the letters discovered at Lachish and Arad from the last days of Judean independence.

After the eclipse of the Assyrian empire with the fall of Nineveh in 612 B.C. (celebrated in the Book of Nahum), the dominant powers in the Middle East were Egypt of the Twenty-sixth Dynasty and the Babylonian kingdom founded by Nabopolassar in 626 B.C. Josiah, last great king of Judah, died at

109

Megiddo in 609 B.C. trying to prevent the passage of the Egyptian forces on their way to bolster Assyria and thus maintain the balance of power in the region. The Syro-Palestinian corridor then passed under the control of Neco II of the Twenty-sixth Dynasty. After the death of Josiah, "the people of the land" put his younger son Jehoahaz—the first lion cub of Ezek. 19:3–4—on the throne, but after three months he was deposed by Neco, who set up his half-brother Eliakim as his puppet in Jerusalem, renaming him Jehoiakim. The Egyptians continued to control the region until their decisive defeat by the Babylonians at Carchemish on the upper Euphrates in 605 B.C. At that point Judah, together with the other small states of the region, became a Babylonian vassal. During the reign of Nebuchadnezzar II (605–562 B.C.) the Babylonians remained the dominant power, though their hegemony was continually challenged by Egypt which they never succeeded in completely subduing. A year after Carchemish, Nebuchadnezzar campaigned in Palestine, the principal object of his attention being the Philistine city of Ashkelon on the Mediterranean coast. A few years later he attempted unsuccessfully to conquer Egypt, and his withdrawal around 600 B.C. inspired Jehoiakim to withhold tribute. The Babylonians responded with punitive raids, using auxiliaries from the neighboring states of Moab, Ammon, and Syria (or perhaps Edom, II Kings 24:1–2). They followed this up a year later with a full-scale attack on Jerusalem, the capture of which is recorded in the Babylonian Chronicle.

While these events were in progress, Jehoiachin succeeded his father on the throne, but after reigning only three months, he was deported to Babylon with his family (Ezek. 17:1–4; 19:5–9). Nebuchadnezzar, the first of the two great eagles of Ezekiel, then placed his uncle Mattaniah, renamed Zedekiah, on the throne as a Babylonian puppet. Zedekiah (598–587 B.C.) seems not to have remained loyal to the Babylonian overlord very long, since we hear of an anti-Babylonian league convening in Jerusalem in the early years of his reign with representatives from all the states condemned by Ezekiel in chapters 25—32, with the exception of Egypt and Philistia (Jer. 27:1–3). Egypt was probably involved in any case, acting a role comparable to that of the superpowers today in relation to their clients. The idea of joint action may, in fact, have been inspired by the accession of Psammeticus II in 595 B.C., a vigorous ruler whose plans included the reassertion of Egyptian control in the Syro-

110

Palestinian region. The Philistine cities may have been unable to participate on account of Babylonian military control of the coastal area.

Since the neighboring states that did send representatives failed to support Judah when the Babylonians eventually moved against Jerusalem, and did not have to bear the brunt of the Babylonian campaigns in the west (especially Ammon, see 21:18–23), the animus expressed in the oracles against these nations is easily understandable. The prediction of the end of Babylonian rule within two years announced by the prophet Hananiah in the temple (Jer. 28) may have been inspired by problems experienced by Nebuchadnezzar with the Elamites on the eastern side of the empire, problems aggravated by a revolt in the army (ca. 596–594 B.C.). Shortly thereafter, Ezekiel was called to prophesy and to pursue in the diaspora the same policy of nonresistance to Babylonian rule that Jeremiah was advocating in Jerusalem. Ezekiel provides glimpses of the war party that surrounded Zedekiah (8:7–13; 11:1–7) and the prophetic support that gave it religious sanction (13:1–16). Anti-Babylonian prophets were also active in the diaspora (see Jer. 29:15–23), lending powerful support to expectations that Ezekiel believed to be illusory. The war party at the court eventually prevailed, impelling Zedekiah to rebel in 591/590 B.C., no doubt encouraged by the prospect of support from Psammeticus II, who passed through Palestine about that time. Ezekiel's attitude toward the rebellion is clearly stated (e.g., 17:5–21; 21:25–27). Judah is a "rebellious house," Babylon, significantly, is not among the nations condemned, and Egyptian support is not only illusory but pernicious in its religious influence (8:7–13; 16:26; 17:7–10, 15–18; 23:27). And, of course, the tragic outcome of the rebellion, including the fate of Zedekiah himself (12:10–15; 17:19–21), is the subject of practically all the prophecies in the first part of the book.

After the fall and sack of Jerusalem, the mass executions at Riblah (6:14), and the deportations, the Babylonians appointed Gedaliah, a Judean nobleman, as viceroy of the conquered province, with his headquarters at Mizpah, generally identified with Tell en-Naṣbeh about eight miles north of Jerusalem. The appointment of a native, designed to reconcile the province to Babylonian rule, persuaded many of the refugees who had fled to the Transjordanian region to return (Jer. 40:11). But the nationalist movement had not been entirely suppressed. One of

111

the repatriates, a descendant of the royal house named Ishmael, attempted to seize power with the backing of the Ammonite king Baalis. The assassination of Gedaliah and his Babylonian militia at Mizpah did not, however, lead to a popular uprising, and Ishmael was obliged to take refuge once again in Ammon (Jer. 41).

After several of the survivors of the failed coup, fearing reprisals, had fled to Egypt (Jer. 41:16–18), the Babylonians may have launched a punitive campaign against the rebels and their supporters. Josephus (*Ant.* 10.180–182) reports that Nebuchadnezzar attacked Moab and Ammon and planned further moves against Egypt which continued to support anti-Babylonian factions in the neighboring states. The third deportation in the twenty-third year of Nebuchadnezzar (582/581 B.C.), of which Jeremiah speaks (Jer. 52:30), may belong in this period of unrest. Josephus also reports a thirteen-year-long Babylonian siege of Tyre (587–573 B.C.) which was ultimately unsuccessful, though Tyre did eventually accept vassal status. We do not know whether the predictions of Babylonian conquest of Egypt pronounced by Jeremiah (Jer. 43:8–13) and Ezekiel (Ezek. 29:17–20) were fulfilled, and if they were, in what way, though the Babylonian Chronicle records a Babylonian attempt to invade the country in Nebuchadnezzar's thirty-seventh year (568/567 B.C.). The frequency of dates attached to the anti-Egyptian sayings in Ezekiel may indicate the need to authenticate predictions which, at the time of writing, were fulfilled only partially, if at all.

Ezekiel 25:1–7
Ammon

The first four of the sayings, directed successively against Ammonites, Moabites, Edomites, and Philistines, are much less colorful and much more formulaic than the series against Tyre and Egypt, which suggests that they originally formed a distinct collection. Ammon is one of several Aramean states that were formed around the beginning of the Iron Age (ca. 1200 B.C.). Its location corresponds roughly to the kingdom of Jordan, and its principal city, Rabbah, is situated near the Jordanian capital, Amman. Hostility between Ammonites and Israelites goes back to the time of the settlement of Israelite tribes in the Transjordanian region. Conquered by David, Ammon recovered its independence after the division of the kingdoms, certainly by the eighth century B.C. (see Amos 1:13–15). Ammonites took part in the Babylonian-sponsored raids on Judean territory during Jehoiakim's reign (II Kings 24:2). Though it certainly came within the Babylonian sphere of influence and activity, and had taken part in the anti-Babylonian conspiracy of 595/594 B.C. (Jer. 27:1–3), Ammon escaped the retribution dealt out to Judah (Ezek. 21:18–23, 28–32). The Ammonite king Baalis was behind the attempted coup of Ishmael and the assassination of Gedaliah (Jer. 40:13—41:18). The oracle is undated but was composed after the Babylonian conquest and at a time when the Kedarite Arab tribes were beginning to gain control over a broad strip of land from the Sinai to the Transjordanian region. Ammonite hostility continued down to the time of Nehemiah, one of whose worst enemies was Tobiah the Ammonite.

Ezekiel 25:8–11
Moab

The story of Lot's incest with his two daughters, transparently a political spoof on Moabites and Ammonites (Gen. 19:30–38), testifies to the close ethnic relations between the two peoples and between them and Israelites. The kingdom of Moab, which emerged about the same time as Ammon, occupied the territory east of the Dead Sea bordered on the south by Edom and on the north by Ammon. At odds with its Cisjordanian neighbor from the earliest times (Num. 22—25; Judg. 3:12–30), Moab was conquered first by David (II Sam. 8:2) and later by Omri of the kingdom of Samaria (II Kings 3:4). The Moabite stone, discovered in A.D. 1868, records how Moab won back its independence from Omri's son, Ahab. The long anti-Moabite discourse in Jeremiah 48 may have been occasioned by the Babylonian-sponsored raids mentioned earlier (see also Isa. 15:1—16:14), though this type of saying could be adapted and

113

expanded to fit changing historical situations. (This is particularly clear from the conclusion of the anti-Moabite oracle in Isa. 16:13–14.)

Two of the towns mentioned here—Baal-meon and Kiriathaim—also occur on the Moabite stone. All three have been identified with Transjordanian sites, but none of the identifications is secure. The oracle predicts that Moab too will fall to the Kedarites and will cease to exist as an independent political entity, as indeed happened. The story of Ruth, the proselyte from Moab, was meant to demonstrate, in defiance of the law in Deut. 23:1–8, that even age-old, inveterate enmities can be overcome in the shared worship of Israel's God.

Ezekiel 25:12–14
Edom

Edom, located east and south of the Dead Sea down to the Gulf of Aqaba, attained statehood at the beginning of the Iron Age and earlier than Israel (Gen. 36:31); hence Esau (= Edom) is Jacob's elder brother. Prophetic oracles against Edom (Isa. 21:11–12; Jer. 49:7–22; Amos 1:11–12; Obad. 1–14; Mal. 1:2–5) are particularly virulent, no doubt on account of the close kinship between Israelite and Edomite reflected in the Jacob-Esau narrative cycle, a relationship that appears to have been consolidated by treaty (see Deut. 23:7; Amos 1:9). The story of the relations between these two peoples is one of unending feud; so much so that by the Roman period "Edom" could serve as a code name for Rome, much like "Babylon" in Revelation. The Edomites were especially reviled for having taken advantage of the Babylonian conquest to occupy the southern part of Judah. This situation is reflected in numerous biblical texts (in addition to prophetic oracles, Ps. 137:7–9 and Lam. 4:21–22), in lists of place-names in postexilic texts, and in the archaeological record. The ostraca from the last days of Judah discovered at Arad near Beersheba attest to Edomite penetration into the Negeb and refer to the evil they had wrought. The judgment on Edom has been expanded by a later hand (v. 14), perhaps from as late as the Maccabean period.

114

Ezekiel 25:15–17
Philistines

Inhabitants of the southern coastal plain, the Philistines included Cherethites (Cretans?) established to the southeast of the major Philistine centers. (I Sam. 30:14). Though defeated by David, they preserved their identity and continued to be a thorn in the side of the neighboring Kingdom of Judah (see Isa. 14:28–32; Jer. 47; Amos 1:6–8; Joel 3:4–8; Zeph. 2:5–7). Though the Philistine cities also suffered from the Babylonian armies, they were able to profit from the destruction and deportations in Judah, taking over part of Judean territory after 598 B.C. Close political and cultural ties existed between the Philistine cities and the Phoenicians, as is clear from prophetic denunciations (e.g., Jer. 47:4; Joel 3:4) and archaeological sites excavated in the Philistine region.

Ezekiel 26:1—28:19
Tyre

The seven sayings directed against Tyre are by no means all of the same kind. The first four, grouped under the heading "The word of Yahweh came to me" (26:1), are roughly equal in length, relatively colorless, and put together according to the same formula. They therefore parallel the four preceding aimed at Judah's immediate neighbors. The last three (27:1–36; 28:1–10, 11–23) are conscious literary creations of a quite different order which have little in common with the conventional form of the prophetic oracle. The incomplete date at the beginning of the series, the year in which Jerusalem fell to the Babylonians, probably refers to the first four sayings. The prediction of the siege of Tyre ending in its complete destruction 115 provides an interesting case of the disconfirmation of prophecy, for by the time of the last anti-Egyptian saying, dated sixteen years later (29:17–20), it was well known that the attempt of Nebuchadnezzar to reduce the city had failed. This is not the only instance of unfulfilled prediction (see, e.g., Amos 7:11; II Kings 22:20), and it may serve to illustrate the important point that prediction *in itself* was not of the essence of prophecy.

The Phoenician cities on the Mediterranean coast of what is now Lebanon provide an excellent illustration of the decisive influence of physical environment on cultural and political development. Hemmed in by mountains along a narrow littoral, but with excellent harbors, the Phoenicians took to the sea, rivaling the Greeks in exploration, commerce, and colonization. The resulting cosmopolitan character of the cities contributed to their reputation for literacy and culture, and it is hardly accidental that the alphabet, the most decisive breakthrough in written communication in antiquity, developed in that environment. The principal Phoenician city during the first millennium B.C. was Tyre. Situated on an island (now a peninsula) about half a mile off the coast, it had the benefit of two good harbors, to the north and to the south. Its relations with the Israelite kingdoms were close and generally friendly. One of its greatest kings, Hiram, supplied the plans and much of the material and skilled labor for the construction of Solomon's temple. He also played an essential role in the development of maritime trade during the period of the united monarchy (I Kings 9:26–28; 10:11; II Chron. 8:17). A later Tyrian king, Ittobaal, was the ally of Omri, the powerful ruler of the Northern Kingdom in the ninth century B.C. The alliance was sealed by the marriage of his daughter Jezebel to Omri's son, Ahab, a *mariage de convenance* which led to what must be one of the earliest examples of religious warfare in history. Together with all other western states, Tyre fell under the Assyrian shadow in the following century. Though forced to pay tribute, it was never taken, a circumstance that must have generated a strong sense of security and invincibility. The first to penetrate its walls was, in fact, Alexander, who succeeded only after building a causeway out from the mainland.

Tyre Will Be Inundated (26:1–21)

The first of the four related sayings (vs. 1–6) castigates the Tyrians for gloating over the destruction of Jerusalem and anticipating profit from the disappearance of a commercial competitor. There were no doubt Tyrian trading posts in

Jerusalem—they were still there in Nehemiah's day (Neh. 13:16)—and in Babylon, and news of the disaster would have traveled fast. The description of Jerusalem as "the gate of the peoples" may refer to tolls exacted by the city for the import and transfer of goods, including such typical Phoenician wares as glass and dyed cloth. Judgment will come on the Tyrians too, in the shape of a foreign invasion like the waves of the sea. Tyre's vaunted defenses will be breached, she will be turned into a bare rock (the Hebrew for Tyre, *ṣor*, also means "rock"), and her suburbs ("daughters") on the mainland will be overrun.

Tyre took part, with Judah, in plans for concerted action against Nebuchadnezzar in 595/594 B.C. (Jer. 27:3). Resentment at Tyre's failure to come to Judah's assistance during the campaign which ended with the destruction of Jerusalem is apparent in the next saying (vs. 7–14) which may date from the beginning of the thirteen-year-long siege following upon the devastation of Judah. The use of horses and chariots would have been effective only in the first stage against the mainland quarter of the city. For the rest, Ezekiel falls back on the conventional description of a siege (cf. 4:1–3): earthen rampart, wall of shields like the Roman *testudo,* battering rams, and so forth. It will be the beginning of the end for the vaunted affluence and culture of Tyre. Tyre did eventually submit to the Babylonians, but the siege was not successful and the defenses held. Nebuchadnezzar will have to take it out on the Egyptians instead (29:17–20).

The next saying (vs. 15–18) describes the consternation of the other Phoenician maritime cities at the fall of Tyre and puts into their mouth a lament which has unfortunately been corrupted and annotated in transmission almost beyond recognition. It is, however, at least clear that it speaks of the city's destruction. As we have seen, this did not happen in Ezekiel's day, and we must leave open the possibility that some of these sayings were edited and expanded after the reduction of the city by Alexander in July 332 B.C. It bears repeating that prophetic sayings were not copyrighted, and this kind of saying in particular could be recycled to fit the changing international situation.

In the fourth and last saying of this first series (vs. 19–21) the fall of Tyre is given broader significance by transposition into the idiom of mythology. The basic motif is the familiar one of descent to the underworld, more fully developed in connection

117

with Egypt (32:17–32). Tyre will be submerged by the waters of the cosmic flood, the abyss *(tehom)* or watery chaos from which the created world emerged at the beginning of time and to which it reverted at the great deluge (Gen. 1:2; 6—8). Alongside this primal image of divine judgment is that of the realm of the dead, the pit or netherworld, below the surface of the earth. The passage to this land populated by the ancient dead and the proud civilizations that they built is a one-way journey. It stands in contrast to "the land of the living" where alone—paradoxically for the contemporary Christian or Jew—God's presence is experienced (cf. Ps. 27:13; 116:9; 142:5). There is as yet no idea of a blessed immortality, though we may detect intimations here and there in the Old Testament that even death cannot withstand the power and energy of the living God. We may find a clue along these lines to the broader significance of this common language of myth in the context of prophetic denunciation. Tyre may be taken to represent the pursuit—through affluence, political prominence, even culture—of a security and an autonomy that contradict the nature of created reality. Notwithstanding the promise with which it ends, the account of the deluge as an undoing of creation suggests that order is always under threat from disorder, "chaos come again." Jeremiah translates this into the language of prophetic judgment:

> I looked on the earth, and lo, it was waste and void;
>   and to the heavens, and they had no light.
> I looked on the mountains, and lo, they were quaking,
>   and all the hills moved to and fro.
> I looked, and lo, there was no man,
>   and all the birds of the air had fled.
> I looked, and lo, the fruitful land was a desert,
>   and all its cities were laid in ruins
> before Yahweh, before his fierce anger.
>   Jeremiah 4:23–26, RSV

To know this is to suspect all pretensions to autonomy, all aspirations to security and permanence reinforced by the accumulation of wealth and material goods. The point will be made even more clearly in the three poems that follow.

118 A Shipwreck Observed (27:1–36)

A second and much longer lament follows. It exploits the image of Tyre as a galleon weighed down with cargo which goes down with all hands in sight of land. The working out of the metaphor allows for the interesting literary device of a lament within the lament spoken by the observers of the tragedy on shore (vs. 32–36). Mention of trading partners on board the doomed ship provided the occasion for inserting a long catalog of these partners and their wares which, however inappropriate from the literary point of view, is a major source of information on Levantine trade in antiquity.

The lament begins by describing the good ship Tyre: keel of fir planks from Hermon, mast from a cedar of Lebanon, oars of oak from Bashan east of the Jordan, deck of pine imported from Cyprus, sail of fine Egyptian linen, deck awning of imported cloth from Elishah (perhaps identical with Alashia, an ancient name for Cyprus). The vessel must have been of the "round ship" or merchantman type, as opposed to the long boat or war galley, both represented on Assyrian reliefs, Carthaginian stelae, and Phoenician coins of a somewhat later period. Her oarsmen hailed from Sidon and Arvad (now Ruad), Phoenician cities to the north, and her pilots from Zemer (Sumra?). The elders of the ancient city of Gebal (Byblos) served in the menial capacity of caulkers. The emphasis is clearly on the ascendancy of Tyre over the cities of Phoenicia which came to an end with the exhausting struggle for survival against the Babylonians.

Insertion of the long trade directory (vs. 10–25) was suggested by the allusion to bartering in the previous verse (v. 9) in which, however, the ship metaphor has been left behind. It begins with a list of mercenaries drawn from as far afield as Iran, Asia Minor (if Lud is identical with Lydia), and North Africa (Put), as well as places nearer home such as Arvad. Tyre was well known for its use of mercenaries. It could afford to pay them, and its own pool of conscripts was limited. The catalog of trading partners and their wares takes in a broad arc from the western Mediterranean to Mesopotamia and from Asia Minor to the Arabian peninsula. The reputation of the Phoenicians as fearless mariners and traders was well established long before Ezekiel's day. Herodotus (*History* 4.42) reports that Phoenician sailors circumnavigated the African continent during the prophet's lifetime, returning to base after an absence of three years. Later still, they would feel their way up the Atlantic coast to Brittany and Cornwall in search of tin, essential for the manufacture of bronze objects.

119

The list begins with Tarshish and ends with ships of Tarshish (vs. 12, 25a). Tarshish has been variously identified with Tartessus in Spain, Nora in Sardinia, and Tarsus, birthplace of Paul, in Cilicia. Its mineral ore products would be consistent with a trading post in Spain but would not exclude other candidates. Spain is also supported by the story of Jonah, the biblical Sinbad the Sailor, who was commanded to go to Nineveh in the far east but instead booked a passage at Joppa (Yafo near Tel Aviv) for Tarshish, presumably in the far west (Jonah 1:3). "Tarshish ships" (see also I Kings 10:22; 22:48; II Chron. 9:21; Isa. 2:16; 23:1, 14; 60:9) was probably a technical term for oceangoing vessels designed to carry ore. In the Isaian diatribe against Tyre (Isa. 23:1, 14) they are also associated with the city. Javan stands for the mainland and Ionian Greeks, principal trade rivals of the Tyrians. The next three names—which we will meet again in the Gog-Magog passage (38:1–6)—represent Asia Minor. After the Island of Rhodes (Dedan in Hebrew), the "many coastlands" probably alludes to Africa, source of ivory and slaves. We may note in passing that other anti-Tyrian sayings in prophetic books make much of the city's involvement in the slave trade, including trade in Jewish slaves (Amos 1:9–10; Joel 3:4–8). The important Red Sea trade, in which the Phoenicians had been involved for centuries (see, e.g., I Kings 9:26–28; 10:11), is represented by Edom, the Kedarite Arabs, Sheba (Saba), and Raamah in the southern Arabian peninsula. Apart from typical Bedouin products like embroidery and saddleclothes, the imports from these regions included precious stones, coral, agate, and, perhaps most important of all, spices. Judah and Israel are at the center of the list, providing agricultural products as they doubtless had done for centuries. From northern Mesopotamia came high-quality garments and rugs.

The point of the insertion is to emphasize the self-confidence of the city, bred of affluence, commercial skill, and advanced technology. Like other highly developed societies and empires that have followed, it sees itself as at the center of the world, drawing on the resources of less fortunate peoples. The point of the lament, as it continues after the insert (vs. 25b–36), is that arrogant self-sufficiency of this kind bears within it the seeds of its own destruction. Returning to the metaphor with which the poem began, we find that the ship no sooner cleared the harbor mole than it was struck by the force of the

120

east wind and capsized, losing all hands on board. The implication seems to be that it was overloaded, implying in its turn that a combination of surfeit and overconfidence would bring about the ruin of the city. It was left for the observers on shore and on board the other vessels in the harbor to go through the motions of ritual mourning—wailing, throwing dust on the head, cutting off locks of hair, putting on sackcloth—and to intone a lament inspired more by astonishment and awe than by genuine sorrow.

The lament within the lament begins in somewhat the same way as the main poem:

> Who is like unto Tyre
> In the midst of the sea?

It goes on to recall the material benefits the city brought not to itself but to other nations—no doubt an ironic touch. It then goes on to speak of the shipwreck and, an additional refinement, the effect of the spectacle on the observers, meaning the other Phoenician cities, for they could not help thinking of their own prospects. They are not gloating over the destruction of the city. The merchants do not hiss (v. 36, RSV) but whistle through their teeth, to this day a typical Mediterranean reaction of amazement and consternation. The city that symbolized supreme self-confidence and permanence had simply ceased to exist. And so the poem ends in the same way as the previous collection of sayings (26:21).

The Godlike King of Tyre (28:1–10)

The poem that follows is addressed to the prince of Tyre, perhaps Ittobaal II, Ezekiel's contemporary, though the allusions are typical rather than realistic. It is undated but presumably was composed toward the beginning, or at any rate before the end, of Nebuchadnezzar's siege (587–574 B.C.). Play on the contrast between divine pretensions and human reality perhaps allows us to describe it as satire. Unlike the preceding poem, it is not heavily metaphorical, but some continuity is maintained by repetition of the motif "in the heart of the seas" (27:4, 25, 26, 27; 28:2, 8). Typically, the accusation of arrogance—literally, "highness of heart" (cf. Prov. 16:5)—is backed by the accused's own words. Another prophet puts similar aspirations in the mouth of the proud king of Babylon:

121

> I will ascend to heaven;
> above the stars of God
> I will set my throne on high;
> I will sit on the mount of assembly in the far north;
> I will ascend above the heights of the clouds,
> I will make myself like the Most High.
> Isaiah 14:13–14, RSV

The Most High is Elyon, an epithet of El, the supreme deity of the Canaanite pantheon. The king of Tyre makes the same claim to divine status ("I am El") and to the same position ("I occupy the seat of the gods"). There is a further twist to the claim, since the divine residence is transferred from the mountain in the far north—Jebel Aqra north of Ugarit, the Olympus of the Phoenician pantheon—to the city of Tyre "in the heart of the seas." The claim to divine status is associated with the possession of wisdom, a term that includes the kind of intellectual problem solving that the biblical tradition associates with Solomon (I Kings 4:29–34; 10:3–4) and a range of technological skills. The example of Solomon also reminds us that it is also the quality which allows a ruler to govern and judge prudently and justly. There is therefore a touch of irony in the comparison with Daniel, the wise and just king known to us from the Ugaritic texts (cf. 14:14, 20). For the king of Tyre has used his wisdom, the reality of which is not questioned, not for the creation of a just society but for the acquisition of wealth.

There is a curious paradox about wisdom as described in the Old Testament which is worth noting at this point. It can be observed in the splendidly written narratives dealing with the succession to David's throne, in which it occurs with such frequency as to constitute a major theme. Thus, when Amnon, first in line of succession, desires to possess himself of his half-sister Tamar, he has recourse to Jonadab, David's nephew, described as "a very wise man" (II Sam. 13:3). Making use of this wisdom, he devises a plan whereby Amnon's evil design can be accomplished. The ruse is successful, but its very success leads in the course of time to Amnon's death at the hands of Absalom. A few years later the army commander Joab, wishing to end Absalom's exile, employs a wise woman, whose wisdom consists in skillful speech, to lure David into granting this request. The ruse, again, is successful, but the return of Absalom leads to his rebellion and death (II Sam. 14—18). The same pattern underlies the story of the Man, the Woman, and the Snake in the

Garden of Eden (Gen. 2—3). The tree of the knowledge of good and evil, described as desirable for conferring wisdom (Gen. 3:6), is off limits to the Man and the Woman, but the Snake, the most cunning of creatures, persuades them to eat of its fruit in the expectation of attaining divine status. The wisdom was (and is) real, no question about that, but it proves to be death-dealing. As one of the Jewish sages put it, "He whose wisdom exceeds his fear of sin, his wisdom will not endure" (*m. 'Abot* 3.10).

So, we are told, it will be with this city famed throughout the world for its intellectual and technological preeminence. Because Tyre, represented by its ruler, has aspired to godlike status, judgment is at hand, to be administered by the Babylonians, "most terrible of the nations" (cf. 30:11; 31:12; 32:12). No moralizing is needed to bring out the implication of these pretensions in our contemporary situation, pretensions that, as always in the prophetic tradition ("The Egyptians are men, and not God," Isa. 31:3, RSV), come up sooner or later against the reality of the human condition and the obligation to acknowledge it.

The King of Tyre in Eden (28:11–19)

As in chapter 26, a lament *(qinah)* follows denunciation of the proud city, a genre that, for obvious reasons, came into its own during those crucial and tragic years (see especially Lamentations). The actual form of the lament is not always detectable because of later amplification (especially the list of precious stones) and occasional obscurity of expression. The structure and the intent of the poem are, nevertheless, fairly easy to follow, especially with the help of the parallel version of the myth of the First Man in Genesis 2—3.

The lament is over the king of Tyre, but it is also addressed to him. This is what we would expect in the context of a funeral service during which the attributes of the deceased are memorialized. The first of these, translated "signet of perfection" in RSV, is obscure. All we can say is that the signet ring *(hotem)* symbolizes royalty (cf. Jer. 22:24; Hag. 2:23). The First Man is created perfect in wisdom and beauty, which is not stated explicitly in the Genesis version, though the wisdom of the Man is hinted at in the naming of the animals. The omission is amply rectified in traditional Jewish commentary on the passage, and in those patristic and medieval commentators who list

123

the preternatural gifts which Adam enjoyed, only to lose after his sin. The location, the Garden of Eden, is the same in both; both speak of precious stones (Gen. 2:11–12), though there is no mention in Genesis of the holy mountain of God. The mountain at the center of the world is a familiar mythological motif. Both the Egyptian pyramid and the Mesopotamian ziggurat, or stepped temple, are stylized representations of the first mound to appear after the subsidence of the floodwaters. Whereas the Man in Genesis is naked, in the lament he is clothed in a garment which, like the high-priestly chasuble, is adorned with precious stones. (The Old Greek version of Ezek. 29:13 has twelve of these, not nine as in the Hebrew, corresponding to the description of the high-priestly vestments in Exod. 28:17–20.) The First Man has therefore both royal and priestly status, corresponding to ancient representations of kingship. Each of the stones has its own particular significance related to one of the twelve signs of the zodiac.

In contrast to Genesis 3, with its dramatic and symbolic detail, its cast of characters and its psychological profundity, Ezekiel's poem does not seek to explain the invasion of evil. The First Man was blameless in his conduct until iniquity was found in him. As in the Priestly account of the early history of the human race (Gen. 6:11–13), sin takes the form of violence compounded by pride and self-sufficiency. Since the poem connects this with commerce, the characteristic activity of the city, we are invited to think of the kind of cutthroat competition that earned Tyre its ascendancy as a maritime power.

The punishment is ejection from the garden in which, as in Genesis, the cherub or guardian deity plays a role. The fire which comes out from within the city is also reminiscent of the flaming sword which debarred the way to the tree of life (Gen. 3:24). The conclusion is the same as the other lament: you have come to a dreadful end and shall be no more forever.

It would be natural to assume that this lament draws on the familiar story of the Garden of Eden in Genesis, but it is equally possible to read both as distinct but related forms of an ancient mythic narrative well known in the ancient Near East. Whereas here it serves to convey a political message, the Genesis version is given a universal significance precisely by being placed at the beginning of the biblical story. In this, as in other instances, the first question to ask is not, Did it really happen? but, What does it mean? It invites attention to its symbolic meaning as a diagnosis of the human situation from a perspective that is both theologically and psychologically profound. Leaving aside the fate of Tyre, a matter of past history, what both versions convey is that sin emerges out of our interaction with the environment and in society—personal and sexual relations, the family, the larger political community. Both speak, in different ways, of the corruption of wisdom (see Ezek. 28:17), let us say of the human capacity for knowledge, mastery, and the quest for the fullness of life. Both take seriously the consequences of deviating from the original purpose of creation while affirming the possibility of restoration.

Sidon: Concluding Remarks (28:20–26)

The last of the series, exclusive of the anti-Egyptian sayings, is directed against Sidon. The judgment is couched in quite general terms: pestilence, blood, the sword, framed by the familiar formulaic language of Ezekiel: Behold, I am against you; you will know that I am Yahweh. We have the impression that Sidon was included simply because it is generally linked with Tyre in prophetic invective (Isa. 23:1–14; Jer. 25:22; Joel 3:4; Zech. 9:2), and perhaps also to make up the number seven. One of the principal Phoenician cities—with Tyre, Arvad (Ruad), and Gebal (Byblos)—Sidon is located on the Lebanese coast about equidistant from Tyre to the south and Beirut to the north. Because of its more exposed position, it suffered more directly from the Assyrians than Tyre and was even destroyed by Esarhaddon. Sidon was one of the coconspirators against Nebuchadnezzar in 595/594 B.C. (Jer. 27:3), and its king was subsequently deported to Babylon along with other western rulers, including Jehoiachin of Judah. It seems, however, to have emerged relatively intact and was thus able to take over the lead role from Tyre after the eclipse of the Babylonian empire. By dint of close cooperation with the Persians, especially by providing a Mediterranean fleet, it maintained its ascendancy until the rebellion of Tennes against Artaxerxes III, when it was destroyed in 351 B.C. Unlike Tyre, it submitted to Alexander and continued to play an important role in the politics of the region under his successors.

The series concludes with a remark on the beneficial effects on Israel of their God's control of international affairs (v. 24). This is no cause for self-congratulation but an occasion for acknowledging him as he is. The briers and thorns which he picks

125

out of their flesh are identified in the targum as wicked kings and vexatious rulers. The final summing up, almost certainly from a later hand (vs. 25–26), anticipates the message of hope and restoration delivered in the postcatastrophe years (cf. especially 39:25–29). It envisages the return of the deportees scattered throughout the world and the secure possession of the land, a theme of great importance in the book.

Ezekiel 29:1—32:32
Egypt

The seven anti-Egyptian units (29:1–16; 29:17–21; 30:1–19; 30:20–26; 31:1–18; 32:1–16; 32:17–32) are structurally distinct and parallel the seven anti-Tyrian sayings. All except one (30:1–19) are precisely dated, and the dates are in chronological order, with the sole exception of the second (29:17). It is possible that the original collection consisted of only five, the second (out of chronological order) and the third (undated) having been added subsequently for reasons about which we can only speculate. The entire collection of foreign nation oracles is, at any rate, organized in sevens, as we have seen. The much greater length at which Egypt is taken to task, and the absence of Babylon from the list, can both be explained by Ezekiel's construal of the political events of the twenty-two years of his active ministry, events that reached their climax in the fall of Jerusalem and the end of the Judean state. Taking his cue from Jeremiah, Ezekiel saw Babylon as the instrument of divine judgment on Judah and its neighbors, and of these, Egypt was not only the most powerful but the most persistent in opposing Babylonian imperial expansion. The frequency of dates in this section, much higher than elsewhere in the book, testifies to the need to authenticate and verify predictions made during the crucial period just before and after the fall of Jerusalem.

With the exception of 29:17–21, dated April 571 B.C., the latest date in the book, the anti-Egyptian sayings cover a period of about twenty-six months. With the exception of the second, just mentioned, they all date after the beginning of the siege in January 588 B.C. (Ezek. 24:1; also II Kings 25:1; Jer. 39:1; 52:4). The third (30:1–19), however, is undated, and the month is

126

missing in the seventh and last (32:1–19). The first, fourth, and fifth fall together within the first six months of 587 B.C., therefore during the siege, while the sixth (32:1–16), and perhaps also the seventh (32:17–32), are dated twenty-one months later, therefore after the fall of the city. The late date of the second oracle is explained by Nebuchadnezzar's failure to reduce Tyre after a thirteen-year siege which ended in 574/573 B.C. It predicts that his failure will be compensated by the occupation and sack of Egypt and therefore, in a certain sense, attempts to explain the nonfulfillment of previous sayings predicting the destruction of Tyre.

The sequence of events may be set out for convenience as follows:

January (Tebeth)	588	Beginning of the siege
Spring	588	Accession of Hophra; temporary raising of the siege by the Egyptians
January (Tebeth)	587	First saying (Ezek. 29:1–16)
April (Nisan)	587	Fourth saying (Ezek. 30:20–26)
May/June (Sivan)	587	Fifth saying (Ezek. 31:1–18)
August (Ab)	586	City and temple burned
February (Adar)	585	Sixth saying (Ezek. 32:1–16)
(no month)	585	Seventh saying (Ezek. 32:17–32)
April (Nisan)	571	Second saying (Ezek. 29:17–21)

As spare as it is, this outline is not free of difficulties. There are problems involved in synchronizing the chronological indications in the biblical sources (II Kings, II Chronicles, Jeremiah, Ezekiel), and the results have to be squared with Babylonian and Egyptian chronology. We have to allow for the possibility of different systems of reckoning, and the date of the fall of Jerusalem (587 or 586 B.C.) is still disputed. But for our purpose the *relative* chronology is secure enough to enable us to grasp the situation envisaged by the sayings and therefore the principles according to which Ezekiel construes and interprets contemporary events.

The Great Dragon Is Dead (29:1–16)

The first of the seven anti-Egyptian sayings is dated to early January 587 B.C., almost exactly a year into the siege and a little more than half a year before its end. Hophra (Apries) had succeeded Psammeticus II in the spring of the previous year, and almost immediately sent an army whose approach led to a temporary raising of the siege (Jer. 37:3–10; 34:21). It was during this brief respite that Jeremiah, attempting to leave the city to claim property that he had purchased at Anathoth, was arrested as a deserter and thrown into prison (Jer. 37:11–15).

The indictment of the Pharaoh and his people was probably inspired by the false hopes raised by Egyptian intervention at this point, but this was only the latest chapter in a long history which, for Ezekiel, began with Israel's sojourn in "the house of bondage" (Ezek. 20:5–8). During long periods of its history Israel lay within the Egyptian sphere of influence, a situation that, viewed from the prophetic perspective, was insidious and compromising (see especially 16:26; 23:3, 8, 19–21). It was also Egypt, in the person of Psammeticus II, the second great eagle, that had persuaded Zedekiah to break his oath of allegiance to the Babylonians and was therefore coresponsible for the disasters that followed (17:7–21).

The judgment on the Pharaoh is in verse (vs. 3–6a) and is justified in two articles of indictment which follow (vs. 6b–9a, 9b–12). These are, surprisingly, rounded off with a promise that Egypt will be restored after judgment, if on a much reduced scale (vs. 13–16). The unit was probably not composed all at the same time, but it is presented as a literary unity under the rubric "The word of Yahweh came to me" and may be interpreted as such.

In the poem, Pharaoh is addressed as the great dragon that lurks in the reaches of the Nile delta. As is clear from the detailed description in Job 41, the "dragon" (generally *tannin* but here and at 32:3 *tannim*) is the crocodile in its natural habitat. The image is obviously appropriate, especially in view of crocodile cults associated with the divine ruler in Egypt. But Tannin is also, together with Leviathan (Lothan in the Ugaritic texts), Rahab, and others, one of those mysterious and fearful

128

projections of monstrous evil which, in the Hebrew imagination, lurked in the dark waters that surrounded the narrow circuit of the inhabited, more or less civilized world. Though priestly theology insisted that these were created by God (Gen. 1:21; Ps. 148:7), there was always a sense that evil was only controlled, held at bay, by the act of creation, that its irruption into the orderly world of human society was always possible. As Robert Graves well put it in his poem "Vanity":

> Be assured, the Dragon is not dead
> But once more from the pools of peace
> Shall rear his fabulous green head.

These are the agents of death which, in ancient Canaanite poetry recovered from Ugarit, wage war against Baal in the endlessly recurring struggle between life-bestowing fertility and death-dealing aridity. The mythological drama was taken over by poet and prophet in Israel into the realm of Israel's historical drama, the paradigm of which was the conflict and victory at the Red Sea:

> Awake, awake, put on strength,
>   O arm of Yahweh;
> awake as in days of old,
>   the generations of long ago.
> Was it not thou that didst cut Rahab in pieces,
>   that didst pierce the dragon [Tannin]?
> Was it not thou that didst dry up the sea,
>   the waters of the great deep;
> that didst make the depths of the sea a way
>   for the redeemed to pass over?
>   Isaiah 51:9–10, RSV

As the great dragon, Hophra therefore was only the most recent embodiment or agent of evil forces by which Israel had always been threatened.

Typically, Ezekiel quotes the accused's own words in his indictment. As the king of Tyre claimed divine status (28:2), so the Egyptian king claims ownership of the Nile, source of Egypt's existence, by virtue of his own creative act. The aspiration to divine status is even clearer if we maintain the Hebrew which, translated literally, reads "My Nile is mine; I have made myself." For then we would have an echo of Heliopolitan theology according to which Atum, later identified with Re the sun-god, is described as self-begotten. These pretensions are deflated in the ensuing description of a crocodile hunt using

129

hooks, to which no doubt bait was attached. By this means, the crocodile will be pulled out of the water and left as carrion on the dry land. The fish sticking to its scales are no doubt meant to associate the people of Egypt—or their allies—with the Pharaoh's fate.

So far we can detect no allusion to the contemporary historical circumstances suggested by the date. The first of the two explanations (vs. 6b–9a) describes the Egyptians as a walking stick or crutch provided for the—presumably disabled—ally Judah. Being made of thin papyrus reed, it broke as soon as weight was put on it, injuring the user even further. The same image was used, also with reference to Egypt, by the Assyrian official trying to browbeat Hezekiah into surrendering more than a century earlier: "You are relying now on Egypt, that broken reed of a staff, which will pierce the hand of anyone who leans on it" (II Kings 18:21; Isa. 36:6). The final judgment will be by the invader's sword which will turn the land into a shambles.

The second indictment (vs. 9b–12) enlarges on the first, extending the destruction over the entire land from Migdol in the north to Syene and the border of Cush in the south. Migdol was probably known to Ezekiel as one of the early Jewish diaspora settlements in the Delta region, not far from Pelusium (Jer. 44:1; 46:14). Syene (modern Aswan), just north of the first cataract, marked the southern limit. It was close to the site of another Jewish settlement on the island of Jeb known from the Elephantine papyri. The alternative mark, at the border of Cush (Nubia), would take in the area between the first and the second cataract, also claimed by Egypt. The threat of forty years devastation and exile uses the conventional language of judgment. It is difficult to imagine that the seer intended it to be taken as a literal prediction that everything would be all right by the year 547 B.C.

The final prediction of restoration, surprising in view of Ezekiel's anti-Egyptian animus, may have been appended at a later stage. Egypt will be restored, no longer as a threatening, dominating power but confined to its place of origin in Pathros, a name that signifies the south land, the upper reaches of the Nile valley (cf. Isa. 11:11; Jer. 29:14; 44:1, 15). The historical tradition reflected here is of Thebes as the center of government in the early dynastic period. The reason for this surprising twist to the condemnation of contemporary Egypt is probably to be sought in the great expansion of the Jewish diaspora in Egypt beginning in the sixth century B.C., if not earlier (Jer. 43—44). Jeremiah's indictment of Egypt also ends with a word of hope for the future (Jer. 46:26), and later still, probably much later, another seer speaks of the worship of Yahweh in that land, cities in which Hebrew will be spoken, and of the Egyptians as Yahweh's people (Isa. 19:18–25). The blessing of Abraham will overflow Israel and descend on all peoples, a prophetic insight, often forgotten, which will be taken up by early Christianity.

Egypt in Exchange for Tyre (29:17–21)

The second anti-Egyptian saying, the latest of those dated in the book, was composed in April (Nisan) 571 B.C. It acknowledges that the siege of Tyre had failed. Heads and shoulders had been rubbed bare, probably as a result of carrying heavy baskets of earth and wearing armor and helmets continuously for so long. For the common soldier, then and for long afterward, the prospect of loot was the only compensation for the dangers and hardships that were incurred. This was doubtless also the easiest way to pay the many mercenaries who marched with Nebuchadnezzar in his western campaigns. Failure to penetrate the defenses of the island fortress meant that pay was thirteen years in arrears. The implication, surely somewhat ironic, is that justice must be done; the laborer is worthy of his hire (see, e.g., Lev. 19:13). Hence the promise, in the oracle that follows, that Nebuchadnezzar will have Egypt to plunder in lieu of Tyre, by which means he will finally be able to pay off his overworked men.

The most surprising touch is this: "They worked for me, says the Lord Yahweh." *I* sent them against Tyre; *my* prophet foretold its destruction. I am therefore under obligation to give them something in exchange, and Egypt lies at hand.

The most interesting thing about this second saying is the frank acknowledgment that previous prophecies of the fall and destruction of Tyre had not been fulfilled. The thirteen-year-long siege of which we hear in Josephus ended sometime between 574 and 572 B.C. By that time the situation had changed considerably and a new assessment was called for, including a reinterpretation and even annulment of previous assertions. While there is nothing quite comparable to Ezek. 29:17–21 in the prophetic literature, the idea of a progressive updating of predictive utterances is not unparalleled. A long discourse di-

131

rected against Moab in the Isaian collection, for example, is followed by a later updating:

> This is the word which Yahweh spoke concerning Moab in the past. But now Yahweh says, "In three years, like the years of a hireling, the glory of Moab will be brought into contempt."
>
> Isaiah 16:13–14, RSV

That Yahweh retains his freedom of action even after his prophet has spoken is the disconcerting and (for the prophet in question) unpalatable truth conveyed by the Jonah legend. As Jonah saw it, all he had to do was to proclaim, "Yet forty days, and Nineveh shall be overthrown" (Jonah 3:4, RSV) and wait for it to happen. The king of Nineveh *(sic)*, theologically somewhat more perceptive, wondered aloud whether God might change his mind (repent) and turn from his fierce anger; and that is what he did. The Ezekiel saying makes the point even more strongly, since the Tyrians, unlike the people of Nineveh, were not saved by repenting. Needless to say, this relativization of predictive prophecy renders the task of discerning between authentic and inauthentic prophecy more complicated. It also warns that prophecy cannot and should not serve as a ready-made means of construing world events in the present and the future. The problem with prophecy, now as then, is that it is always necessary but never by itself sufficient.

We have no information on the conquest and occupation of Egypt by Nebuchadnezzar in the ten years that elapsed between this prediction and his death. Our principal source, Herodotus (*History* 2.161–169), records the disturbances which accompanied the deposition of Hophra and the usurpation of his successor Amasis about 568 B.C. and in which Lybians and Greeks were involved but not Babylonians. A fragmentary Babylonian record speaks of Nebuchadnezzar marching against Egypt in his thirty-seventh year, which would be about that time, but it says nothing about the outcome of that campaign. The issue cannot be decided one way or the other.

The two concluding remarks addressed to the prophet (v. 21) may be connected, in the sense that judgment on Egypt will both benefit Israel and vindicate Ezekiel himself whose reputation may have been harmed by the non-fulfillment of the oracles against Tyre (cf. earlier misgivings, 12:22, 27). The same mixed metaphor of a horn sprouting occurs in Ps. 132:17. The horn symbolizes strength and therefore rule. Alexander was

132

known among the Semites as "he of the horns," and in the vision of the beasts in Daniel (7:7–8) the horns stand for rulers. The accompanying verb (stem: *ṣ m ḥ*) is meant to recall the Hebrew substantive *ṣemaḥ* (translated "branch" in RSV) which was used from the time of the Babylonian exile as a kind of code name for the Davidic ruler, present or future (see, e.g., Jer. 23:5–6; 33:14–16; Zech. 6:12). It is therefore possible to read the first statement as an affirmation of the future restoration of the Davidic monarchy, which certainly was part of Ezekiel's vision of the future (cf. 34:23–24). The "opening of the lips" can hardly refer to the loss of speech that ended some fifteen years earlier (33:22). It must therefore mean that a time will come when the prophet will speak to his people with confidence (what the New Testament calls *parrhēsia*), free of the doubts, probably including self-doubts, of the present uncertain moment.

The Day of Egypt (30:1–19)

The third unit is the only one without a date, and we should not assume that it is covered by the date of the first (29:1), much less the second (29:17). It is composed of four oracular sayings each introduced by "Thus says Yahweh" (vs. 2, 6, 10, 13) which may not all be contemporary. Any attempt at dating must be speculative, since there is little if any correlation with known historical events; only the third of the four oracles alludes to an invasion of Egypt by Nebuchadnezzar.

The opening poem on the Day of Yahweh, linked to the preceding saying by verbal association, restates the theme already developed in the sermon in chapter 7. The idea that history is moving toward a moment of resolution, in which the moral and religious ambiguities of the present will be dissolved by a decisive divine intervention, courses through the entire prophetic collection (e.g., Amos 5:18–20; Isa. 2:12–17; Jer. 30:7; Zeph. 1:14–18; Joel 1:15; 2:1–2). It is an idea that has retained its vitality throughout Christian history, though often (and at no time less than the present) overshadowed by the attempt to pinpoint the moment and vitiated by failure to grasp the metaphoric nature of the language in which it is described. The poem goes on to describe one such moment of resolution which will affect Egypt and Cush (Nubia) its southern neighbor. The language draws on the ancient motif of divine intervention in battle, including the divinely inspired panic of which we hear in the epic narratives of the Philistine wars (I Sam. 4:7–8; 14:15).

133

As in chapter 7, the result will be the collapse of the entire social fabric and descent into chaos.

The second oracle (vs. 6–9) extends the judgment to the allies or mercenaries of Egypt of whom a later commentator has given a partial list in the note at v. 5. Four of the names—Cush, Put, Lud, and Cub—are similar in sound, and two or more of them are often found together (see Ezek. 27:10 and 38:5; also Isa. 66:19; Jer. 46:9). Cush-Nubia, between the first and the second cataract, has always played an important role in Egyptian history, especially under the Twenty-fifth Dynasty (715–663 B.C.) whose pharaohs were Nubian in origin. Put, son of Ham and brother of Egypt in "the table of the nations" (Gen. 10:6), refers to Cyrenaica, the region around Tripoli. Lud probably stands for settlements of Lydian mercenaries, comparable to the Jewish military settlement on the island of Elephantine near Aswan. Herodotus, who refers to them, also records a treaty between Pharaoh Amasis and the fabulously wealthy Croesus, last ruler of the Lydian kingdom. Cub is probably a textual error for Lub, meaning Lybia, which is how some of the ancient versions understand it. The Hebrew *kol-ha'ereb*, literally "the entire mob" (cf. Jer. 25:20; 50:37), is often read as *kol-ha'arab*, meaning "all the Arabs," but this does not seem to be necessary. The last category may simply refer to allies in general, but it is tempting to refer "those of the land of the covenant" to Jewish mercenaries who had enlisted in the Egyptian armies.

Using the language of the first unit (29:1–16), the oracle predicts the devastation of Egypt from one end to the other (Migdol to Syene, cf. 29:10) and the destruction of its cities. To this has been added a later comment in prose which speaks of messengers of doom going by ship up the Nile to bring news of disaster to the Nubians (v. 9). It recalls, and is no doubt meant to recall, the saying of Isaiah about Nubian messengers, traveling by the same means but in the opposite direction, with proposals for an alliance against Assyria (Isa. 18). It may serve to remind us, as we read these texts, that there are lines of continuity within the prophetic tradition, an ongoing process of reappropriation and reinterpretation which is part of the total meaning.

134

Only in the third oracle (vs. 10–12) do we hear again the prediction of Babylonian conquest. It is worded in such a way as to make clear that the God of Israel is master of both history and nature. Nebuchadnezzar acts as his agent, and it is he himself who will dry up the Nile, the source of Egypt's existence. On the problematic question of the fulfillment of these predictions something was said earlier. According to one reading of biblical prophecy, history confirms religious belief, but we would have to add that belief must often be sustained in spite of history. The connection is inescapable, but there is no easy way to formulate it.

The final oracle (vs. 13–19) employs the literary device, exemplified in other prophetic books (e.g., Micah 1:10–15), of amplifying by means of a list of toponyms. They are arranged in no clearly discernible order. With the exceptions of Memphis and Thebes, capitals of Lower and Upper Egypt respectively and generally familiar, all of the city names are in the region of the Nile delta, and most of them could have been picked up from Jeremiah. Memphis (Noph) is mentioned first as the capital of Egypt during the Old Kingdom and center of the cult of Ptah, the creator-deity and of the worship of the bull-god Apis. As such, its importance was revived by Pharaoh Amasis. Pathros designates Upper Egypt, and Zoan, known to the Greeks as Tanis, was the ancient capital of the Hyksos and of Ramses II in the eastern delta. Thebes (No), the spectacular remains of which at Karnak and Luxor are on every visitor's list, was the principal cult center of the god Amon during the Middle and New Kingdoms. The targum identifies the Hebrew place-name at Alexandria, no doubt because of its great importance at that time for the Jewish diaspora. Sin is generally identified with Pelusium on the Mediterranean coast near Port Said. An important frontier post, it was to be the scene of the Egyptian defeat by the Persians in 525 B.C. and, later still, of the assassination of Pompey. On is Heliopolis, the city of the sun, about six miles northwest of Cairo. As the name suggests, it was dedicated to the worship of the sun-god Re-Atum. Pibeseth or Bubastis, also near Cairo, was the city of the goddess Bastet and a famous center of pilgrimage. Tehaphnehes or Tahpanes or Daphnai to the Greeks, on the Suez Canal, is mentioned often in Jeremiah as one of the principal settlements of the Jewish diaspora in Egypt. Apart from showing off a knowledge of Egyptian topography, the list makes the same important point as the story of the city and tower of Babel, namely, the intimate connection and insidious collusion between political power and religion. The history of Israel, then and now, is proof that the point is

135

made not just for the benefit of "the others," and the same can be said, with even greater reason, of the history of Christianity.

Pharaoh's Broken Arm (30:20–26)

The following short prose oracle is dated in late April (Nisan) 587 B.C., about three months after the first (29:1) and with several months of the siege still to run. The Egyptian troops sent by Hophra, perhaps led by him personally, had been forced to withdraw during the previous year, but there were doubtless still some in the doomed city, and among their compatriots in exile, who were looking for last-minute salvation from that quarter. The point of the oracle is to dispel such hopes. The image by means of which the point is made is decidedly unpleasant, even sadistic. Yahweh has broken Pharaoh's arm, Pharaoh will not receive medical attention to enable him to take up arms again, and, just to make sure, Yahweh will break it again and the other one also for good measure. Pharaoh will stand moaning with pain in the presence of his conqueror. We must surely regret the use of violent and distasteful imagery in the Old Testament, of a kind that is particularly frequent in this type of prophetic saying. (Other examples are the dishonoring of Nineveh and its women in the Book of Nahum, and Moab drowning in a dung pit in Isa. 25:10–12.) Rather than attempting to justify this kind of thing—for example, on the grounds that the motivation is strictly religious—we should admit frankly that no view of biblical inspiration need entail the conclusion that the Bible is theologically perfect. If it were not so, how could we avoid endorsing, for example, the command to commit genocide on the Amalekites and the indigenous population of Canaan (Exod. 17:14–16; Deut. 7:1–2; 25:17–19)? There are matters in the Bible which are time- and culture-conditioned, there are high points and low points, and, above all, there are developments in the way divine action and appropriate human reaction are perceived and described. If we are not to fall back on allegory and accommodation, these must be taken into account in our own response to the texts.

This fourth anti-Egyptian saying, which, as brief as it is, is remarkably repetitious, discourages delusive hopes by assuring the prophet's audience that Hophra will be in no position to resume the offensive against the Babylonians. On the contrary, Egypt itself will be attacked by them and they will suffer the same fate as Israel: foreign conquest, occupation, and dispersion among the nations.

The Felling of the Great Cedar (31:1–18)

The fifth saying is dated almost two months later, in late May or early June (Sivan) of 587 B.C. Addressed to the Pharaoh and his people, it takes the form of a poem (vs. 2–9), similar in some respects to the lament over the king of Tyre (28:11–19) but without the uneven (3 + 2) verse form demanded by the *qinah*. The poem is followed by two oracles: the first consisting of the indictment (vs. 10–14) and the second describing the descent into the underworld of the Pharaoh and his people (vs. 15–18).

Using the language of allegory, the poet-prophet compares Egypt to a cedar of Lebanon, the tallest and most impressive tree known to the people of the Near East. The great tree metaphor was used more than once by Ezekiel (see 17:3, 22–24; 19:10–14), and we will find it recurring, in similar descriptive terms, in the dream of Nebuchadnezzar in Daniel (Dan. 4:1–12, 19–27) and in the parable of the mustard seed in the Gospel (Matt. 13:31–32 and parallel). The poet dwells on its thick foliage, its great width and height, the shelter it affords to birds that nest in it, and the shade it gives to animals peacefully going about their business. Its appropriateness as a metaphor for a great nation or its ruler is obvious, and the poet even abandons metaphor to speak of the protection afforded to nations allied with or in vassalage to Egypt (v. 6).

That there is more to the representation than a simple comparison with this well-known conifer is suggested early on in the reference to the source of its size and vigor. Its roots draw their nourishment from the subterranean waters of the abyss, the *tehom,* the boundless circumambient floodwaters covered by darkness at the beginning of time (Gen. 1:2) which inundated the world in the days of Noah (Gen. 7:11; 8:2). The cedar is therefore the world tree, a familiar mythological *topos* (e.g., the tree Yggdrasil of the Norse peoples), planted at the center of the earth and sending its roots down into the underworld. That the nourishing water flows in streams and channels round the place of its planting describes the situation in the Nile delta, but it is also reminiscent of the rivers flowing from Eden which water the surface of the ground and account for the boundless fertility of the place. Ancient and very persistent ideas underlie this description, ideas that have been developed in interesting ways in Jewish and even, to some extent, Christian legend and folklore. It was said that the temple was built over the floodwa-

137

ters, drawing its power from them and at the same time re-
straining them from erupting and flooding the world. It is there,
where he has overcome the forces of chaos, that God sets up his
throne:

> Yahweh sits enthroned over the flood;
> Yahweh sits enthroned as king for ever!
> Psalm 29:10, RSV

Christian mystical interpreters identified the cross of Christ
with the tree in the middle of Eden and therefore in the middle
of the earth. As John Donne put in in one of his last poems:

> We thinke that Paradise and Calvarie,
> Christs Crosse and Adams tree, stood in one place.

It is not surprising, therefore, that Ezekiel refers here also to the
Eden myth (cf. 28:12–19). The Pharaonic tree exceeds in beauty
all the trees of Eden, which are moved to envy, until both it and
they end up in the underworld (vs. 8–9, 16–17).

The image of the great tree whose roots are nourished by
the subterranean waters acknowledges that Egypt draws its
strength from its own rootage in the divine world, the world of
religious knowledge and ritual, including the veneration of the
dead. The reality of this other dimension of reality is not denied;
after all, it had sustained the life and institutions of that people
for some two and a half millennia before Ezekiel's time. The
first of the two oracles appended to the song (vs. 10–14) simply
asserts that it will be cut down and therefore severed from its
life-giving roots. Using the language and themes of the song, it
asserts that it will be delivered over to "a mighty one [literally,
"ram"] of the nations," namely, Nebuchadnezzar, and "the
most terrible of the nations" (cf. 28:7; 30:11; 32:12), namely, the
Babylonians. The same arrogance and self-sufficiency that led to
the wreck of the Tyrian ship also leads to the felling of the
Egyptian cedar. This is a common, almost too familiar theme,
running through prophetic preaching, the writings of the sages,
and the teaching of Jesus: the God of Israel humbles the exalted
and exalts the humble.

The first of the two additional sayings ends by reverting to
verse, with an elegiac reflection on mortality rather untypical
of Ezekiel:

138

> They are all delivered to Death,
> To the Netherworld,
> Among mortals, with those who go down to the Pit.
> Ezekiel 31:14

The second oracle (vs. 15–18) continues in the same vein with the theme, familiar from the Tyre poems (26:19–21), of the descent to the underworld. To describe the place of the dead, the Old Testament, here and elsewhere, uses a variety of expressions. It is Sheol, to which Jacob must go to see his dead son (Gen. 37:35). It is the earth *('ereṣ)*, or the netherworld, or the pit, from which the psalmist prays to be delivered (Ps. 28:1; 63:9). In this respect, Israel shared in the common understanding of the state of the dead of ancient Mesopotamia, which, interestingly and paradoxically in view of the subject matter of the poem, was quite different from the vista of a luminous afterexistence cherished in ancient Egypt. The fullest description of the Mesopotamian view occurs in the Gilgamesh epic, where Enkidu relates an ominous dream presaging his own death. The denizens of the house of darkness are clothed like birds, eat dust and clay, are bereft of light and warmth, and together with the kings and great ones of olden times serve Ereshkigal, the cold queen of the underworld (Gilgamesh 7.31–54). This is the fate of Egypt, the great cedar, though this last oracle dwells more on the effect on nature and the living than on the descent itself. The entire cosmos will mourn, the subterranean waters will be dried up, bringing gloom and infertility on nature, including Lebanon. Even the trees of Eden will go down with it to the pit. The fall of the cedar will be like an earthquake which will terrify all nations and destroy those of them who had taken shelter under it—namely, its allies and vassals. Even in the underworld, Egypt will be dishonored, assigned a place with the uncircumcised—a disgrace for Egyptians who practiced circumcision—and war casualties denied burial. The somber description ends by repeating, in a slightly different form, the initial question and by identifying, once again, those to whom it is addressed, as if to say, See now what has become of Pharaoh and all his mob.

Lament for a Dead Dragon (32:1–16)

The last two sayings are dated after the fall of Jerusalem, 32:1–16 in late February–early March 585 B.C. and 32:17–32 a couple of weeks later. Variations in the early versions were probably due to an attempt to fit them all in before the end of the siege (33:21). The passage now under consideration is presented as a lament *(qinah)* and even ends with a note about its performance, analogous to the lament about the lioness and her cubs (ch. 19). All that remains of it, however, is a single couplet

139

(v. 2) now followed by two oracular sayings (3–10, 11–15) in which faint traces of the limping meter of the lament (3 + 2) are detectable.

The opening couplet plays on the contrast between Egypt's self-image as "a lion among the nations" and the reality. To describe this, Ezekiel reverts to the *tannin,* the crocodile that lurks in the waters of the Nile delta. The rest of the description is obscure, but since "feet" is a euphemism for genitals, the fouling of the waters is probably another example of the kind of satire to which Ezekiel was not averse. Understandably, therefore, the targum paraphrases rather drastically: "You were the mightiest of the nations, and you were like a monster in the seas, and you broke forth with your armies, and made the nations tremble with your auxiliaries, and you destroyed their countries." The lion image may have been suggested by the sphinx, of leonine body, and the phrase "lion of the nations" would have served to dissociate it from "the lion of Judah" (cf. 19:1–9).

The continuation is in verse, in the usual form of prophetic-oracular utterance (vs. 3–8), to which a comment in prose has been appended (vs. 9–11). Taking its cue from the first of the seven anti-Egyptian sayings (29:1–16), it describes a crocodile hunt, with nets in this instance rather than hooks and bait, which ends with the great beast thrown out on dry land as food for scavengers—an echo, perhaps, of the slaying of the monster Tiamat in the Babylonian creation poem *Enuma Elish* (4.95). The anticipated downfall of Egypt elicits imagery of cosmic and apocalyptic dimensions: the land covered with blood even up to the mountains, the darkening of the sun, moon, and stars, reminiscent of the plagues at the beginning of the history that preceded the exodus (Exod. 7:14–24; 10:21–23). The association is strengthened by the prose addition (vs. 9–10) which speaks of an Egyptian exodus into captivity, an event that will inspire fear for their own safety in her allies and satellites. An entire phase of the history of international relations, which in Ezekiel's view had brought nothing but disaster to Israel, is therefore seen to be drawing to an end.

The second oracle (vs. 11–15) identifies the king of Babylon, Nebuchadnezzar, as the agent of divine judgment on Egypt. The entire land will be stripped of its human and animal population, which will allow for the cleansing of its life-giving waters, thus reversing the situation described in the opening couplet.

The grim scenario therefore at least ends on a note of ecological hope. The final statement (v. 16), comparable to the one following the lament over the lioness and the vine (19:14), is in the manner of a rubric enjoining the chanting of the lament by professional mourners from the nations associated with Egypt. It serves to give a sense of concreteness and reality to the events described, as if they had already taken place.

Egypt's Welcome in the Underworld (32:17–32)

The last of the seven sayings is also dated to the twelfth year, but the month is missing in the Hebrew text. The Old Greek version supplies the first month (Nisan), but since this would date it earlier than the preceding sayings, we should probably follow those medieval Jewish commentators who opt for the twelfth month (Adar). It would then follow about two weeks later. The prophet is again told to lament, but what follows is not called a *qinah,* and the meter, where detectable, is of the regular 2 + 2 type, perhaps an alternative lament form as, for example, in Jer. 9:19:

> How are we rúined,
> We are greátly ashámed!

The text of the entire passage, especially the first five verses, is more than usually corrupt, with repetitions, amplifications, and recurrence of stock phrases suggesting much editorial elaboration. The general idea at least is clear: the drama of Egypt's fall ends with a speech of welcome to the underworld delivered by the heroes long dead and accompanied by the ritual lamentations of "the daughters of the nations" mentioned at the end of the previous saying.

The theme of the descent to the underworld, of frequent occurrence in the literature of Semitic and Greek antiquity, was well adapted to the prophetic judgment on world events and the movers and shakers on the world scene. A poem in the Isaian collection, probably from the exilic period, incorporates it into an ironic lament on the king of Babylon:

> Sheol beneath is stirred up
>   to meet you when you come,
> it rouses the shades to greet you,
>   all who were leaders of the earth;
> it raises from their thrones
>   all who were kings of the nations.

141

All of them will speak
    and say to you:
"You too have become as weak as we!
    You have become like us!"
Your pomp is brought down to Sheol,
    the sound of your harps;
maggots are the bed beneath you,
    and worms are your covering.
                    Isaiah 14:9–11, RSV

Ezekiel, then, is told to send down Egypt, by the power of the prophetic word, to the lower earth (cf. 31:14, 16, 18), with those who go down to the pit (cf. 31:14, 16). This land of the dead—Sheol, the pit, the underworld—is the counterpart to the land of the living in which alone the divine presence can be experienced and its redemptive and life-giving possibilities are accessible. Like the Hades of Homer and, for that matter, the Inferno of Dante, this kingdom of the dead has degrees of differentiation. Egypt, proudest of nations, is allotted a place with those slain by the sword—perhaps alluding to those who remained unburied after battle—and the uncircumcised who, on the Israelite analogy, belonged to no ordered community (cf. 31:18). She is therefore in the lowest reaches of the underworld, surrounded by her satellites, as the pyramid-tombs of the Pharaohs were surrounded by those of their principal officers. The differentiation is not based on moral criteria, not directly at any rate. According to this view, the worst fate awaits the dead who remain unburied, and we recall that Egypt was cast out like carrion on the steppe.

These ancient views of postmortem existence, which seem so far removed from those taken for granted by Christian and Jew today, should nevertheless provoke reflection. The denial of death (the title of an influential work by Ernest Becker) works very powerfully throughout our culture, is reflected in the language we use for the different stages of life ("the golden years," e.g.), and comes to expression in our funeral services and mortuary practices—including what someone has referred to as the obscene art of the mortician. The anxiety that the certainty of death—however skillfully camouflaged—induces can, of course, be salutary, but the effort at the conscious and the unconscious level to suppress it can also have a crippling effect. The situation would, we imagine, be rather different in a traditional society where the individual exists at the point of intersection of the living community at the horizontal level and those who have

142

gone before and will come after on the vertical axis. The phrase "to be gathered to the ancestors," of frequent occurrence in the Old Testament (somewhat pedantically paraphrased by one scholar as "aggregation to the totality of the clan"), insinuates the natural element in the process of dying and, correspondingly, deemphasizes the crippling anxiety which the prospect of death more easily provokes in our kind of disgregated culture. A good death is therefore a kind of communion with those who have gone before, an event that can be commemorated and celebrated by those who remain without undue sorrow. A bad death, the sort foreseen for Egypt, is a kind of excommunication, a casting out from the commonwealth in which both the living and the dead have citizenship and franchise.

From this view of solidarity between the living and the dead it is not so great a step to the idea that the power of the God who reigns in the land of the living also extends into the regions beyond death. While this idea is expressed clearly and unambiguously only in the latest phase of the history of Israel in the biblical period, intimations of it can be detected here and there in the psalms, especially where divine justice is the issue or where the experience of God in worship is being described:

> God will ransom my soul from the power of Sheol,
>   for he will receive me.
>> Psalm 49:15, RSV

> When my soul was embittered,
>   when I was pricked in heart,
> I was stupid and ignorant,
>   I was like a beast toward thee.
> Nevertheless I am continually with thee;
>   thou dost hold my right hand.
>> Psalm 73:21–23, RSV

We left Egypt and its satellites as they were being welcomed to the underworld by the dead heroes of the past (32:21). They are first introduced to those already there, the nations who spread terror during their time on earth or, as the targum paraphrases, who exercised tyrannical rule over the land of Israel. Again we note the absence of Babylon. The first three, in fact, are nations that threatened Babylon from the north and the east and that therefore presuppose the perspective of the Babylonian diaspora. The first is Assyria, whose domination came to an end with the fall of Nineveh in 612 B.C., an event

143

celebrated, perhaps proleptically, in the Book of Nahum. Elam, one of the principal opponents of Assyria until its decisive defeat by Ashurbanipal, lay east of the Tigris. By Ezekiel's day it was no longer a force to be reckoned with and was eventually absorbed into the Persian empire, its principal city, Susa, becoming the winter capital of the Persian kings. Meshech and Tubal, corresponding to the *mushku* and *tabal* of Assyrian records, were located in Asia Minor (Phrygia and Cilicia respectively) and therefore represent the threat from the far north. They were mentioned as trading partners of Tyre (27:13), and we shall meet them again in the Gog-Magog passage (chs. 38–39). The last two lie to the south and north of the land of Israel and are therefore often taken to be later additions. Hostility to Edom came to a head during the exilic period (cf. 25:12–14; 35), and we have noted that Sidon became the leading Phoenician city about the same time and remained so throughout the Persian period (cf. 28:20–23). The sight of all these in the underworld will help to reconcile Pharaoh to his fate, for he will acknowledge that he is one of those movers and shakers who have now passed from the scene. Ezekiel recapitulates what might be called the prophetic theology of history, to be taken up in not entirely different circumstances by Augustine in his *City of God.* Ezekiel anticipates, at the same time, the imagery and message of the writers of apocalyptic tracts, from the vision of the beasts from the abyss in Daniel to the condemnation of the Roman Babylon in Revelation.

PART FOUR

The Fall of Jerusalem
EZEKIEL 33

The point has been made more than once that the structure or internal organization of a prophetic book, or for that matter of any biblical book, is an important aspect of its total meaning and therefore one to which the exegete must give careful attention. In the Book of Ezekiel the turning point is the fall of Jerusalem or, more precisely, the moment at which Ezekiel and his fellow deportees receive the news of this event. The date, which is carefully noted (33:21), marks the end of the first part of his prophetic career, a period of some six and a half years. The last two years of this period, corresponding to the siege of the city, are also marked off as especially significant (24:1–2). The collection of sayings against foreign nations, spoken or written at different times, has appropriately filled this two-year gap, since, as we have argued, Ezekiel was barred during that time from addressing his fellow Israelites. It therefore introduces an element of dramatic tension between the announcement of a new phase of prophetic activity (24:25–27) and its inception on the arrival of the fugitive from Jerusalem (33:21–22). Chapter 33, therefore, serves to recapitulate the first phase—as we shall see in detail in what follows—and at the same time initiates a new phase corresponding to the quite different situation obtaining after the fall of the city.

Ezekiel 33:1–9
The Prophet as Sentry—Again

By paralleling the appointment of the prophet as sentry at the beginning of his career (3:16–21), this first passage recapitulates the period of ministry at a time of crisis—the six and a half years from Tammuz 593 to Tebeth 587/586 B.C. In all probability, 3:16–21 was appended, by no means inappropriately, to the call narrative and is therefore dependent on the version that is before us in this chapter. This version, couched in the form of casuistic law (see the commentary on 3:16–21), begins with a theoretical statement on the extent and limits of the sentry's responsibilities (vs. 1–6). If, in time of war, the sentry appointed by the city officials sees the enemy approaching, warns the inhabitants by a blast on the ram's horn, and they fail to take appropriate action, they alone must bear responsibility for the (probably fatal) consequences. If, on the other hand, the sentry does not warn, he bears responsibility for the consequences. This all seems quite obvious, but the point is to emphasize the nature of prophetic ministry in a time of crisis. If we look back again over the preceding chapters, we shall see that the task is not just to sound the prophetic trumpet blast—like Jonah's "yet forty days, and Nineveh shall be overthrown!" (Jonah 3:4, RSV)—but to recognize and evaluate the situation and to find ways of creating an awareness that will lead to appropriate action. Not all of Ezekiel's methods may be appropriate today, but we cannot help admiring the variety of ways, verbal and nonverbal, in which he attempts to discharge his task.

The statement of principle is then applied to the situation of Ezekiel himself (vs. 7–9), a passage that is reproduced almost verbatim in the call narrative (3:17–19). For those whose ministry consists almost entirely in preaching or ministering to the converted, a not uncommon situation, it may be disconcerting to note that the charge is here concerned exclusively with the unconverted and that in carrying it out the prophet's own life is at stake. The sentry metaphor suggests that the language of living and dying used here refers to physical survival in a war-

146

time situation. But there must be more to it than that, for we hear of the wicked dying "in his iniquity" (vs. 6, 8, 9). The prospect is similar in the presentation of the three generations in chapter 18. While it would be anachronistic to transpose into the language of eternal salvation and reprobation, there is at least the sense that any meaningful kind of life involves association with God, a condition of which is obedience to his life-giving laws (cf. 20:11, 13, 21). There is also at least an intimation concealed in the phrase "dying in one's iniquity" that there is a certain moral and spiritual dimension to death and that therefore it makes a difference whether one dies in association with or dissociation from God. We shall see that the same questions arise in the following section.

Ezekiel 33:10-20
How Can We Survive?

The theme of living and dying is taken up again in the question posed to the prophet by his fellow exiles, a question reminiscent of the community laments in the psalms. The frequency of these consultations and disputations between the prophet and his public, usually introduced by quoting the words of the latter (12:9, 22, 27; 14:1; 18:2, 19, 25, 29; 20:1; 21:7; 24:19), suggests a specific social location, a *Sitz im Leben* in the Babylonian diaspora, perhaps a rudimentary synagogue setting which allowed—as the synagogue still does—for both prayer and instruction. The teaching contained in the present passage reproduces more or less exactly the remarks appended to the case history of the three generations (i.e., 33:12–16 = 18:21–24 and 33:17–20 = 18:25–30*a*). Very probably, however, the present version, which gives the occasion and setting for the teaching, was the source for the version in chapter 18. It will be noted that that chapter interrupts the series of allegories which begins in chapter 15. In speaking of the weight of the past and of the possibilities for the future, 33:10–20 also fits the immediate postcatastrophe situation and serves as a point of transition between judgment (chs. 1—24) and restoration (chs. 34—48).   147

The despairing cry of the community shows that the disaster has at last brought home to them the consciousness of sin, the devastating effects of which call into question the possibility of survival. It seems, then, that Ezekiel's preaching has at last begun to take effect and that they are disposed to listen. The immediate response is a statement of God's ultimate purpose, beyond all prophetic denunciations and condemnations: I have no pleasure in the death of the wicked (see also 18:23, 32). There is always an opening for repentance, for "turning," and precisely this is the answer to their question.

Comparison with 18:21–24 shows that here too the present version is more complete and systematic, beginning with a general statement of principle (v. 12), not in the parallel version, which is then applied to the actual cases of a righteous and a wicked person (vs. 13–16). The principle enunciates the reality of conversion, the act of choosing either evil or good. There is no accumulation of merit which can minimize or annul that act of choice, nor is there an accumulated weight of sin which can inhibit (literally, "cause to stumble") at the moment of choosing the good. There is always the possibility of redirecting one's life, which is the basic idea behind what both the Old and the New Testament have to say about repentance.

The exemplification of the principle in concrete case histories, typical of Ezekiel's teaching, is presented in inverse order in 18:21–24. The case histories of the righteous and the wicked are introduced by decrees of acquittal and condemnation respectively, characteristic of priestly forensic usage but also deliberately reminiscent of prophetic formulations, especially those of Ezekiel himself. There is therefore no predetermination, no closing off the possibility of change, even after the verdict has been announced by either priest or prophet. There is no assurance of salvation, no confidence in past merits, which can be invoked in the act of turning to sin. What is important is always the present orientation of one's life. This is as true of the reprobate as it is of the righteous; and to make sure that the act of "turning" is well understood, that it is a matter of doing rather than aspiring, examples are given: restoring the poor man's pledge (cf. Exod. 22:25–27), returning stolen property— in a word, observing the life-giving statutes. We see that this liberating and demystifying moral teaching responds to the despairing question of Ezekiel's contemporaries by both removing the burden of the past and opening up the possibility of a different future.

The teaching also answers the question, already posed, about the divine moral governance of the world (vs. 17–20; cf. 18:25–30*a*). There is no carryover of moral accountability from one generation to the next, no accumulation of guilt laid on the shoulders of the present generation by its predecessors. There are no theological alibis, though we may feel it necessary to add that there can be constraints and limitations on freedom of moral choice—physical, psychological, and social—of which Ezekiel and his age were unaware.

Ezekiel 33:21–22
The Fall of Jerusalem Announced

We have seen that the fall of Jerusalem marks the great divide in Ezekiel's career, bringing to an end six and a half years of sentry duty—warning, threatening, condemning—and inaugurating a period of at least fifteen years of reconstruction. The account of the arrival of a refugee from Judah bearing the news links directly with a prediction made at the beginning of the siege about two years earlier (24:25–27). In the Hebrew text it is dated in the tenth month of the twelfth year of Jehoiachin, which would be mid-January 585 B.C. But since it would be difficult to explain why it took seventeen months for the news to reach Babylon (cf. II Kings 25:8–9; Jer. 52:12), most commentators emend to the eleventh year, a change that requires minimum alteration of the Hebrew text. We then have a reasonable interval of about five months, and we recall that Ezra's journey in the opposite direction took four months (Ezra 7:9; 8:31). The bearer of the news is called a survivor *(palit)*, a term that is used elsewhere in Ezekiel for a deportee (6:8–10; 14:22). We would therefore be inclined to think not of a stray fugitive from the Babylonian armies ravaging the homeland but of the arrival of the mass deportation that followed the taking of the city (II Kings 25:11)—a conclusion that would also explain the use of the article (the deportee) with a collective noun.

Ezekiel reports that he had entered a state of trance the previous evening, the fourth of the month Tebeth, and that by the time the news reached him the following morning his aphasia had ended and he was able to speak. This too had been

149

predicted at the beginning of the siege (24:27). We find here one more indication that the entire period from the prophetic commissioning is now being recapitulated, for we have seen that loss of speech, accompanied by seclusion in his house, has also been incorporated into the call narrative (3:24–27). It will already be apparent that the interpretation of Ezekiel's silence is one of the most intractable problems of the book. Taken by itself, 33:21–22 might suggest that the affliction, if that is what it was, was of short duration, like that of Zechariah, father of John the Baptist (Luke 1:20–22, 64). It certainly could not have lasted for the entire period from the call. We have taken the view, based on 24:25–27, that its duration corresponded to the two years of the siege and that, whatever its nature, it prevented Ezekiel from communicating with his fellow deportees. We therefore have a hiatus between the first and the second period of the prophet's activity, one that has been filled by the prophecies directed against foreign nations. It is very doubtful whether we can get beyond these structuring features to discover the clinical or metaphorical nature of this highly significant silence. The main point is to grasp the sense of release into a new and quite different phase of activity when the news finally arrived.

Ezekiel 33:23–29
A Disputed Claim to the Land of Israel

The expropriation of ancestral holdings following the removal of several thousand Judeans into captivity remained a sensitive issue during the exilic period, becoming one of the principal sources of tension between the "Babylonians" and the "Palestinians" and causing severe social problems once some of the former began to return during the early Persian period. We saw that after the first deportation those who remained behind justified the takeover by arguing that the deportees had, in effect, been expelled from the cult community—as a result of sin, understood—and had therefore forfeited title to real estate (11:14–15). The situation following the second deportation was exacerbated by the Babylonian policy of handing over vacated holdings to the landless peasants in order to maintain a viable agrarian economy in the province (Jer. 39:10). Since there were many in the diaspora who entertained hopes of returning in the not too distant future, the issue was one of immediate and pressing concern.

The force of the argument presented by those who had escaped deportation is not immediately obvious. It may seem at first reading that they are basing their claim either on need or on strength in numbers—if Abraham could do it on his own, we who are many may be confident of success. But not only would this be remarkably inept, the appeal to Abraham requires a theological argument comparable to that of their predecessors after the first deportation. The point of the contrast between the one and the many will be seen more clearly if we turn to a prophetic saying of the early Persian period:

> Look to Abraham your father
>   and to Sarah who bore you;
> for when he was but one I called him,
>   and I blessed him and made him many.
>   Isaiah 51:2, RSV

They are therefore claiming, in effect, to be the great nation which, according to the divine promise to Abraham, would descend from him and inherit the land (Gen. 12:1–3, 7; 13:14–17; 15:17–21; 17:5–8; 22:15–18). The implications of this claim, and the counterclaim of the Babylonian diaspora, would not become apparent for some time. In retrospect, however, we can detect here the seeds of sectarianism as it developed in the time of the Second Temple, with different groups within the restored community claiming to be the legitimate successors of the old Israel.

Ezekiel's reply is in the customary form of indictment and verdict, arranged elegantly in four groupings of three brief statements. The first charge is eating meat without draining the blood (Gen. 9:4; Lev. 19:26) or, if the text is slightly emended, eating on the mountains (cf. 18:6). It is followed by the accusation of idolatry which, as often in Ezekiel, is linked with bloodshed (e.g., 22:1–16). The next three charges reflect the social disorder and anomie in Judah in the wake of the Babylonian conquest, including the failed coup of Ishmael (Jer. 41). The verdict (vs. 27–29) threatens further destruction by the sword, wild beasts, and pestilence, a variation on a theme often heard in the first part of the book. It was probably not far off the mark,

151

especially in view of the reprisals that followed the assassination of Gedaliah, the Babylonian viceroy in the province (Jer. 52:30).

The incident may serve to remind us of the passionate concern of Ezekiel with the land of Israel, one of the major themes, perhaps *the* major theme of the book. It may be surprising to learn that the designation "the land of Israel" *('ereṣ yiśra'el),* in common use today, occurs for the first time in Ezekiel (40:2; 47:18) and very rarely elsewhere (I Chron. 22:2; II Chron. 2:17), apart from the more restrictive allusion to the Northern Kingdom. By preference, however, Ezekiel speaks of "the soil of Israel" *('admat yiśra'el),* a phrase that occurs eighteen times in the book and nowhere else in the Hebrew Bible. (The title "holy land," literally "holy soil," used preferentially by Christians, occurs only once, at Zech. 2:12.) The soil of Israel is personified and addressed directly (7:2; 21:2–3; 36:6), its fate is a matter of the deepest concern, and the promise of restoration is first and foremost the promise of return to it:

> You shall know that I am Yahweh, when I bring you onto the soil of Israel, the country which I swore to give to your fathers.
> Ezekiel 20:42

> I will bring you home onto the soil of Israel.
> Ezekiel 37:12

The idea that land as a physical reality can carry such theological weight is difficult for the contemporary Christian to grasp, though it was not so during the early centuries of the church's history; and the failure to grasp it is perhaps the greatest obstacle to the Christian's understanding of Judaism in its historical and contemporary reality. For Ezekiel, this physical reality is the visible sign of the covenant and the promise. It is for Israel to possess, but the disputation recorded at this point in the book shows that its possession can never be taken for granted.

Ezekiel 33:30–33
Prophecy as Entertainment

152

The account of this turning point in Ezekiel's career begins with the prophet as sentry and ends with the prophet as unwilling entertainer. Popular reaction to the fulfillment of his predictions is described in realistic terms colored with a sense of sad irony. Ezekiel is now the big success story in the diaspora communities. People are standing around in the shade talking about him; everyone is saying, "You have got to come and hear this man." And so they come as never before and sit around him (the targum adds, characteristically, "as students") as they would a minstrel or a flute player or any popular entertainer. Some commentators have found evidence here and elsewhere (I Sam. 10:5; II Kings 3:15) that prophets chanted their oracles, but the evidence is not compelling, and the analogy in any case is as much with the content as with the performance. Unlike other popular assessments of prophets—as windbags (Jer. 5:13) or holy fools (II Kings 9:11; Hos. 9:7; Jer. 29:26)—the people's attitude is benign; they listen eagerly, but his words go in one ear and out the other.

Unlike some contemporary media-assisted pulpit entertainers, Ezekiel was not taken in by the apparent success of his preaching, as he might well have been after a long history of failure. He knew only too well that the test of success is not what people say (the "loving words" in their mouth, v. 31) but what they do to change the basic orientation of their lives. They hear only what they want to hear, what reinforces their own self-interest—a promise of future success and prosperity with no strings attached. So only when the predictions are verified, when reality catches up with them (as it has a habit of doing), will they appreciate the force of the prophetic word. The same message is conveyed in Jesus' parable of the sower, among the hearers of which were those whose main concern was "the cares of the world and the delight in riches" (Matt. 13:1–23, RSV). Listening to the word is a dangerous exercise, for it exposes the hearer to the prospect of a fundamental change of attitude and conduct of life.

PART FIVE

Resurrection and Restoration

EZEKIEL 34—37

Ezekiel 34:1–31
The Good Shepherd

The present section consists of a complex of oracles introduced by the customary "Thus says Yahweh" (vs. 2, 10, 11, 17, 20) and united by the theme of shepherding. Those who use such opening and concluding formulae to distinguish between "primary" and "secondary" levels of composition would argue that the collection has been augmented at several points and therefore they designate at least vs. 7–9 and 31, possibly also vs. 25–30, as later additions. In this instance it does not seem worthwhile to argue the point, for the theme is developed in a logical and coherent way without notable inconsistencies. There seems to be no close connection with what precedes and follows, though its location at this point may have been suggested by the disastrous situation in postbellum Judah as described in 33:23–29 and ch. 35.

That the shepherd's task is no longer familiar to most people in our Western societies does not constitute a serious barrier to understanding, since the metaphorical import is made abundantly clear. Our term "pastoral" embodies the same metaphor, and therefore the theme may be restated as *pastoral responsibility,* allowing the adjective the broader connotation of public office of any kind involving responsibility for people.

As so often in Ezekiel, the development of the metaphor seems to have been suggested by the preaching of Jeremiah (in

Jer. 23:1–8). Both begin with a woe oracle, rulers are condemned for much the same reasons, and there is a promise of restoration involving a descendant of David ruling over a reunited Israel. The Jeremiah passage should be read in conjunction with this section which will be seen to constitute, in effect, a new and expanded version of the same theme.

By the time of Ezekiel, shepherding was a well-established metaphor for governing and, since gods were routinely represented in the ancient Near East as absolute monarchs, one that could easily be transferred to deity. Already in the third millennium B.C. the Sumerians applied it to both kings and gods (e.g., the shepherd-god Dumuzi), and it appears quite frequently in royal inscriptions (e.g., of Hammurabi, king of Babylon). In Israel there was an obvious and convenient connection with the narrative tradition about David's occupation before entering Saul's service (I Sam. 16:11; 17:15, 34–37; II Sam. 7:7–8; Ps. 78:70–71). The metaphor has proved to be very durable, in spite of the fact that it may be thought to have unflattering implications for those cast in the role of sheep. Hymnals and prayers in common use would provide ample proof. Perhaps a certain pastoral allure or nostalgia may explain the popularity of Psalm 23 ("The Lord is my shepherd"), and, for the more literate, there is the romantic image of the shepherd in poets from Spenser and Shakespeare to Burns and Wordsworth. The reality, we may be sure, was rather different. The shepherd's job no doubt had periods of boredom and relative inactivity, but it could also be dangerous. There were thieves to contend with (Gen. 31:39) and beasts of prey, including the lion (I Sam. 17:34–35; Isa. 31:4; Micah 5:8)—generally with the help of nothing more than a stick or similar primitive weapon and maybe a dog (Job 30:1). The shepherd had to give an exact reckoning for the animals confided to him (Lev. 27:32; Jer. 33:13; Ezek. 20:37) and either pay for any that were missing or produce a part of the carcass if one had been killed (Exod. 22:13; Amos 3:12).

The first two oracles (vs. 2–10) fall into the customary sequence of indictment and verdict. They are addressed to the shepherds of Israel, meaning the kings who ruled throughout the history of the kingdoms but especially in the last years of Judah (cf. chs. 19; 21:25–26). Ezekiel stands here within a long tradition of prophetic opposition to monarchy. Various strands of this tradition have been brought together in the portrait of Samuel, who anointed and eventually rejected Saul, David's tragic predecessor. The early prophets in the Northern Kingdom, of whom Elijah is the best known, were not opposed to monarchy in itself but only the kind of hereditary and absolute monarchy that excluded what might be called the charismatic principle. The degree to which this principle remained alive in the Kingdom of Israel may perhaps be gauged by the fact that eight of its nineteen rulers were assassinated. Hosea, for whom the "original sin" of Israel was the passage to monarchy (Hos. 10:9), continued the same tradition, eventually incorporated into the Deuteronomic program which insisted that the king was also under the law (Deut. 17:14–20). The historian of the kingdoms, finally, makes it abundantly clear that the monarchy was the principal architect of Israel's ruin.

Ezekiel indicts the "shepherds" on the counts of venality, self-interest, and the exploitation of those for whom they were responsible. He then goes on to charge them with dereliction of duty. What that duty consisted in was well understood not just in Israel but in the ancient Near East in general. In the prologue to his famous law code, Hammurabi declares that he was appointed by the gods "to promote the welfare of the people, cause justice to prevail in the land, to destroy the wicked and evil that the strong might not oppress the weak." In one of the Ugaritic epics from the Late Bronze Age a king's son charges his father with neglecting his royal responsibilities:

> You judge not the cause of the widow,
> Nor adjudicate the case of the wretched;
> You do not drive out them that prey on the poor,
> Feed not the fatherless before you
> Nor the widow behind your back.

Ezekiel's shepherds are guilty of the same dereliction of duty. They have no care for the weak, the sick and crippled, the straying and lost sheep. Public office of any kind is a pastoral responsibility, an opportunity for service, not for personal gain and glory. The result of their neglect is that the sheep are scattered, which is to say that Israel's rulers bear responsibility for the exile. The ensuing situation is encapsulated in the phrase "sheep without a shepherd" (cf. I Kings 22:17; Matt. 9:36). Given the gregarious nature of this rather feckless animal, a sheep without a shepherd is a sheep in big trouble. Pastoral office is a response to needs that call out for selfless dedication and unremitting solicitude.

157

Since these sayings date from after the fall of Jerusalem, when the "shepherds" had disappeared from the scene, several commentators conclude that the verdict (vs. 7–10) can only refer to Gedaliah, appointed by the Babylonians to rule the conquered province. But the sentence is in the plural, and there is no evidence that Gedaliah was accorded royal status. The allusion is therefore still to past rulers, since the effects of their misrule persist. The targum avoids the problem by identifying the shepherds with leaders in a broader and more general sense, a conclusion that we may accept as at least true to the spirit of the passage.

The perspective shifts to the future in the oracle that follows (vs. 11–16). In it, Yahweh vows to go himself in search of the sheep which scattered on a cloudy, dark day—an obvious allusion to the political disasters of the recent past. The language reminds us of the imagery of Psalm 23 which is not all peaceful, sunlit pastures. For the presence of the good shepherd takes away fear even in the worst situations.

Even as I walk through the death-dark canyon
I will fear no evil.

> Psalm 23:4

The scattered sheep will be reassembled and brought back to their own land, where they will graze in security on the mountains and by the flowing streams. In all of this, Yahweh will exhibit the character of true pastoring:

The lost I will seek,
The stray I will bring back,
The broken-limbed I will bind up,
The sick I will nourish back to health,
The sleek and the strong I will watch over.

> Ezekiel 34:16

(The last line assumes a slight emendation, but if we read "destroy" with the Hebrew text for "watch over," it would anticipate judgment on the sleek sheep who are pushing the weak ones around, vs. 20–21.)

The metaphor of God as good shepherd has carried over into the teaching of Jesus. His parable of the straying sheep (Matt. 18:12–14; Luke 15:3–7) provides a powerful and sustaining image of divine mercy toward the sinner. Jesus himself sends his disciples to the lost sheep of the house of Israel (Matt. 10:6; 15:24) and takes pity on the crowd who are like sheep

158

without a shepherd (Matt. 9:36). These and similar hints are gathered together into the Johannine discourse on the good shepherd, certainly dependent on Ezekiel, which can serve as a paradigm of pastoral ministry: the good shepherd walks ahead of his sheep; he knows them individually and they recognize his voice; where necessary, he will defend them against attack even at risk of injury or death (John 10:1–18). The same discourse also highlights the necessity of discriminating between authentic and inauthentic "shepherds" and recalls the description of false prophets as wolves disguised as sheep (Matt. 7:15), a striking image that has lost none of its force in the contemporary world of media-disseminated religion.

The oracle concludes by abandoning metaphor to introduce the concept of justice *(mishpaṭ),* the quality essential in any kind of leadership role, civic or religious. It also serves to link with the saying that follows (vs. 17–24) which illustrates how this quality is to be exercised.

So far we have been presented with the prospect of a reunited Israel in its own land, one flock guided and protected by its shepherd. Now we learn that there are distinctions to be made within the flock: between the sleek and the lean sheep, between rams and he-goats. The accusation of trampling down the pastureland to which the weaker sheep are restricted, fouling the water they have to drink, and pushing them out of the flock is addressed presumably to the sleek sheep and the he-goats. The figurative language is easily transposed into an accusation of economic and political exploitation within the postbellum Judean community. The social and economic upheaval following the Babylonian conquest, and especially following the assassination of Gedaliah and his entourage (Jer. 41), is no doubt the scenario alluded to here. Such a situation is the antithesis of a community founded, as all communities religious as well as civil must be, on justice, equity, and law. The same language is adopted in the judgment scene in Matt. 25:31–46 in which the shepherd separates the sheep from the goats. Disconcertingly, perhaps, the criterion of discrimination is not religious orthodoxy or orthopraxy but care for the weak and disadvantaged—the hungry, thirsty, and sick, the prisoner and the stranger.

The need for order, justice, and the protection of the weak 159 against the strong leads to the announcement that Yahweh will "raise up" his servant David as the one shepherd or prince *(naśi')* of his flock (vs. 23–24). After more than four centuries the Davidic dynasty was extinguished, with the exile first of Jehoiachin and then of his uncle Mattaniah (Zedekiah). The hope of its eventual restoration was, however, kept alive in the homeland and during the diaspora, and attempts were actually made to restore it: Ishmael, shortly after the fall of Jerusalem; and Zerubbabel, grandson of Jehoiachin, in the early Persian period. Neither of the attempts came to anything. The Jeremian passage on which Ezekiel's shepherd discourse appears to be based (Jer. 23:1–8) also predicts the "raising up" of a future Davidic ruler who will rule wisely, exercising justice and righteousness over a reunited Israel. He is designated by the title "righteous shoot" *(ṣemah ṣaddiq)* and is given the symbolic name "Yahweh our righteousness" *(YHWH ṣidqenu)*, containing perhaps an ironic pun on the name of the miserable Zedekiah (see also Jer. 33:14–26). The reference to David as "servant" (see also Ezek. 37:24; Jer. 33:21–22, 26; Zech. 3:8) also suggests a connection with the "servant of Yahweh" of Isa. 42:1–4, a spirit-endowed individual who will impose justice but without the violence and arbitrary exercise of power usually associated with kingship. The code name *ṣemah* (shoot) seems to have been well known as a designation for this "once and future king," turning up some years later in connection with the messianic expectations that focused on the person of Zerubbabel during the reign of Darius (Zech. 3:8; 6:12). Much later still, it will be used as a messianic designation for Jesus, but it will then be understood—by way of the Greek translation word *anatolē*—not as a plant rising from the ground but as a star rising through the sky (Matt. 2:2; Luke 1:78).

The final section (vs. 25–31) merges the prospect of the restoration of order and justice under the Davidic ruler into a cosmic vision of a world in which there will be no more beasts of prey, no more oppression and enslavement, no more hunger because nature will give of her fullness, a world, above all, in which fear will have been abolished. (We need only pause and reflect for a moment what it would be like to live without fear.) This will be achieved through a "covenant of peace" (v. 25)— the same phrase occurs later in Ezekiel (37:26) and in Second Isaiah (Isa. 54:10). In the biblical sense, peace is not just the absence of hostility. It stands for a positive state of harmony and accord, especially between parties to an agreement. A covenant of peace is therefore, quite simply, "a covenant that works"

160

(Taylor, *Ezekiel*, p. 224). This dream of a return to paradise, an abjuration of violence among peoples, and, beyond that, a total harmony within nature keeps on recurring throughout the Old Testament and the literature of the ancient Near East. An earlier prophet, Hosea, looked forward to a covenant that would not only end war but reestablish a lost harmony with nature at every level (Hos. 2:18–23). Isaiah associated the coming of the just ruler with a new age in which the lion would lie down with the lamb, the leopard with the kid (Isa. 11:6–9). Like Adam in paradise, Jesus spent forty days in the wilderness with the wild beasts (Mark 1:13). The practical reason tells us it is illusory and impossible, but a generation that has to contemplate the possibility of unparalleled ecological disaster and thermonuclear war should not be the first to abandon this eschatological goal.

Ezekiel 35:1—36:15
Mountains of Edom, Mountains of Israel

Another diatribe against Edom seems to interrupt the projection of a restored Israel, but as we read on, we note that it forms one panel of a diptych, the address to the mountains of Israel (36:1–15) being the other. It may also have been suggested by the prediction of the removal of wild beasts in 34:25, and it will be apparent from the anti-Edomite oracle in 25:12–14 that in the years following the fall of Jerusalem, Edom was *the* enemy. While it would be risky to distinguish between the original content of a prophetic text and later additions to it on the basis of a distinction between verse and prose, prophetic oracles were generally composed and delivered in verse and were often transmitted with commentary either from the original author or a later tradent. In the present instance, we can detect four stanzas of three verses each in the 3 + 3 meter (v. 35:3–4, 9, 15). All except the first stanza end with what we have called the acknowledgment formula ("You will know that I am Yahweh"), and the theme is the devastation of the land and cities of Edom. In between, reasons are given for this harsh judgment ("because . . . ," 35:5, 10) and the verdict is expanded upon ("therefore . . . ," 35:6, 11).

The prophecy begins with the hostile stare directed against

Edom here named Seir or Mt. Seir. This alternative designation (cf. Gen. 36:8–9; Deut. 1:2; Ezek. 25:8), similar in sound to the Hebrew word for "hair," accounts for the description of Esau as hirsute in the Genesis narrative (Gen. 25:25; 27:11). In like manner, the name Edom, probably named for the red sandstone characteristic of the region, accounts for Esau's ruddy complexion and the "red pottage" (borsch?) for which he surrendered his birthright (Gen. 25:25, 30). These and similar etymological *jeux d'esprit* illustrate the popular nature of a narrative that skillfully combines the old folklore motif of sibling rivalry with the history of two closely related ethnic groups.

Together with other anti-Edomite sayings in the prophetic corpus (see commentary on 25:12–14), the present oracle predicts devastation and ruin. Edomite encroachments during Judah's death agonies were never forgotten. Together with Amalek, Edom could be used as a kind of code name for any evil oppressor long after the nation itself had passed from the scene. Edom will be dealt with according to the law of retaliation: you are guilty of blood, so blood will pursue you (35:6; cf. Gen. 9:6); I will deal with you according to your own anger, envy, and hatred (35:11). The quotation outlining Edom's design on both Judah and Israel—a surprising formulation in view of the political situation at that time—strikes a particularly bitter chord, since this land, devastated as it is, is still Yahweh's land which he had entrusted to his people as their inheritance. The design will not succeed, for Edom will suffer the same fare as her neighbor, only for her there will be no reversal of fortune.

The Jacob-Esau rivalry also serves to make a point in an early Christian text which has caused a great deal of discussion and debate. In Romans 9, Paul is arguing that physical descent from the ancestors, beginning with Abraham, is not the essential qualification for membership in Israel. What is essential, he claims, is appropriation through faith of the promise made to the ancestors. This he attempts to demonstrate by scriptural arguments. One of them runs as follows:

> And not only so, but also when Rebecca had conceived children by one man, our forefather Isaac, though they were not yet born and had done nothing either good or bad, in order that God's purpose of election might continue, not because of works but because of his call, she was told, "The elder will serve the younger." As it is written, "Jacob I loved, but Esau I hated."
>
> Romans 9:10–13, RSV

162

It will be readily appreciated that this text has played a major role in the classical doctrine of divine predestination. For the fate of the siblings was decided by divine decree before their birth, and, following the second scriptural quotation, it foreordains to well-being in the one case and reprobation in the other. It is indeed a clever argument, combining a divine oracle received by Rebecca during her difficult confinement (Gen. 25:23) with an anti-Edomite saying at the beginning of the postexilic prophet Malachi (Mal. 1:2–3). The problem is to know how any traditional and biblical concept of God can be reconciled with hatred conceived antecedently to an individual's existence. The argument does not appeal to divine foreknowledge; in fact, it seems to exclude it. Some commentators have tried to draw the sting by observing that in biblical usage "hate" can have a relative sense, as in the saying about hating father and mother (Luke 14:26, with which compare Matt. 10:27). Others have pointed out that Malachi was referring not to individuals but to the two peoples and their history of antagonism—a correct observation but irrelevant, since what is at stake is *Paul's* understanding and use of the text. It would be more to the point to recall that Paul is not speaking here of eternal salvation and reprobation but of the identity of the true Israel. He is saying that membership in the house of Israel is not determined, and from the beginning was never determined, primarily by sociological law and custom, including primogeniture. The election of Israel, and the eventual extension of franchise in Israel to Gentiles—a point also supported by biblical arguments (Rom. 9:24–26)—are inscrutable, free acts of God totally unmerited by the recipients. There is no questioning why this is so. God is free to give or to withhold. How unsearchable are his judgments and how inscrutable his ways (Rom. 11:33)!

We return to Ezek. 36:1–15, the second panel of the diptych, which is also the counterpart to the condemnation of the mountains of Israel earlier in the book (ch. 6). Edom's spurious claim to the ancient heights, referring primarily to the highlands of the Judean Negeb, is quoted. We are then given a realistic description of the state of the country after the conquest, the southern and western parts of which, as we know, had been overrun by Edomites and Philistines respectively ("the remnant of the nations," 36:3–4). Since judgment has already been passed on these peoples (25:12–17), Ezekiel moves

163

on at once to predict a flourishing of nature in preparation for the exiles' homecoming. The land will be repopulated, the cities will be rebuilt, and it will be better than before. We have to bear in mind that it was prophecies like this which in the course of time gave the repatriates the courage to start again. As unrealistic and even fantastic as some of the biblical restoration prophecies may appear, they have proved capable of sustaining hope and the will to survive and rebuild.

The final oracle (36:13–15) answers the charge of the neighboring peoples that the land devours its inhabitants, a curious allegation reminiscent of the Priestly version of the report of the spies before the conquest of Canaan (Num. 13:32). The present context suggests not so much barrenness and infertility as a long history of deportation and depopulation, beginning with the northern tribes after the Assyrian conquest. With the return from the Babylonian exile, this reproach will no longer be heard.

Ezekiel 36:16–38
Internal Renewal

The promise of restoration continues with a discourse. The nucleus of it is a long oracle (vs. 22–32) followed by two short ones (vs. 33–36, 37–38) which serve as appendixes or footnotes and which may have been added, by Ezekiel or a later editor, to complete the picture. The thematic continuity with the preceding sayings is maintained by reference to return to the land (cf. 34:13; 36:8), the provision of sustenance after the return (cf. 34:13–14, 27, 29), repopulation (cf. 36:10–12), and the silencing of the taunts of neighboring peoples (cf. 34:29; 36:6–7, 15). It concludes by returning to the original theme of the sheep and shepherd, thus suggesting that the entire section is to be read as a unity (cf. the allusion to David as the one shepherd toward the end of the following chapter, 37:24).

The oracle is introduced by a retrospect on Israel's life in the land before the catastrophe (vs. 16–21). The Israelites were cast out of the land because they had polluted it by their conduct, summarized, as previously (22:4), by the twinned terms bloodshed and idolatry. One of the priestly authors of the ritual

164

law in the Pentateuch gave the same reason for the expulsion of the pre-Israelite peoples (Lev. 18:24–25), and Ezekiel, as a priest, follows his lead. The basic metaphor in 36:17, which we encountered earlier (7:19–20), is menstrual blood which pollutes by contact. Anxiety to prevent pollution from this source eventuated—in the Mishnaic tractate *Niddah* and its commentaries—in a mass of legislation of quite formidable complexity. The biblical legislation (Lev. 15:19–30; 18:19), with which Ezekiel was of course familiar (cf. Ezek. 18:6; 22:10), aimed primarily at preventing defilement of the sanctuary (e.g., Lev. 15:31; Num. 19:20); and the intimate association between sanctuary and land will go some way to explaining the use of the metaphor in the present context.

For anyone not brought up in an active Jewish environment, or in a traditional society in which taboos of this kind are still operative, the *niddah* metaphor will probably appear odd, even repugnant. This is not the place to discuss the rationale for the ritual laws of purity, the subject of endless debate among biblical and Talmudic scholars and anthropologists (e.g., Mary Douglas' well-known study *Purity and Danger,* with a chapter on the abominations of Leviticus). It will be enough for the present purpose to note that, in the biblical context, they are taken to reflect the holiness of God and therefore, *grasped in their totality,* constitute a form of *imitatio Dei* peculiar to Israel.

Ezekiel, then, takes over the Levitical explanation of exile as the result of polluting the land, with the emphasis on idolatry and arbitrary violence. The taunt addressed to the deportees, that Yahweh had proved powerless to prevent the deportation, illustrates the urgency of coming up with a theological explanation. The literature of that age provides a variety of solutions to the problem. In the Egyptian diaspora, people were arguing that the proscription of the Asherah cult by Josiah was responsible—an interesting case, since it is perhaps the only instance in the Old Testament where women are heard on the subject of religion (Jer. 44:15–19). The historian of the monarchy (known, inelegantly, as the Deuteronomistic Historian) defended the justice of the punishment on the grounds that they had been warned by prophets sent for that purpose by God. Second Isaiah (Isa. 40—55) countered the charge of divine powerlessness with a new affirmation of Yahweh as sole creator and guarantor of prophecy. Ezekiel's explanation is consonant with his own background. In the same vein, he adds that the return from exile will not be by merit of the deportees but by virtue of Yahweh's concern for his holy name; and we have seen that the sanctification of the name *(kiddush hashem)* is the driving force behind the entire history of Israel (ch. 20). This, again, signals a truth which, in spite of the first petition of the Lord's Prayer, is overlooked more easily by the Christian than by the Jew. Paul was aware of it. Sin is not just failure to conform to a moral code but a falling short of the glory of God (Rom. 3:23). That the object of existence is the "sanctification" of God—the acknowledgment of God as he is with all its ramifications—can never be sufficiently emphasized.

The restoration oracle (vs. 22–32) begins by making the same point. The return from exile is not on account of Israel's merits; it is not even, basically, for the sake of Israel but rather to vindicate the holy name of God. Compared with the reassurances of Second Isaiah, this may seem cold comfort. In the last analysis, Israel is the means by which God has chosen to "cause his name to be hallowed" (v. 23). This is what Israel is for. Yet the fact remains that Israel will indeed return to its own land. That this political fact of the repatriation of an exiled people takes its significance from an internal renewal is underlined by a kind of ring composition in the next few verses (vs. 24–28):

> I will take you from the nations, gather you from all the lands, and bring you to your own land.
> I will sprinkle pure water upon you and purify you from all your impurities, and from all your idols I will purify you.
> I will give you a new heart, and a new spirit I will place within you; and I will remove the heart of stone from your body and give you a heart of flesh.
> I will place my spirit within you and cause you to walk in my statutes and carefully observe my ordinances.
> You will dwell in the land which I gave to your ancestors; you will be a people for me and I will be God for you.

The process of internal renewal begins with an external act: the sprinkling of pure water. Lustrations are a familiar feature of religious rituals and were used in Israel both before and after significant religious acts. Purification by water was essential for terminating states of ritual uncleanness brought about, for example, by skin disease or bodily discharge (e.g., Lev. 14:52; 22:4–6). Perhaps more relevant in this instance is the sprinkling with water mixed with the ashes of the red heifer (Num. 19).

166

The targum makes the connection explicitly: "I will forgive your sins, as though you had been purified by the waters of sprinkling and by the ashes of the heifer sin-offering." The passage is also quoted in a saying attributed to Rabbi Akiba:

> Blessed are ye, O Israel. Before whom are ye made clean and who makes you clean? Your father in heaven; as it is written: And I will sprinkle clean water upon you and ye shall be clean. And again it says, O Lord, the hope *(mikveh)* of Israel. (Jer. 17:13)—as the mikveh (ritual bath) cleanses the unclean, so does the Holy One (blessed be He!) cleanse Israel.
>
> *m. Yoma* 8.9

The symbolic cleansing with water is not just a routine ritual act. It signifies the end of a period of disorder (dirt) and the beginning of a new phase of existence. This is clearly the sense in the present passage: abjuration of a disorderly and idolatrous past and a fresh start. The Qumran community will take this a step farther by insisting that the new age can be experienced only by those who belong to their ranks after undergoing the rite of purification by water. But they also insist that this rite must be accompanied by repentance and a sincere change of heart: "He [the unrepentant] will not be made guiltless by atonement and he will not be purified in waters for purification; he will not sanctify himself in seas or rivers, nor will he be purified in all the waters of cleansing" (1QS 4.4–5). Whatever the historical antecedents of Christian baptism, whether an initiatory cleansing of the Qumran type, or proselyte baptism, or a combination of different features, the basic pattern is already detectable in Ezekiel's promise to the deportees.

The purification by water is symbolically efficacious only if accompanied by an inner transformation, to which Ezekiel now turns. The experience of those terrible years seems to have induced a deep sense of bondage to sin which colors the piety of Judaism throughout the Second Temple period. (Read, e.g., the communal confessions of sin in Ezra 9 and Neh. 9.) Jeremiah asks whether his contemporaries, hardened in their ways, can any more change than the Ethiopian can change the color of his skin or the leopard its spots (Jer. 13:23). Anticipating Augustine and Luther, he broods on the human heart deceitful above all things and desperately corrupt (Jer. 17:9). Only a miracle of grace, a new initiative beyond the demonstrated moral capacities of the individual, could effect an inner transformation. Ezekiel uses the language of a new heart and a new spirit (as

167

already, 11:19–20) and even speaks of the necessity of a heart transplant if they are to have a "heart of flesh," that is, a genuinely receptive disposition, an inner core which is spiritually alive. But to this must be added a transfusion of the divine spirit without which the human impulse to action, to change, cannot be sustained. Allusions to the spirit of God can be found in the earliest writings of the Old Testament, but it is not surprising that it is only from this time that we have consistent attestation to the divine spirit as the agent of inner transformation (see also Ezek. 37:14; 39:29; Isa. 44:3; 59:21; Joel 2:28–29). It is therefore understandable that early Christianity associated baptism with the giving of the spirit:

> You did not receive the spirit of slavery to fall back into fear, but you have received the spirit of sonship. When we cry, "Abba! Father!" it is the Spirit himself bearing witness with our spirit that we are children of God.
>
> Romans 8:15–16, RSV

The result of this new divine initiative is an enabling of the will expressed in the observance of the life-giving commandments; then, at last, the covenant will be a reality: "You will be a people for me and I will be God for you"—a formula of frequent occurrence in Ezekiel (11:20; 14:11; 34:31; 37:23). According to the theology of the priest-theologians shared by Ezekiel, the covenant was made first with the postdiluvian generation (Gen. 9:8–17), then with the ancestors represented by Abraham (Gen. 17). Both are *everlasting covenants,* that is, covenants which, once made, are indefectible. Throughout subsequent history, therefore, it is only a question of God *remembering* his covenant (Gen. 9:15–16; cf. Ezek. 16:60). To the more ancient covenant formulations which concentrate on the promise of land, the priests added the promise of divine presence which, in their view, implied presence in the sanctuary. We can therefore more easily understand the intimate association in Ezekiel between land and sanctuary as involved in the covenant relationship (e.g., 37:26–27). Here too the promise of land is associated with a reaffirmation of the covenant presence (v. 28).

168   In spite of this thematic continuity, the deep sense of sin and failure of which we were speaking seems to have led to the conviction of the need for a new divine initiative, a different basis for the relationship—in effect, a new dispensation. Some-

thing of this is apparent in what is probably an exilic strand of Deuteronomy which speaks explicitly of the covenant in the land of Moab, that is, prior to entry into the land, as a new covenant with respect to the covenant at Horeb (Deut. 29:1). But it comes to clearest expression in a passage in Jeremiah that Ezekiel almost certainly had in mind at this point:

> Behold, the days are coming, says the LORD, when I will make a new covenant with the house of Israel and the house of Judah, not like the covenant which I made with their fathers when I took them by the hand to bring them out of the land of Egypt, my covenant which they broke, though I was their husband, says the LORD. But this is the covenant which I will make with the house of Israel after those days, says the LORD: I will put my law within them, and I will write it upon their hearts; and I will be their God, and they shall be my people. And no longer shall each man teach his neighbor and each his brother, saying, "Know the LORD," for they shall all know me, from the least of them to the greatest, says the LORD; for I will forgive their iniquity, and I will remember their sin no more.
>
> Jeremiah 31:31–34, RSV

This promise of a new basis for the relationship, which is reformulated by Ezekiel, creates a dialectic between the idea of continuity and permanence ("the everlasting covenant") and the insight that new situations can arise calling for new dispensations. This was clearly the view of the Qumran sectarians who thought of themselves as constituting the new covenant. Early Christianity also celebrated the new covenant in the death of Jesus, entry into which was through baptism and the conferring of the Spirit. The Christian appropriation of the term has regrettably given rise to the view that Judaism, the religion of the old covenant, has been superseded by Christianity. Perhaps we should say, rather, that the dialectic remains, and that Judaism and Christianity constitute two distinct but related dispensations.

The two brief concluding oracles (vs. 33–36, 37–38) enlarge on the promise of return to the land which, given the situation, must have been a daunting prospect. The most pressing needs would be the rebuilding of the cities (cf. Isa. 44:26, 28; 49:17; 54:11–12) and the repopulation of the land (cf. Isa. 49:19; 54:1–3). The history of Judah during the Persian period shows that these needs were still being met at the time of Nehemiah, who carried out a drastic plan for repopulating Jerusalem (Neh. 11). The agrarian economy of the province would also have to

169

be put on a new footing. This also would be done, though not without great hardships, as we know from later biblical sources. To describe the end result, the oracle reverts to the image of the Garden of Eden (28:11–19; 31:8, 9, 16, 18; cf. Isa. 51:3). The neighboring peoples will be obliged to swallow their taunts and to acknowledge that this was the work of Yahweh—a theme that also features prominently in Nehemiah (e.g., Neh. 6:16). The last saying returns to the original image of the sheep and shepherd by comparing the repatriates to the flocks set aside for sacrifice which in earlier and happier times must have congested the streets of Jerusalem. The targum adds another dimension, probably implied in the Hebrew text, by identifying these "human flocks" with the purified people who will come to Jerusalem to celebrate Passover.

Ezekiel 37:1–14
The Bones of the Dead Come Alive

Though this section has neither heading nor date, it occupies an important place in the book as the third of four vision narratives, all introduced by the phrase "The hand of Yahweh was on me," indicating the state of trance in which the vision was experienced. The first, following the inaugural vision (3:22–27), and the third (37:1–14) take place in the same location, the plain or valley near the exilic settlements. Whereas the first, in which Ezekiel is told to go into seclusion, signifies the absence of prophetic inspiration and therefore death, the third is a call to life out of death through the prophetic word. There is a similar correspondence between the second (chs. 8—11), heralding the destruction of the temple, and the fourth (chs. 40—48) in which the new temple is graphically portrayed.

Typically for Ezekiel, this vision narrative (vs. 1–10) is followed by an explanation (vs. 11–14). The explanation identifies the bones as the whole house of Israel and thus points forward to the following saying dealing with the eventual reunification of the dispersed tribes. The discouragement of the deportees is expressed in a dirgelike quotation reminiscent of psalms of communal lamentation. Allowing for a slight emendation in the third verse *(nigzar nolenu* for *nigzarnu lanu),* it runs as follows:

Our bones are dried up,
Our hope has perished,
Our life thread has been cut.

The metaphor of dessicated bones, expressive of physical and spiritual debility, occurs frequently in poetry (e.g., Isa. 66:14; Job 21:24). Taken up in a deliberately literal fashion, it has been developed into a suggestive scenario of a field that had witnessed combat or slaughter, rather like a Brady photograph of a Civil War battlefield. As so often happens in Ezekiel, we hear an echo of the preaching of Jeremiah:

At that time, the bones of the kings of Judah, the bones of its princes, the bones of the priests, the bones of the prophets, and the bones of the inhabitants of Jerusalem shall be brought out of their tombs; and they shall be spread before the sun and the moon and all the host of heaven, which they have loved and served, which they have gone after, and which they have sought and worshiped; and they shall not be gathered or buried; they shall be as dung on the surface of the ground.

Jeremiah 8:1–2, RSV

In spite of the possibility of contamination by contact with the dead (Num. 19:16–18; II Kings 23:14, 16; Ezek. 39:15–16), Ezekiel is led in trance through the field, wondering at the great number of the bones of those long dead. The question that he hears addressed to him—"Mortal, can these bones live?"—seems to call for only one answer. Ezekiel, however, does not answer, since he knows that the power of God extends even into the realm of death. He is then commanded to proclaim a message not to the obtuse, as in his inaugural vision, but to the dead, summoning them back to life. He does so, and it comes to pass before his eyes.

Much, but by no means all, early Christian interpretation of this famous passage found in it proof of the bodily resurrection, a belief well established in Judaism by the beginning of the common era. It is generally thought that the first clear indication of this belief in the biblical literature occurs in Daniel in connection with the fate of those who suffered death during the persecution of the Seleucid king Antiochus IV in the period 167–164 B.C.:

171

Many of those who sleep in the dust of the earth shall awake, some to everlasting life, and some to shame and everlasting contempt. And those who are wise shall shine like the brightness of the firmament; and those who turn many to righteousness, like the stars for ever and ever.

Daniel 12:2–3, RSV

While it is natural to assume that martyrdom would be seen to demand a solution of this nature, it is unlikely that such ideas arose spontaneously at that precise point in time. Writing about a century earlier, a distinguished and controversial sage seems to be familiar with them (in what precise form, it is difficult to say) and, true to form, expresses himself skeptically:

Who knows whether the spirit of man goes upward and the spirit of the beast goes down to the earth?

Ecclesiastes 3:21, RSV

By that time, also, the quite different idea of the immortality of the soul, as propounded by the Orphic schools and Plato, was well established, though we have to wait some time for the first clear signs of its adoption in Judaism. Both Judaism and Christianity, therefore, inherited an uneasy combination of two quite different forms of belief respecting the postmortem fate of the individual: the corporeal resurrection of the dead and the immortality of the soul as the indestructible core of personality. The synthesis is expressed graphically by the artist who depicted Ezekiel's vision on the north wall of the synagogue at Dura-Europos, a Roman outpost on the Euphrates destroyed by the Persians in the middle of the third century A.D. Touched by God's hand, the prophet stands among severed limbs against a background of a mountain split by an earthquake, while four psyches (winged female figures), corresponding to the four winds from which the spirit is summoned, descend to bring life to the *disjecta membra*. It would not be difficult to match the implied emphasis on individual resurrection with more or less contemporary texts from both Jewish and Christian sources.

We have seen that, in answering the question put to him, Ezekiel does not rule out the possibility of resuscitation, of a reversal of the natural life-death sequence. He does not affirm it either, since belief in the postmortem survival of the individual was not part of Israelite faith at that time; even considerably later the author of Job raises it as a possible solution only to dismiss it (Job 7:9–10, 21; 14:7–12). He leaves it up to God—

172   "Lord Yahweh, thou knowest"—who is the living God, the source of life, he who kills and restores to life (Deut. 32:39). That death was not an insuperable obstacle to the life-bestowing

power of God was also illustrated by well-known stories of restoration of the dead to life through the intercession of Elijah and Elisha (I Kings 17:17–24; II Kings 4:18–37). Of particular interest is a posthumous miracle of Elisha:

> So Elisha died, and they buried him. Now bands of Moabites used to invade the land in the spring of the year. And as a man was being buried, lo, a marauding band was seen and the man was cast into the grave of Elisha; and as soon as the man touched the bones of Elisha, he revived, and stood on his feet.
>
> II Kings 13:20–21, RSV

While the modern, critical reader will inevitably raise questions about the historicity of narratives such as these, they at least testify to the belief that the power of God could triumph over death, which of course is quite different from the contemporary Christian and Jewish belief in the survival of death in a postmortem existence. While, therefore, Ezekiel's vision certainly deals with the restoration of Israel—as the explanation in vs. 11–14 makes abundantly clear—it would probably be mistaken to exclude systematically any hint of the postmortem destiny of the individual.

Returning now to the text, we note that the narrative is held together by the key term *ruaḥ.* It occurs ten times in all and here, as elsewhere, can be translated "spirit," "breath," or "wind" according to the context. It was the *spirit* that led Ezekiel out into the plain strewn with the bones of the slain. He is to proclaim that God will bring them together and instill life-giving *breath* in them. The result of the prophesying, accompanied by a noise and a rattling (or perhaps an earthquake, as in the Dura panel), is accomplished in two stages. The first (vs. 7–8) is the assembling of the bones into skeletons and the transformation of the skeletons into cadavers with sinews, flesh, and skin. Only then (vs. 9–10) is Ezekiel commanded to summon the life-giving *breath* from the four *winds* to give life to this array of zombies. There takes place, therefore, a reenactment of the primal act of creation, when God formed humanity from the dust of the ground and breathed into its nostrils the breath of life (Gen. 2:7). The explanation (vs. 11–14), which, surprisingly, shifts the scene from a battlefield to a cemetery, applies the process to the community. It is the spirit activated through prophetic preaching which bonds the community together and gives it the will to live and accept its future. When that future

173

becomes reality with the return to the land, the community will finally acknowledge the truth of the prophetic word.

Ezekiel 37:15–28
Reunification

The prospect of an eventual union between the northern tribes and Judah must have seemed as unrealistic in Ezekiel's day as the unification of the churches will appear to most contemporary Christians. The northern and central tribes had gone their own way, formed their own kingdom, and set up their own separate centers of worship three and a half centuries earlier. Then, in the eighth century, the Northern Kingdom— otherwise known as Ephraim or, since Omri, the kingdom of Samaria—was absorbed into the Assyrian empire, many of its inhabitants were deported, foreigners were brought in, and to all intents and purposes the ten tribes disappeared from history, thus giving rise to endless and pointless speculations on the location of "the lost tribes of Israel." Yet the ideal of eventual reunification was never completely lost from sight. During the reign of Hezekiah, the first Judean king to reign without a counterpart in the north, we hear of attempts to incorporate the survivors of the Assyrian conquest (II Chron. 30:1–12). The eclipse of the Assyrian empire in the seventh century made it possible for Josiah to attempt the reconquest of the irredentist provinces to the north and their return to Jerusalemite orthodoxy, an attempt that ended with his death at Megiddo (II Kings 23:15–20, 29). The ideal of reunion keeps emerging in the prophetic writings (e.g., Hos. 1:10–11; Isa. 11:12–13), especially in Jeremiah (Jer. 3:6–18; 30:1–3, 8–9), who in this respect also appears to have been Ezekiel's mentor:

> In those days the house of Judah shall join the house of Israel, and together they shall come from the land of the north to the land that I gave your fathers for a heritage.
>
> Jeremiah 3:18, RSV

174 Ezekiel himself never loses sight of it. We have seen that he was called to "bear the punishment" of both Israel and Judah (4:5–6); that he speaks of the restoration of Samaria, the elder

sister (16:46–58); that he uses by preference the term "Israel" rather than "Judah," sometimes "the entire house of Israel" (11:15; 37:11); and that in his review of the religious history of the people in chapter 20 he makes no distinction between north and south. The use of twelve-tribal symbolism, from Chronicles and Ezra to Qumran and the New Testament, demonstrates that the idea of recovering a lost unity remained as an essential aspect of the self-understanding of the several Judaisms that emerged throughout the Second Commonwealth. And so it was also with early Christianity.

One conclusion that can be drawn by the Christian reader of the Old Testament is that the ecumenical movement, which has lost some of its urgency in recent years, has its biblical basis in the unity of Israel acted out and proclaimed by Ezekiel after the fall of Jerusalem. Given the apparently endemic tendency to factionalism, divisiveness, and in-group mentality, the prospect of healing the great schisms of the eleventh and sixteenth centuries must seem remote and unrealistic. And, as Karl Barth pointed out during the Second Vatican Council, beyond the issue of church unity there lies the one basic and immensely problematic issue of Christian-Jewish relations grounded historically in that other schism of the first two centuries of the era. The attainment of a lost unity may be an eschatological goal but one that no Christian body professing allegiance to the biblical tradition can afford to neglect.

Returning now to the text, we see that, once again, Ezekiel communicates his message by means of mimetic action (cf. ch. 4—5). He takes two pieces of wood, which are intended to serve as tablets, and writes on them the names of their respective owners—Judah and confederates on the one, Joseph and associated tribes on the other. As is made clear in the ancestral narratives (Gen. 48:8–22), Joseph stands for the tribes of Ephraim and Manasseh which settled the central highlands and became in due course the nucleus of the Northern Kingdom. The name is occasionally used for this political entity (Amos 5:6, 15; 6:6), but since it is somewhat unusual, a glossator has added "Ephraim" in parentheses. The prophet then joins the two together, probably concealing the ends of both with his fists. As is usual in this kind of playacting, the audience requests an explanation (cf. 12:9; 21:7; 24:19). The answer comes in the form of a prophetic oracle. Yahweh proposes to reunite the twelve tribes now dispersed in foreign countries, bring them

175

back to their own land, and constitute them as a purified people under a single ruler. How, given the fate of the northern tribes, this was thought to be possible, we do not know. Perhaps Ezekiel had in mind the survivors of the mixed population to the north of whom we hear from time to time (e.g., Jer. 41:4-8). Sometime after the return from captivity some of these, who profess to worship Yahweh, will make an unsuccessful bid to share in the rebuilding of the Jerusalem temple (Ezra 4:1-2). To judge by the names of their deities (e.g., Anath-Bethel), the somewhat less "orthodox" Jewish settlers at Elephantine in Upper Egypt during the early Persian period also hailed from the former kingdom of Samaria. But it seems likely that Ezekiel is acting out and proclaiming an eschatological goal the fulfillment of which, in ways not then imaginable, would be brought about by God. Ezekiel's public is therefore being asked to accept on prophetic warranty that this is an essential aspect of God's plan for the future of his people.

The final section (vs. 24-28) fills out this picture of a future united people. Several indications in the text—for example, different words for the ruler and the temple—have persuaded many of the commentators that it has been expanded at a later point in time either by Ezekiel himself (a possibility often overlooked) or by an editor. This may well be the case, but since the end result is self-consistent and consistent with the book as a whole, it may be taken as it stands. It foresees a fourfold honoring of ancient promises—ruler, land, covenant, and temple. When speaking of foreign and contemporary or recent Judean rulers, Ezekiel generally uses the standard term *melek* ("king"), less frequently *naśi'* ("prince"). Thus, Jehoiachin and Zedekiah are referred to as both *melek* and *naśi'* (1:2; 12:10, 12; 17:16; 19:1; 21:25). The future Davidic ruler, however, is almost invariably designated *naśi'*, the only exceptions being in the present chapter (vs. 22, 24). The reason, no doubt, is to emphasize the quite different role of political office conformable to the kind of community Israel is called to be. In this respect, Ezekiel adopts the ideology and political theory of the authors of Deuteronomy (see Deut. 17:14-20). The same implication is carried by the designation "servant" used of the Davidic ruler (vs. 24, 25). "Servant" is an honorific title, but it also implies the view that public office has to be seen in terms of service rather than self-advancement or domination. In this respect, there may

176

well be a connection with the first of the so-called "servant songs" in Second Isaiah (Isa. 42:1–4; see commentary on 34:23–24). The conclusion is perfectly clear that Israel is to show forth a model of political community quite different from contemporary realities.

The juxtaposition of obedience to the law and dwelling in the land carries the same message and, at the same time, excludes in advance the exploitation of such biblical passages in support of territorial claims. The land of Israel is very properly an essential ingredient of Jewish self-understanding and one that Christians have found difficult to appreciate, but it is clear from the major biblical statements—especially in Deuteronomy and the Priestly material—that possession of the land is in function of a purpose that transcends territoriality, as it is also contingent on fidelity to the covenant. Understandably, the promise of an indefectible covenant of peace or reconciliation was much in people's minds during that critical transitional period (cf. Isa. 54:10; 55:3; 61:8; see commentary on 34:25). It is, in the first place, the Priestly tradition which speaks of an indefectible covenant (Gen. 9:16; 17:7, 13, 19) and which adds to the ancient promise of land and peoplehood that of the divine presence. According to this way of thinking, shared by Ezekiel, the divine presence is mediated through the temple and the cultic acts carried out in it. The climactic promise is therefore the establishment of the sanctuary among them, an eventuality that is spelled out in detail in the final vision of the book (chs. 40—48). It is worth noting that, in addition to the usual term *miqdash* ("sanctuary"; cf. 5:11; 8:6; 9:6), Ezekiel also uses, here and nowhere else, the term *mishkan* ("dwelling place"), thematically associated with the wilderness tent which, according to the Priestly view, housed the ark of the covenant. By the time of writing, the wilderness tent had become a powerful symbol of the divine presence animating and guiding a united people in its journey through history. Later Jewish teachers will speak of the *shekinah* as signifying this idea of divine immanence, in keeping with which the targum translates the beginning of v. 27 as "I will make my *shekinah* dwell among them." Taking over the same symbolic language, the author of the Fourth Gospel will speak of the Word which became flesh and "tented" among us (John 1:14), meaning that, according to Christian experience, the *shekinah* is now located

177

in Jesus the Son. In Ezekiel all of these promises are subsumed in the sanctification of Israel, the visible sign of which is the sanctuary in their midst. The conclusion therefore links up with the final vision in chapters 40–48 which will give specific form and substance to the promise.

PART SIX

Gog of the Land of Magog

EZEKIEL 38—39

In spite of occasional unevenness, the Gog passage tells a fairly clear and consistent story. Gog of the land of Magog, princely lord of Meshech and Tubal, will lead an army of confederates in an attack from the north on the unsuspecting Israelites, newly recovered from war and living peacefully and prosperously in their newly repopulated but undefended land. While this army will have its own ideas about the prospects of plunder and loot, ideas shared by others who witness the attack, the operation is really being directed by Yahweh for his own ends, principally the manifestation of his glory and holiness. Therefore, in fulfillment of prophecy, Gog and his hosts will be destroyed in the land of Israel after being visited by various disasters, including pestilence and earthquake. Their bodies will remain as carrion on the mountains of Israel, and their abandoned weapons will keep the Israelites in firewood for seven years. Birds and beasts of prey will be summoned to feast on the corpses in a great sacrificial meal prepared by Yahweh. Alternatively, it will take seven months to bury the slain in the Valley of Hamon-gog, east of the Dead Sea, and thus purify the land. This spectacular conclusion to the invasion will convince the nations witnessing it that the Israelites were exiled not because their God was powerless to prevent it but on account of their sins. Then, finally, the restoration will be complete, they will live securely in their land in possession of the divine spirit poured out on them, and they will acknowledge the hand of God in all that has happened.

The first and perhaps most difficult question about this passage concerns its place in the book. There are clear indications that the abundant material preserved from Ezekiel's preaching and the editorial comment on it have been arranged according to a meaningful structure (see the Introduction). The logical sequence would seem to require that chapters 38—39 precede the section that deals with restoration in chapters 34—37, as in fact they do in one late LXX attestation (the J. H. Scheide papyri, second to fourth century A.D.). The finale of the Gog passage, 39:25-29, would serve very well as a prologue to the more detailed account of the restoration of Israel in chapters 34—37, the fate of the slain enemy's remains would make a fitting contrast with the resuscitation of the dry bones, and the promise concerning the sanctuary with which chapters 34—37 ends would lead smoothly into the vision of the new temple in chapters 40—48. The present position of the God episode is therefore something of a problem.

While any solution will be speculative, it may be that, since the Gog narrative presupposes return to the land but does not speak of a rebuilt temple, this was thought to be the most appropriate point at which to fit it in. Another possibility is suggested by Josephus, who, among the very little that he says about Ezekiel in his history, tells us that Ezekiel left behind two books (*Ant.* 10.79-80). Since we know nothing of a pseudepigraphal work attributed to the prophet with which Josephus may have been familiar, it may be that chapters 40—48, the description of the new temple and related matters, at one time circulated as a separate publication. In that case, chapters 38—39 may have been simply appended to the first book (chs. 1—37) in keeping with a tendency, clearly observable in other prophetic books, to end with the prospect of a future consummation (Isa. 66:24; Joel 3; Amos 9:11-15; Obad. 15-21; Zeph. 3:8-20; Zech. 14).

There can be little doubt that the Gog episode has undergone considerable expansion in the course of transmission. The result is seven sayings each introduced by the customary formula "Thus says the Lord Yahweh" (38:1-9, 10-13, 14-16, 17-23; 39:1-16, 17-24, 25-29). The repetition of the language of the first saying in the two sayings that follow suggests serial composition, and the abandoning of the slain as carrion (39:4-5, 17-20) is not easily reconciled with their careful collection and burial (39:11-16). Allusion to the prophets of former days (38:17; cf. Zech. 1:4-6) suggests a date for the section beginning here considerably later than Ezekiel. Yet there remains enough

180

of language and theme characteristic of Ezekiel to justify assigning the basic narrative to him, though a glance at the commentaries will convince the reader of the difficulty of distinguishing between what is "primary" and "secondary." In any event, nothing prevents us from interpreting the passage as it stands, as a reasonably coherent and self-consistent narrative.

Numerous attempts have been made to date this narrative by identifying the protagonist with a historical figure. All are inconclusive for the simple reason that the description of Gog lacks the precision necessary for establishing any conclusion of the kind. A wide range of candidates has, nevertheless, been put forward, ranging chronologically from Babylon personified (based on a complicated cryptographic system) to the Seleucid king Antiochus Eupator in the second century B.C. The favorite candidate has always been Alexander the Great in the fourth century B.C., which, however, has the disadvantage of putting him at the head of an improbable coalition including Persia, his principal opponent (38:5). It is safe to say that none of these attempts to break Gog's incognito has been successful, but it is equally true and important to add that, throughout the ages, people who live by the biblical tradition, and who find themselves confronted with overwhelming evil, have applied the text to themselves and drawn strength and comfort from it. It is therefore not surprising that the targum identifies Magog with Rome and Gog with the Roman emperor, or that Augustine, preparing for the final assault of the barbarians, identified the hordes from the north with the Goths. This kind of reactualization of biblical texts has lost none of its validity today. It must, however, be carefully distinguished from the unfortunate tendency in some Christian denominations to extract detailed predictions of the future from etymologies, numerical calculations, and the like, generally of a quite implausible kind. So it is still necessary to repeat that *ro'sh meshech* (38:2) has nothing to do, etymologically or otherwise, with Russia and Moscow and that therefore some other means will have to be found to identify the evil empire described in these chapters.

The Gog narrative is often said to be the earliest example in the biblical writings of apocalyptic, but this description is not entirely accurate. As the name suggests, the apocalyptic genre deals with revelations, generally mediated by angelic beings, of secret information about the heavenly world and, occasionally, the course of future events. Eschatology, on the other hand, has

181

to do with the final phase of history in general or a particular epoch of history, including the end of individual existence and the postmortem destiny of the individual. Apocalyptic therefore may, but need not, be eschatological in character, but where it is, it is generally characterized by a precise determination of historical epochs preceding the final consummation.

The difference between the two terms may be seen more clearly if we compare Ezekiel 38—39 with the account of the last phase of history in Revelation 20. In the latter the seer foresees a millennium during which Satan will be restrained in the bottomless pit while the resurrected saints share in the reign of Christ. This will be followed by a period of unspecified length during which Satan will be on the loose and will marshal Gog and Magog in a last assault on Jerusalem. The attack will be foiled by fire from heaven, the forces of evil will be thrown into the lake of fire and sulphur, and the final judgment will follow.

Obviously, this scenario has certain features in common with the Ezekiel passage on which it draws, but there are also significant differences, especially the role of a heavenly intermediary and the determination of time. At first reading, Ezekiel 38—39 might appear to the reader who is familiar with the Bible to be a farrago or collage of biblical phrases and motifs. On closer inspection, however, it will be seen that the author has skillfully drawn together into a consecutive narrative several major themes of prophetic eschatology. These may be set out as follows:

The enemy will attack from the north (Jer. 1:13–15; 4:5–18; 6:22; Joel 2:20)

Their invasion will lead to a final war in which Yahweh fights for Israel (Isa. 17:12–14; Hab. 3:8; Zech. 14:3–4)

This final conflict will be accompanied by earthquake and cosmic convulsions (Isa. 24:19–23; Nah. 1:4–5; Joel 4:15–16)

It will take place in the land of Israel (Isa. 14:24–25), in fact, in or near Jerusalem (Zech. 14:1–5)

Following the defeat of the enemy, their weapons will be destroyed or used as fuel (Isa. 9:5)

God's people will celebrate with a sacrificial banquet (Isa. 34:5–8; Jer. 46:10; Zeph. 1:7–8)

There are some indications, in both the prophetic writings and the psalms, that several of these themes may have been brought together in mythic recital and cultic celebration long before Ezekiel. If so, Ezekiel 38–39 moved a step farther by giving them a distinctly narrative form which can be seen as transitional between prophetic eschatology and the apocalyptic visions of Daniel and the Book of Revelation. Hence the importance of these chapters in the evolution of the biblical view of the tension between good and evil in human affairs and its eventual resolution.

Ezekiel 38:1–9
Gog and His Allies

The first proclamation, addressed to Gog, expresses hostile intent but also Yahweh's design to bring him and his forces against Israel newly recovered from war, repopulated, and enjoying peace and prosperity. Gog is addressed as from the land of Magog and princely ruler of Meshech and Tubal. In the ethnic genealogy of Genesis 10, Magog is the second of the Japhethite nations (v. 2; also I Chron. 1:5). No satisfactory explanation of this name has been proposed, which may suggest an artificial formation from the name Gog, a twinning by assonance rather like Eldad and Medad in Num. 11:26–30. The meaning and identification of Gog have been the subject of interminable discussion. The Old Greek and Samaritan versions read "Gog" for "Agag," king of the hated Amalekites, at Num. 24:7, and king Gog makes another unexpected appearance in the LXX of Amos 7:1, but neither of these reinterpretations throws any light on the name as it appears here. Similar forms (Gaga, Gagi) have been noted in the Amarna tablets from the early fourteenth century B.C. and in Assyrian records, and it has even been suggested that the name is a personification of the Sumerian *gūg*, darkness. The most likely, but by no means certain, identification is with a certain Gūgu mentioned in the annals of the Assyrian king Ashurbanipal, probably the Lydian king Gyges (ca. 680–650 B.C.) of whose half-legendary exploits we hear in Herodotus and in Plato's *Republic*. If this is correct, it does not necessarily imply that the biblical author knew of the identification of this or the other ethnic or geographical names in the narrative, most of which could have been picked up from Genesis 10. However he came by it, it suggests less a historical personage than a symbol of overwhelming, evil power. As we have seen, Rev. 20:7–10 accentuates this symbolic equivalent in its description of Satan leading Gog and Magog (both now personal names) in the final assault of evil following the thousand years' reign of the Messiah. Later still, Gog will be identified successively with Ethiopians (*Sibylline Oracles* 3.319, 512), Goths, the Muslim invaders of Europe, the Mongols, Stalin, Hitler, and so on.

Gog is further described as "chief prince" of Meshech and Tubal. There are only two proper names here, since *ro'sh* ("chief, head") is nowhere attested as such. It has no more connection with Russia (a name of Norse extraction) than Meshech has with Moscow. There is an evil empire here, but it is not the USSR. We have already encountered these two peoples in the list of Tyre's trading partners (27:13) and as denizens of the underworld (32:26), and they are also listed together as "sons" of Japheth in Gen. 10:2. They are probably identical with the Mushki and Tabal of Assyrian records (Moschoi and Tibarenoi in Herodotus), tribes of the central Anatolian highlands. Gog is described as a wild beast that must be trapped, subdued with hooks, and made to obey, for the invasion of unsuspecting Israel is part of God's plan in which he has a role to play (see also vs. 16–17).

Gog of Magog is accompanied by heavily armed troops of seven other nations. The names of all the nations, with the exception of Persia, occur in the ethnic genealogies of Genesis 10 (vs. 2–3, 6), and several crop up at earlier points in Ezekiel: Persia and Put in a list of Tyrian mercenaries (27:10), Bethtogarmah as a trading partner of the same city (27:14), Cush in one of the anti-Egyptian sayings (30:4, 5, 9). Cush corresponds to the Sudan and Ethiopia, Put a region along the North African littoral. Gomer is usually identified with the Gimirrai of Assyrian inscriptions, or the Cimmerians, originally from the southern Russian steppe, later settled south of the Black Sea. Togarmah is probably Til Garimmu located, according to Assyrian annals, in the foothills of the Caucasus. "The far reaches of the north" cannot apply to Persia, Cush, and Put. We must therefore conclude either that these have been added at a later point (as Zimmerli, *Ezekiel*, 2:306) or that "the far reaches of

184

the north" stands in apposition to Beth-togarmah. But the repetition of this phrase in the narrative (38:15; 39:2) suggests the broader motif of the north as the cardinal point of danger and disaster. In this respect too, Ezekiel seems to have drawn on the early preaching of Jeremiah (Jer. 1:13–15; 4:5–31; 5:15–17).

The description is therefore of a gathering of fierce, barbarian nations along the rim of the known world. That Ezekiel does not have a precise event in mind is also clear from the indications of time—after many days, in the latter years. It will happen after return to and settlement in the land, but it foresees not so much a purely historical event as rather the final resolution of the conflict between good and evil. In this respect, as noted earlier, chapters 38—39 mark an important transitional stage in the emergence of a fully apocalyptic view of history of the kind encountered in the visions of Daniel.

Ezekiel 38:10–16
The Enemy War Plans

The following sayings (vs. 10–13, 14–16) make extensive use of the language of the first, and are therefore generally read as editorial comment on it. The first of the two, presumably still addressed to Gog, foresees that he will take things into his own hands, his main objective being plunder. The rhetorical questions addressed to the northern predator by spectators in the wings (for the names, see 27:12, 20, 22) betray a disposition to share in the anticipated loot. The description of the peaceful and secure state of the province of Judah corresponds not at all with the situation there during the Persian period. Jerusalem remained, however, undefended and unwalled until the administration of Nehemiah in the second half of the fifth century B.C., and there were those who believed that its defense should be left entirely to God (Zech. 2:5–9). The description of Jerusalem as "the navel of the earth" derives from pre-Israelite mythic representations of a kind found practically everywhere in the ancient world, including Israel itself (cf. Judg. 9:37 with reference to Gerizim; also Mt. Tabor). The navel is identical in significance with the cosmic mountain, the point of attachment of earth to heaven, the focal point of creation. As such, it provided

185

a rich source of symbolism of birth and death and rebirth. The second saying emphasizes once again that, in spite of Gog's own intentions, what is to follow will be under divine control, serving the ultimate purpose of demonstrating the reality and holiness of Yahweh as the true God (cf. 20:41; 28:22, 25; 36:23; 39:27). It may seem too banal to quote the old adage "Man proposes, but God disposes," but our experience confirms that there may be forces at work that move in a quite different direction from that of our conscious aims and intentions. The implication here is that the same principle applies on the political level, a point made earlier by Isaiah with respect to the Assyrians (Isa. 10:5–11) and by Habakkuk with respect to the Babylonians (Hab. 1:5–11).

Ezekiel 38:17–23
Later Fulfillment of the Prophecy

The sequence of thought is difficult to make out at this point. Allusion to "my servants the prophets of Israel" (v. 7, RSV) suggests a period when prophecy was already considered to be a thing of the past, as in the similar retrospective mention of "the former prophets" in the postexilic Zechariah (Zech. 1:4–6). The designation "his servants the prophets" occurs in the exilic history of the kingdoms (II Kings 9:7; 17:13) and in prose passages in Jeremiah originating in the same circles (Jer. 7:25; 26:5; 29:19; 35:15; 44:4). Here too the allusion is retrospective, taking in the entire sequence of prophetic witness from Moses, fountainhead of prophecy, to the time of writing. This opening verse, therefore, is addressed to a historical figure who was thought to fulfill the earlier predictions of a disastrous invasion principally, no doubt, those of Jeremiah and Ezekiel himself. It illustrates how assiduously the prophets continued to be read, interpreted, and applied to the changing historical circumstances of each age. It goes without saying that this process is fraught with ambiguity and misunderstanding, but it remains nevertheless an essential ingredient in the self-definition of both Christianity and Judaism.

186

The description of the event continues in the language of prophetic eschatology (vs. 18–23). It is "the day of which I have spoken" (39:8, RSV), the Day of Yahweh announced by earlier prophets from the time of Amos. Divine judgment on Gog will be in the form of a cosmic upheaval—earthquake, torrential rain, hail, fire and brimstone. A divinely inspired panic will lead the enemy to turn their weapons on each other—a familiar motif in the old narratives of the wars of Yahweh (e.g., Judg. 7:22; I Sam. 14:20). And by means of this demonstration of irresistible power Yahweh's greatness and holiness will be made known to the nations of the world. What are we to make of this language, so frequent in Ezekiel, which overwhelms the reader with its accumulation of images of death and destruction? There are, fortunately, other voices to be heard which reveal other aspects of the divine reality. In Ezekiel, the intensity of negative emotion springs from a deep sense of the reality and power of evil to which corresponds an equally strong conviction of the reality of divine judgment. There is also in passages like this the underlying idea that rampant evil unlooses forces that rage beyond human control and reach out beyond human society into the natural environment. This, at least, is an idea that can be grasped more easily today than at any time in previous history.

Ezekiel 39:1–16
Defeat of the Invaders and Disposal of the Slain

This third summons to prophesy against Gog introduces the fifth oracle in the series. Since it repeats the terminology of the original prophecy, it is generally thought to be an editorial expansion, which is possible but by no means certain. The new element is the prediction that the corpses of the slain will be left as carrion for the scavenger birds and animals to feed on, an image that will shortly be developed into the eschatological motif of the sacrificial banquet prepared by Yahweh (vs. 17–20). Another facet of this traditional representation is the destruction of weapons of war which will provide a seven-year supply of fuel for the survivors. Perhaps no aspect of prophetic preaching has had, and continues to have, such appeal as this appar-

187

ently forever to be disappointed anticipation of the abolition of war. We hear it with especial clarity in Isaiah:

> They shall beat their swords into plowshares,
> and their spears into pruning hooks;
> nation shall not lift up sword against nation,
> neither shall they learn war any more.
> Isaiah 2:4, RSV

> Every boot of the tramping warrior in battle tumult,
> and every garment rolled in blood
> will be burned as fuel for the fire.
> Isaiah 9:5, RSV

Ezekiel's projection of the future for Israel and, through Israel, for the world leaves no room for illusions about the capacity of human societies for bringing this about. He does not provide prescriptions for conflict resolution but simply declares the attainment of peace as an eschatological goal which only God can bring to fruition.

The disposal of the corpses by burial (vs. 11–16) was probably added as a more acceptable alternative by an editor concerned with the need for maintaining the ritual purity of the land. The location of the mass burial is unclear. It is in a valley known after the burial as Hamon-gog, originally either as Oberim (the passers-by) or Abarim. The sea east of which, or opposite which, it is situated could be the Mediterranean (usually known as the Great Sea) or the Dead Sea (later referred to as the Eastern Sea, 47:18), or the Sea of Galilee. The contribution of a later commentator, who refers us to a city called Hamonah, is not very helpful since the name is a fictitious adaptation of Hamon-gog. If the sea in question is the Dead Sea, we might think of Abarim in Moab (Num. 27:12; 33:47–48; Deut. 32:49) which is both east of and opposite the Dead Sea. But Abarim is not within the boundaries of Israel according to the description of the land in the last section of the book (chs. 40—48), and it would be surprising if this unhallowed burial were to be located at the site of Moses' burial. More probable, therefore, is a location in the Valley of Hinnom (later Gehenna), the refuse dump south of Jerusalem, which is both east of the Mediterranean and opposite the Dead Sea. It would not be surprising if the author got the idea from Jeremiah, who renamed this place of ill omen the Valley of Slaughter on account of the apostate Israelites to be buried there after the destruction of the city (Jer. 7:30–34).

There are so many dead that their burial will take seven months. The care with which this operation is carried out is due to the need to avoid contamination of the land (cf. Num. 19:11–13) and probably reflects actual practice after military action. Corpses are buried immediately, and after a period of time, work details survey the area carefully and place markers beside human remains which are then also buried. Concern for ritual purity, of the individual, the land, the temple, will be increasingly in evidence throughout the Second Temple period, and is to this day one of the distinguishing marks of Jewish allegiance.

Ezekiel 39:17–24
A Feast for the Birds of Prey

The sixth oracle invites birds and beasts to feed on the carrion; clearly a quite different scenario, though both are combined in the Jeremian sermon just referred to (Jer. 7:30–34). This motif, which plays on the double meaning of the verb *zabaḥ* ("sacrificed, slaughtered"), was well established in prophetic preaching of judgment (e.g., Isa. 34:5–8; Jer. 46:10). There is also a hint of the mythological theme of feasting on the flesh of Leviathan (e.g., Ps. 74:13–14), a theme that will reappear in rabbinic representations of the eschatological banquet. The same image, clearly dependent on Ezekiel, will be taken up by the author of Revelation: an angel standing in the sun summons the birds of midheaven to this grim supper prepared by God (Rev. 19:17–18). As incongruous as it may seem, the eucharistic language of the New Testament also echoes the language used here—the summons to the Lord's table (v. 20; cf. 44:16 and Mal. 1:7, 12); eating flesh and drinking blood—and in doing so, expresses the eschatological aspect of the eucharistic meal.

As so often in Ezekiel, the saying ends with the acknowledgment by the nations of the power and glory of Israel's God. It returns once again (cf. 36:16–21) to the theological explanation of the recent disasters, clearly a dominant issue in the diaspora community, to judge by the writings that have survived from that time.

Ezekiel 39:25–29
Summary of Ezekiel's Message of Hope

This last paragraph, which has nothing to do with Gog, summarizes the message of Ezekiel after the fall of Jerusalem, using for the most part the same turns of phrase that occur in chapters 34—39. The same assurances, even the same expressions, also feature prominently in the so-called Book of Consolation in Jeremiah (ch. 30—31; 33), for the most part from the exilic period. Leaving aside the matter of literary dependence, we may reasonably suppose that both represent a summary of the preaching that was going on in the diaspora communities in the years following the great disaster. "I will restore the fortunes [of Jacob]" is a formulaic, comprehensive expression for restoration, of frequent occurrence in the Book of Consolation (Jer. 30:3, 18; 31:23; 33:7, 11, 26). While Ezekiel does not often refer to Israel as Jacob, the designation is often heard in Second Isaiah. It reminds us that the Jacob narrative cycle in Genesis, which pivots on exile to Mesopotamia and return to the land, reflects the experience and aspirations of that diaspora generation. The promise of mercy unbounded on all of Israel, including the northern tribes, is also a prominent theme in the section of Jeremiah to which we alluded (Jer. 30:18; 31:20; 33:26). Yahweh's concern for his holy name and the vindication of his holiness recapitulates a prominent feature in Ezekiel's explanation of the exile (cf. 36:20–23), the obverse of which is that Israel will continue to *bear* its shame (rather than *forget* in RSV) or, in other words, not lose sight of the mistakes of the past. Secure possession of the land "with none to make them afraid" is clearly a cardinal point in prophetic preaching at that time (cf. Ezek. 34:28; Jer. 30:10; 33:16)—an intimation of what must be the ultimate eschatological hope, the removal of fear. The prediction that none shall be left among the nations or, in other words, the end of the diaspora, was not of course fulfilled. Many, probably most, did not take up the offer of Cyrus to return to the homeland in 538 B.C. and the diaspora remained, what it still is, a permanent feature of Jewish life.

The metaphor of seeing or not seeing God's face is associated from the beginnings of Israel's history with the experience of worship:

> Thou hast said, "Seek ye my face." . . .
> "Thy face, LORD, do I seek."
> Hide not thy face from me.
>   Psalm 27:8–9, RSV

To say that during the exile Yahweh hid his face from his people (as in Ezek. 39:23–24) implies, therefore, the impossibility of worshiping in the traditional way. The long, dark period during which Yahweh's face remained hidden has therefore come to an end with the outpouring of the spirit (cf. 36:26–27) and the restoration of temple worship. The way is therefore prepared for the final vision in which this promise is given body and substance.

PART SEVEN

Vision of the New Temple and Commonwealth

EZEKIEL 40—48

The last section of the book records another visionary trans-location from the Babylonian diaspora to Jerusalem. Like Dante following in Virgil's steps, Ezekiel is led on a tour of the temple which begins and ends at its eastern gate. There he witnesses the return of the divine effulgence which had left the old temple shortly before its destruction. He is given detailed instructions for the temple personnel, offerings, festivals, the civic ruler, and the allotment of land. Back at the eastern gate, he is shown a stream flowing from the temple down to the Dead Sea which waters and fertilizes the barren Judean wilderness. The vision ends with a description of tribal territories and the new Jerusalem.

While this last vision has a character all its own, there can be no doubt that it is structurally and thematically an integral part of the book. The narrator (leaving aside for the moment the question of authorship) himself notes this as he witnesses the eturn of the *kabod* from the east:

> The vision I saw was like the vision which I had seen when he came to destroy the city, and like the vision which I had seen by the river Chebar.
>
> Ezekiel 43:3, RSV

The Book of Ezekiel opens with the vision of the heavenly temple (ch. 1), in a second vision (chs. 8—11) the corruption and consequent destruction of the old temple is announced, and now the new temple built according to heavenly specifications is described. In close correspondence with this structure, the return of the divine effulgence is unintelligible without the

193

previous account of how it left the temple before the destruction (10:3–5, 15–19; 11:22–23). The need for a new form of worship is also implicit in Ezekiel's survey of the religious history of Israel which, as noted earlier, ends with a new exodus (20:33–38). In this respect, he is following a tradition that sees Mt. Zion and its sanctuary as the goal of the long journey that began in Egypt:

> Thou wilt bring them in, and plant them on thy own mountain,
> the place, O LORD, which thou hast made for thy abode,
> the sanctuary, O LORD, which thy hands have established.
> Exodus 15:17, RSV

The possibility that chapters 40—48 at one time followed immediately after chapter 37, which ends with the promise of a newly established sanctuary, was suggested earlier. It is also possible that these chapters circulated independently of the rest of the book, and it is virtually certain that the vision narrative was expanded after the return to the land. The fact remains that it is integrally and structurally part of the book and therefore requires to be read and interpreted in that literary context.

If we take in the larger context of the Hebrew Bible, we note a remarkably close parallelism with the Priestly version of the Sinai event, according to which Moses saw a vision of the divine effulgence and received detailed specifications for the construction of the tent (tabernacle) and ark together with their furnishings (Exod. 24:15b–18a; 25—31). Everything had to be made according to the pattern or model (*tabnit* in Hebrew) revealed to him (Exod. 25:9, 40). There can be no doubt that the two vision narratives, of a kind unique in the Hebrew Bible, are closely related. Ezekiel himself was part of that priestly world of symbolic meanings which represents the creation of the world as a temple of praise, pivots on the establishment of true worship at Sinai, and concludes with the setting up of the sanctuary in the promised land (Gen. 1:1—2:4; Exod. 25—31; Josh. 18—19). On the matter of chronological priority, which is, in any case, of secondary importance, there is no consensus. At a considerably later time the author of Chronicles will transfer the honor of receiving the heavenly model from Moses to David, who passed it on to Solomon (I Chron. 28:11–19). Then the Qumran community will present—in the Temple Scroll from the eleventh cave—a somewhat different and more detailed description of the sanctuary as revealed to Moses after

194

the apostasy of the golden calf. Still later, the seer of Patmos, whose debt to Ezekiel is apparent throughout his work, will speak of the new Jerusalem descending from heaven, a city in which there will no longer be need for a temple, since the divine effulgence will penetrate and pervade the entire city and its inhabitants (Rev. 21).

This motif of temple or city built according to a celestial prototype is by no means confined to the biblical writings. Gudea, ruler of the Sumerian city of Lagash, was shown in a dream the model according to which the temple of Ningirsu was to be built. In these and similar representations, as in the Platonic world of ideas, correspondence with a preexistent pattern assures the reality and validity of human institutions. The correspondence extends not just to the material building but also to the worship carried out in it. Temple worship is thus seen as a participation in the heavenly liturgy from the beginning to the end of time. This idea too is attested in the Hebrew Bible (e.g., the temple vision of Isaiah 6 and several of the psalms) and is reflected at numerous points in Jewish and Christian worship.

The vision narrative also contains a great number of stipulations about temple worship and other matters some of which correspond to and others differ from statutes and ordinances in the Pentateuch. The discrepancies concern such matters as the offering for the first month (Ezek. 45:18; cf. Num. 28:11), the liturgical calendar (Ezek. 45:18–25; 46:1–15; cf. Num. 28—29), Levitical territory (Ezek. 45:5; 48:13–14; cf. Num. 35:1–8), and the laws of inheritance (Ezek. 46:16–18; cf. Num. 36). It is understandable that these caused much concern and even raised doubts as to the canonical status of Ezekiel. A well-known rabbinic tradition tells how, when the book was in danger of being withdrawn, Hananiah ben Hezekiah shut himself in his upper chamber with three hundred jars of oil and labored to reconcile these stipulations with the Torah (*b. Menahoth* 45a). Hananiah's burning of the midnight oil obviously paid off, since the book remained in public use, though we hear that the study of its beginning and end—that is, the *merkabah* vision and the temple vision—was permitted only to those who had reached the age of thirty. It is also possible that comparison with Pentateuchal law led to some omissions from the original draft of the vision narrative. Ezekiel 43:12, for example, announces the law of the temple, but no such law follows immediately after this announcement.

195

Different Methods of Interpreting the Vision

Ezekiel 40—48 is not at all typical of prophetic vision narratives, which is one reason why several scholars, preeminently C. C. Torrey, have dated it to the Hellenistic period (third century B.C. or later). One conspicuous feature, not encountered earlier, is the presence of a supernatural intermediary who acts and speaks in the vision. We will encounter this feature again in the night visions of the postexilic Zechariah, and it will occur routinely in accounts of vision experiences in the Greco-Roman period. This "angel-interpreter" also acts as a kind of supernatural tour guide, anticipating the account of celestial journeys in the Enoch literature and, much later, Dante's tour of hell, purgatory, and heaven. What sets Ezekiel's vision apart from all others in the prophetic literature, however, is the great mass of legislative material and architectural detail that it contains. It is not surprising, therefore, that several commentators have read it as a blueprint for the temple to be rebuilt and the commonwealth to be reestablished after the return from exile.

We know very little indeed about the temple that was rebuilt under the leadership of Zerubbabel and the high priest Jeshua during the reign of the Persian king Darius (late sixth century B.C.), and what we do know has nothing in common with Ezekiel's temple. The books of Ezra and Nehemiah speak of the building materials in general terms (Ezra 5:8; 6:4) and refer to rooms and courtyards (Neh. 8:16; 10:37–39; 12:25, 44; 13:4–9, 12–13). It was certainly on a smaller scale than Solomon's temple (see Hag. 2:3), and according to the imperial building permit, it was to be sixty cubits in height and breadth (Ezra 6:3). This notice, however, can hardly fail to arouse suspicion. If we supply sixty cubits for the missing length, we would have a cube, the symbolically perfect structure, like the immense cube in which Gilgamesh survived the flood and the even vaster cube shape of the heavenly Jerusalem in Revelation (Rev. 21:16). It is, of course, possible that the Ezekiel blueprint never got off the drawing board, so to speak, but there still remains the problem of the symbolic and mythic aspects of the narrative which, as we shall see shortly, point in a quite different direction.

196

Christian interpretations of the passage have usually been filtered through the description of the new Jerusalem in Revelation which draws heavily on Ezekiel's vision. At this point the reader is advised to turn to the description of the transformed earth and the descent of the heavenly Jerusalem in Revelation 21—22 which, as we have seen, follows the defeat and destruction of Gog and Magog. As in Ezekiel, the seer is accompanied by a heavenly guide, one of the seven angels, who holds a gold measuring rod in his hand. He is transported to a high mountain and sees the new Jerusalem coming down from heaven. Like Ezekiel's city, it has twelve gates named for the twelve tribes (Rev. 21:12; cf. Ezek. 48:30–35), but there the resemblance ends. It is made all of gold and precious stones, its dimensions are immeasurably greater, and, most significant, it has no temple (Rev. 21:22). Early Christian apologists interpreted the destruction of the temple in A.D. 70 as the fulfillment of a prophecy of Jesus, as punishment for the failure of most contemporary Jews to accept Jesus as their Messiah, and as a sign that the old order had come to an end. It was therefore understandable that the emphasis should pass from the temple to the city and that, in consequence, Ezekiel's temple vision should be interpreted allegorically. The vision of the new Jerusalem continued to inspire millenarian movements throughout Christian history—one thinks of the Montanist movement in the second and third centuries A.D., the Crusades, the Anabaptists, and so down to the present. (A fascinating account of these movements is available in Norman Cohn's *The Pursuit of the Millennium.*)

Christian interpreters, then, tended to read Ezekiel 40—48 with allegorical reference to their own community. The Christian community is God's temple (I Cor. 3:16–17), and the body of the individual Christian is a temple of the Holy Spirit (I Cor. 6:19). The literal and polemical significance of the temple was not, however, lost from sight. As late as the fourth century the emperor Julian proposed to rebuild the Jerusalem temple as a way of refuting the Christian interpretation of its destruction three centuries earlier. Reaction to the failure of this project on the part of Jews and especially Christians demonstrates the persistence of the symbolic significance of the temple even after such a long lapse of time.

There are enough allusions in chapters 40—48 of a mythic-symbolic and idealistic kind to rule out the suggestion that a literal program or blueprint for the future was intended. The first of these is the very high mountain on which the prophet was set down (40:2). We have heard already in the book of this high, lofty, and holy mountain of Yahweh (17:22; 20:40). It is the same as "the mountain of the house of Yahweh which shall be established as the highest of the mountains" (Isa. 2:2 = Micah

197

4:1), a description which, understood literally, hardly fits the ridge, some 2,500 feet high, on which Jerusalem is built. Another Isaian text (Isa. 14:13) speaks of the mount of (divine) assembly in the far north, an expression familiar from the Ugaritic texts and comparable to Mt. Olympus, residence of the ancient Greek pantheon. Elsewhere Ezekiel speaks of Jerusalem as the center of the nations and the navel of the world (5:5; 38:12), and it is clear that here too he is appropriating for Jerusalem/Zion an ancient mythological motif. The same procedure is even more evident in the splendid image of a life-giving stream flowing from the temple and fertilizing the barren wastes of the Judean wilderness (47:1–12). This too is attested elsewhere in the prophetic writings. Isaiah 33:21 speaks of Zion as a place of broad rivers and streams and Zech. 14:8 of living waters flowing from Jerusalem into the Dead Sea and the Mediterranean. The psalmist could think of no more fitting image for the life-bestowing divine presence experienced in worship than a full-flowing river:

> They feast on the abundance of thy house,
>   and thou givest them drink from the river of thy delights.
>   Psalm 36:8, RSV

The Jerusalem of the vision is therefore the real city, the longing for which is intensified by exile, but it is also a symbol, an ideal location, a projection of a future reality that exists only as aspiration and desire.

What more than anything else gives a sense of realism to the vision are the numerous architectural details recorded together with their exact measurements. Unlike the dimensions of the new Jerusalem in Revelation, which is about 1,500 miles in length, breadth, and height, the measurements recorded by the seer's guide are in themselves quite feasible. One of the Zion psalms may provide a clue to this aspect of the vision:

> Walk about Zion, go round about her,
>   number her towers,
> consider well her ramparts,
>   go through her citadels;
> that you may tell the next generation that this is God,
> our God for ever and ever.
> He will be our guide for ever.
>   Psalm 48:12–14, RSV

198

We see that the physical buildings of the city give assurance of the divine presence. The details recorded in the vision, therefore, which may seem tedious to the modern reader, add up to a kind of meditation. We note also in both the psalm and the vision the concern not only to see, consider, and meditate but to transmit to others.

There is also a distinct possibility that the measurements recorded by the guide are units in a complex numerological system. The dimensions of the new Jerusalem in Revelation (Rev. 21:15–21) are all multiples of twelve corresponding to the Christian church as the new Israel. In Ezekiel, the twelve-tribal symbolism is restricted to the city gates (48:30–34). Most of the other measurements are in multiples of five, with a predominance of twenty-five, culminating in the entire sacred enclosure with an area of 25,000 square cubits (48:20). There is certainly an element of deliberate stylization here, but it is difficult to know what we are to make of it. Zimmerli (*Ezekiel,* 2:344) relates it to the initial date, the twenty-fifth year of the exile which is halfway to the jubilee year of freedom (see commentary below). Since the jubilee is really seven septennial periods plus one year ($7 \times 7 + 1$), he speculates that the operative number throughout is, after all, the sacred number seven. This seems to be somewhat overelaborate. It may be idle to argue the case for the number five as significant in its own right, as it was for the Pythagoreans (the sum of the perfect numbers two and three), the ancient Chinese (the five elements and the five blessings), Islam (the *arkan al-Islam,* or five pillars of Islam), Judaism (the fivefold Torah, five books of psalms, five *megilloth*), and no doubt others. The main point is that in their regularity and homogeneity the measurements are part of a symbolic structure of meaning which transcends without entirely leaving behind the physical and historical reality of city and temple.

Ezekiel 40:1–4
Ezekiel Transported in Vision to Jerusalem

As in the initial vision of the chariot throne, there is a double date. The twenty-fifth year of the exile (of King Jehoiachin, 1:2) would be 573 B.C., two decades after Ezekiel's call, and the latest date in the book, with the exception of the oracle predicting the Babylonian conquest of Egypt which is dated two years

199

later (29:17–20). The second date, fourteen years after the fall of Jerusalem, agrees with the first. Assuming use of the priestly Babylonian calendar—as in Ezek. 45:18–25—the tenth day of the first month would correspond to the preparation for Passover, festival of freedom, a correspondence that can hardly be coincidental (cf. Exod. 12:2–3). The twenty-fifth year could be understood as the halfway mark to the fiftieth, or jubilee, year, following the tradition which represents the exile as the sabbatical rest of the land (Lev. 26:34–35; II Chron. 36:21). The jubilee year is the year of liberation (Lev. 25:10; cf. Ezek. 46:17), so that for the discerning reader or hearer the vision is a proleptic experience of freedom from bondage after exodus from exile. Coming, as it was then thought, at the halfway point of exile, it marked the turning point, the *peripateia,* in the fortunes of the exiled community. From now on, they could shake off the past and look confidently to the future.

We may add that the significance of the date, so understood, greatly increases the probability that at least the nucleus of the vision narrative is from Ezekiel himself. Much was certainly added in subsequent years, though it is not always possible to identify editorial elaborations with any assurance. It may be said in general that the original vision which, like the one experienced almost two decades earlier (ch. 8), consists in a guided tour of the temple, has been transformed into a blueprint for the theocratic kingdom to be established after the return. Much about this blueprint was, inevitably, polemical, especially with regard to control of the temple and civic leadership. The literature of the postexilic period reveals the equally inevitable tension that ensued between vision and reality.

In a state of trance Ezekiel found himself again in the land of Israel, facing Jerusalem, perhaps from the Mount of Olives. We note once again the language of indirection characteristic of dream or vision reports—a structure like a city (cf. 1:5, 26–28). His guide is the same mysterious refulgent individual as on the previous occasion (8:2). As with the man clothed in linen holding a writing case (9:2), his function is revealed by the instruments in his hand—a length of twine made of flax for longer measurements and a rod, probably of papyrus, a little over three meters long. He tells the seer to observe carefully with a view to passing on what he sees to his compatriots. Leaving aside 40:45–46, almost certainly an editorial insertion, he will not speak again until he shows Ezekiel the inner sanctuary of the temple (41:4). This silence, so unusual in a guided tour, is an impressive feature of the description that follows.

Ezekiel 40:5–16
The Enclosure Wall and the East Gate

The tour begins and ends at the east gate leading into the outer court of the temple, through which the divine effulgence will reenter (43:1–5). This contrasts with the survey of the corrupt cults practiced in the temple which began at the north gate (8:3). The east gate, on the temple's axis of orientation, led by way of the outer and inner courts directly to the entrance of the building. Ascent by twenty-five steps, seven at the outer gate (40:22, 26), eight at the inner gate (40:31, 34, 37), and ten into the building itself (40:49), enhanced the symbolic representation of divine transcendence. It also suggests comparison with the Mesopotamian ziggurat, a stepped sanctuary which symbolized the first mound to appear from the waters of the deluge. The enclosure wall around the *temenos,* or sacred area, is measured first. It is six long or old cubits (about 3.1 meters) in width and height, and we shall learn later that it is 500 cubits (about 259 meters) on each side (42:15–20). These extraordinary dimensions emphasize the need to safeguard the purity of the enclosed space. We may note in passing that this is the only height measurement given. For the remaining structures, all we have is a ground plan.

Because of its importance as the point of entry for the return of the divine presence, the eastern gate is described in considerable detail. Unfortunately, not all the details here and throughout the tour are clear, and the text is often corrupt and sometimes unintelligible. The reader whose interests go beyond the theological and symbolic significance of the description may be referred to plans available in several of the commentaries (e.g., Cooke, *Ezekiel,* p. 542; Zimmerli, *Ezekiel,* 2:353ff.; and Taylor, *Ezekiel,* pp. 255ff.). Since we have no comparable description of this feature of Solomon's temple, we cannot tell to what extent, if at all, the present account was influenced by it. The major features—three guardrooms on each side of the interior and an open space or plaza opposite the

201

entrance—are, however, similar to Iron Age gate complexes excavated at Megiddo, Hazor, and Gezer. Seven steps led to the gate itself, which was a little over 5 meters across, widening out inside to about 6.7 meters. The threshold of the gate corresponded to the thickness of the wall in which it was set, and the guardrooms facing each other across the inner passage were also about 3.1 meters on each side. These rooms, intended for use by the Levitical temple guards, had doors leading to the outer court. The space between the rooms, about 2.5 meters, was occupied by recessed windows tapering inward to the back wall. The plaza at the west end of the complex measured about 4.1 by 10.4 meters, and the length of the entire gate area east to west including the plaza was almost 26 meters.

Ezekiel 40:17–37
The Outer Court
and Outer and Inner Gates

Following the guide through the east gate, Ezekiel entered the outer court, a space 100 cubits (51.8 meters) across from outer to corresponding inner gate. Along the outer wall were thirty rooms, ten on each side except on the west which was closed off by a large building to be described presently. These rooms, which must not be confused with the sacristies in the inner court (40:44–47), would have been for the use of temple personnel in general (priests, Levites, musicians, scribes, prophets; see, e.g., Jer. 35:1–4 and Neh. 6:10) and perhaps also for private sacrificial meals. A paved surface ran the length of the wall outside the rooms, its outer edge flush with the inner limit of the gate areas.

This outer court formed part of a concentric, quadratic system expressing in spatial symbolism progressive degrees of holiness. The center was the inner sanctuary, the "holy of holies," abode of the effulgence, surrounded by the walls of the three-room sanctuary. Then came the inner, then the outer court, this last separated by an open space (45:2) from the district allotted to the priests, beyond which again lay an area of equal size assigned to the Levites (45:3–5; 48:8–14). A smaller area on the opposite side, the north, included the city and city land for the use of the laity (45:6; 48:15–20), while the territory of the prince lay to the east and west (45:7–8; 48:21–22). On the outer perimeter, finally, were the tribal territories (47:13–23; 48:23–29). In this way, all of Israel was integrated into a hierarchical, cultic order through which irradiated, in different degrees of intensity, the effulgence of the divine presence in the sanctuary. By the same token, as one approached the center, the demands of ritual purity increased, until we reach the point where only the high priest may enter the inner sanctum, and that only once a year on the Day of Expiation (Yom Kippur).

For most people today the idea of the holy is no longer easy to grasp, and consequently this kind of symbolic structure may well appear artificial and unreal. The starting point is a perception or intuition of a reality that is totally different from what we normally recognize as real in our everyday experience. In the tradition of Israel, that other reality is the holy God whose otherness can be perceived through contact with certain individuals and places and in the commission of certain acts, preeminently the act of worship. Characteristic of the priestly class, specialists of the holy par excellence, is the impetus to order the whole of reality along its temporal and spatial axes; hence the importance of the liturgical calendar and the careful attention to the layout of the temple and its precincts in this part of the book. The concern to express this "holiness by association" in these ways, and to preserve it by means of an extremely complex system of ritual legislation, continued in spite of the increasingly lay character of Second Commonwealth Judaism. One of the principal aims of Pharisaism was in fact to extend it to all aspects of everyday life, so that all Israel would be in reality "a kingdom of priests and a holy nation" (Exod. 19:6, RSV). Early Christianity also pursued this aim, what we might call the democratization of the holy, but with decreasing emphasis on ritual obligation. Now the community itself is the holy temple (Eph. 2:19–22) and the individual Christian the shrine in which God's Spirit dwells (I Cor. 3:16–17).

Ezekiel's progress through the outer court is from east to north and then to south. The purpose is to measure and inspect the northern and southern gates which are identical with the east gate in design and dimensions. Worshipers would enter from the east and face the divine presence. There was no gate on the west side, perhaps to prevent access behind the inner

203

sanctuary. Comparison with what is recorded of the layout of Solomon's temple reveals a greater emphasis on holiness in the visionary complex: there is no longer a royal palace in the vicinity, and the detailed description of the gates suggests concern to safeguard the purity of the temple precinct. The concern for holiness will be even greater in the sectarian Temple Scroll in which the building has an additional court and other features designed to prevent ritual contamination.

Access to the inner court was through three gates 100 cubits distant from the corresponding outer gates with which they shared the same dimensions and layout (vs. 28–37). This court was on a higher level reached by eight steps (vs. 31, 34, 37) corresponding to the increasing degree of holiness as one approached closer to the inner sanctuary.

Ezekiel 40:38–47
Facilities for Sacrifice and Temple Personnel

The state of the text does not permit certainty as to the exact location for the messy business of preparing the sacrificial victims. We will be told later that the offerings of the civic ruler are to take place at the main gate to the east (46:2). This, however, appears to be a special case; other indications in the present text (40:40) and elsewhere (Lev. 1:11; II Chron. 4:6) favor the north gate. Rinsing off the entrails and legs of the animal is prescribed in priestly law (Lev. 1:9, 13). There were to be eight tables for depositing the sacrificial meat and four to hold the knives and other implements required. Stipulations for the carrying out of the different kinds of sacrifice—burnt offering, sin and guilt offerings—are detailed in the same law (Lev. 1 and 4—6). Of greater interest is the rationale for these offerings and indeed for the sacrificial system as a whole. The goal of the entire operation may be briefly stated as the restoration of a divinely ordained cosmic order which had been disturbed by sin. But we must add at once that priestly law makes a clear distinction between inadvertent and deliberate sin (sinning "with a high hand," Num. 15:30, RSV). Sacrifice of any kind—

whether sin offering *(ḥaṭṭa't)* or guilt offering *('asham),* the latter for acts requiring restitution—availed only for inadvertent acts. For the one who sinned "with a high hand," there was no atonement by sacrifice. His fate was the social death of exclusion from the community (Num. 15:27–31). This kind of disposition will seem strange to us, since we are accustomed to thinking subjectively and since the idea of an objective, divinely ordained order does not come easily. What it means is that, according to this Levitical theology, the ethical is subsumed in the ritual, yet without losing anything of its importance and urgency. Something of this persisted in early Christianity, especially in the designation of apostasy as beyond the reach of repentance (Heb. 6:4–8). The shedding of (sacrificial) blood is still essential for forgiveness, but the sacrifice is now the self-offering of Jesus himself (cf. Heb. 9:22).

The guide now brings Ezekiel into the inner court, where he sees the rooms for the use of the temple clergy (vs. 44–46). The one beside the south gate facing north was reserved for the Zadokite priests, who alone were permitted to serve at the altar, while the one opposite, beside the north gate, was for the second-order clergy, i.e., Levites, responsible for the day-to-day running of the temple, including guarding the gates and preparing the sacrifices. (See further the comment on 44:10–31.) The inner court was 100 cubits square, and the altar of sacrifice stood in the open space in front of the east end of the building.

Ezekiel 40:48—41:4
The Three-roomed Temple

On the third and highest level, approached by ten steps, stood the temple. The ground plan, corresponding essentially to that of the Solomonic building, also reproduced in Zerubbabel's and Herod's temple, was quite simple and traditional. Most ancient Near Eastern temples were either of the broad room type, with the entrance on the long side, or the long room entered from the short side. The latter type, represented by Late Bronze Age structures excavated at Megiddo and Hazor, had an entrance hall *('ulam,* sometimes translated "vestibule" or "porch") leading into the main hall *(hekal,* sometimes translated "nave"), with an inner sanctuary or cella ("holy of holies") at the far end from the entrance. Progressive degrees of sanctity are represented not only by the steps, as noted earlier, but by the progressive narrowing of the entrances to the three rooms—respectively fourteen, ten, and six cubits.

The entrance hall measured 20 by 12 cubits (10.4 by 6.2 meters), slightly longer than the corresponding dimensions of the Solomonic building (I Kings 6:3). The two pillars by the entrance, presumably one on each side, correspond to the columns Jachin and Boaz of Solomon's temple which, to judge by their detailed description (I Kings 7:15–22, 41–42), played an important role in the symbolic scheme underlying the architectural layout. This particular feature was not peculiar to Israel. We recall that these pillars were of Phoenician manufacture (I Kings 7:41–42) and represent an architectural feature attested in their place of origin (e.g., the temple of Herakles in Tyre, according to Herodotus) and elsewhere in the ancient Near East. "Jachin" is a verbal form meaning "he establishes," which may suggest a symbolic representation of the columns that were thought to support the world and prevent its collapse into the watery chaos below (e.g., Ps. 75:3). Other suggestions have been made, but this one has the advantage of conforming to the broader theme according to which the temple is built over the waters of chaos and the worship carried out in it has the purpose of maintaining the divinely ordained cosmic order. It may also help to explain the association that appears to exist between these columns and covenants made at different points of the history involving the reigning monarch (II Kings 11:14; 23:3). After the Babylonian conquest, Jachin and Boaz were dismantled and carried off as booty to Babylon (II Kings 25:13; Jer. 52:20–23).

The dimensions of the main hall, 40 by 20 cubits (20.8 by 10.4 meters), were identical with those of Solomon's temple (I Kings 6:17). The same for the inner sanctuary, with the exception that here and throughout the vision narrative the dimension of height is lacking. The cella of Solomon's temple was a perfect cube, 20 cubits square. The guide entered and measured it while Ezekiel stood outside, since only the high priest might enter and that only once a year on the Day of Expiation. Nothing is said of the contents of this room, since the divine effulgence had not yet taken possession of it. The inner sanctuary of Solomon's temple was the depository of the ark of the covenant containing the tablets of the law and covered by the

206

wings of the cherubim; it also contained the altar of incense at which the high priest officiated. The author of the Epistle to the Hebrews, evidently quite familiar with these cultic matters, created an interesting allegory by transposing the spatial symbolism of the sanctuary into temporal terms. The main hall is the present age and the inner sanctuary is the age to come into which Jesus, through his sacrificial death, had entered as the high priest of the new dispensation (Heb. 9). In that capacity he has appeared once for all at the end of the present age to put away sin by the sacrifice of himself (Heb. 9:26).

Ezekiel 41:5–26
Other Structures, Features, and Measurements

A new feature now introduced is a stone structure surrounding the temple on the north, south, and east consisting of ninety small rooms arranged in three stories, thirty on each of the three sides. These were broader at the top than at the bottom. It appears that the temple wall was stepped to allow support for the upper levels and to obviate the need to bond these structures with the wall itself, thus, in a sense, violating the sanctity of the temple. Access to these upper levels was by entrances on the north and south leading to a ramp and stairs. The annexes, probably used for storage—the lower ones were only about two meters square—correspond roughly to a feature of the Solomonic temple (I Kings 6:5–6, 8–10). On the west side of the temple area stood a large building, 90 by 70 cubits (about 46.6 by 36.3 meters), which prevented access to the *temenos* from the west side, behind the cella. Nothing is said about its function and it has no counterpart in the description of the First Temple.

The overall measurements now checked off by the angel-guide confirm the perfect symmetry and order of the architecture (vs. 13–15*a*). The total length of the temple, including the three rooms (72 cubits), intervening spaces (13 cubits), rear wall (6 cubits), annexes (4 cubits), and outer wall (5 cubits), came to 100 cubits. The measurement was the same for the restricted area and the western building, inclusive of its walls, and for the east front with the surrounding temple yard.

207

Since the guided tour seemed to have reached its climax with the prophet's arrival at the entrance to the inner sanctuary (41:3–4), it is surprising that he is led once again into the interior of the temple. The following description of decorations and furnishings may therefore be an editorial expansion of the vision narrative inspired by nostalgia for the First Temple. Unfortunately, many of the details are obscure. The walls were paneled, probably with cedar wood, a luxury item familiar throughout Israel's history (I Kings 6:9; 7:3, 7; Jer. 22:14; Hag. 1:4). There were windows with recessed frames (cf. I Kings 6:4), though probably not in the inner sanctuary, since, according to Solomon's dedicatory prayer, the God of Israel has elected to dwell in deep darkness (I Kings 8:12). The decorative motifs that covered the walls were the same as in the First Temple (I Kings 6:29–30): panels with a palm tree surrounded on each side by a cherub, probably in ivory or gold inlay. These cherubs had on the one side a human face and on the other a lion face. The motif is the familiar one of the tree of life surrounded by animals, an Eden motif, warding off the powers of evil and death—for the temple is, first and foremost, the place of life. Directly in front of the entrance to the cella was a sort of altar or table, made of wood and standing over one and a half meters high, for the showbread, or bread of the Presence, of which we hear in the wilderness sanctuary (Exod. 25:23–30; Lev. 24:5–9) and the First Temple (I Kings 6:20–22). The twelve loaves placed on the table before the Presence and changed every week symbolized the commitment of the twelve tribes to support the sanctuary. The doors leading into both the main hall and the inner sanctuary had two leaves, probably attached to a post set into a central pivot hole. Along the facade of the entrance hall was a cornice or awning (if this is the meaning of the obscure Hebrew word 'ab here and at I Kings 7:6). With this last we are once again in the court surrounding the temple the further description of which follows.

Ezekiel 42:1–20

208 *Sacristies: Final Measurements*

Leaving the building and returning to the inner court, the narrator has his attention directed to additional buildings to the north and to the south. The exact location of these structures is by no means clear. We have already heard of priests' rooms near the north and south gates of the inner court (40:44–46). We cannot discount the possibility that the buildings now to be described represent an alternative version of the temple sacristies which placed greater emphasis on the requirements of holiness. On each side of the temple, north and south, were two buildings facing each other across a passageway 10 cubits wide (ca. 5.2 meters). The one nearer to the temple, adjacent to the temple yard, was twice the length of the one opposite, but the difference was made up by an extension wall which, since it seems to have served no particular function, was probably inserted into the plan for the sake of symmetry. As seen from the observer's perspective in the northern part of the inner court, the buildings were set on terraces or ledges—perhaps to counter the gradient—thus allowing for three stories narrower at the top than at the bottom. The guide, heretofore almost completely silent, is now positively voluble in his explanation of the function of these buildings. They are to serve as sacristies where the priests eat the offerings specially reserved to them and change out of their vestments before leaving this restricted area of holiness. The concern, therefore, is the further distinction between priesthood and laity corresponding architecturally to the distinction between inner and outer court.

The final stage of the visionary tour consists in the measurement and observation of the outer perimeter of the temple area (vs. 15–20). The opening sentence suggests that this phase originally followed the survey of the interior of the temple and therefore followed immediately after 41:15. The sequence of east, north, south, west, if correct, would suggest that the measuring was done from inside the wall in the outer court. But it would be much more natural to measure from the outside, and in fact the Old Greek version (LXX) is probably correct in giving the sequence as east, north, west, south, therefore moving anticlockwise from the starting point. The temple area forms a perfect square, 500 cubits (259 meters) on each side, giving a total area of 250,000 square cubits, rounding off the perfect symmetry of the ground plan based primarily on the number five and its multiples.

Of the greatest importance is the purpose and significance 209
of this perimeter wall: to make a separation and distinction between the holy and the profane. According to the priestly *Weltanschauung,* this distinction is carried over into every as-

pect of life, including diet, bodily states, and all social transactions. In this instance the distinction is not absolute, for, as we have seen, the holiness of the sanctuary is carried over, though in progressively diminishing degree, to the area adjacent to the temple precincts and the land of Israel in general. Within early Christianity, as it developed away from the Jewish matrix, we note a growing conviction that this view of reality is no longer operative in the new commonwealth grounded in the sacrificial death of Jesus. Using traditional cultic-priestly terminology, the author of the Epistle to the Ephesians describes the former state of his Gentile converts and continues as follows:

> But now in Christ Jesus you who once were far off have been brought near in the blood of Christ. For he is our peace [offering], who has made us both one, and has broken down the dividing wall of hostility.
>
> Ephesians 2:13–14, RSV

The language—being brought near, blood, peace offering—derives from the sacrificial system, and the wall that has been broken down is the wall separating the court of the Gentiles from the inner courts of the temple to trespass on which spelled death. The idea of the holy is not thereby abandoned but rather diffused throughout the community. Taken literally, the social implications mark a radical new departure. For, as Paul will say, there are no longer distinctions of status *coram Deo* between Jew and Gentile, free and slave, male and female (Gal. 3:28). After nearly two millennia the Christian churches have still to come to terms with this insight.

Ezekiel 43:1–12
The Return of the kabod

The climactic point of the vision narrative comes when the guide leads Ezekiel back to the starting point at the east gate where he sees the divine effulgence approaching from the east. This itself is described as a vision (v. 3), so that we have the extraordinary situation of a vision within a vision. Such an unprecedented phenomenon raises a troublesome problem that confronts us in much of the prophetic literature and indeed, in a somewhat different way, in poetic production in general: the relation between ecstatic experience and its literary expression. Ezekiel 40—48 is, after all, a literary production incorporating traditional material and sustained meditation, perhaps reflecting the impact of more than one distinct visionary episode. It seems highly unlikely that it represents an immediate, direct, and comprehensive transcription of one visionary event.

The return of the *kabod* is explicitly linked with the account of its departure recorded nineteen years earlier as the Babylonians were about to lay siege to the city (9:3; 10:18–22; 11:22–24) and with the vision by the Chebar a year before that (ch. 1). As on that occasion, it is announced by a noise like that of a great mass of water, the beating wings of the cherubim bearing the Enthroned One through the air (cf. 1:24). As the vision approaches, the ground beneath is lighted by the intense reflected light. Following the path of the rising sun, the effulgence moves from the east along the orientation axis of the temple and enters by the eastern gate into the inner court and thence into the sanctuary. There is an echo here of liturgical procession accompanied by hymns of praise:

> Lift up your heads, O gates!
> and be lifted up, O ancient doors!
> that the King of glory may come in.
> Who is this King of glory?
> The LORD of hosts,
> he is the King of glory!
> Psalm 24:9–10, RSV

Ezekiel is mysteriously borne along by the Spirit into the inner court, where he sees the glory of Yahweh taking possession of his temple. The same is recorded at the dedication of the First Temple: the divine glory filled the temple as the sun fills the heavens with light (I Kings 8:10–13; II Chron. 5:13—6:2). The words addressed to him from the inner sanctuary as he stands outside with his guide beside him are, in fact, the equivalent of a dedication of the sanctuary: "This is the place of my throne and the place of the soles of my feet" (43:7, RSV). The sanctuary is traditionally represented as both the throne (e.g., Jer. 3:17; 17:12) and the footstool of Yahweh (e.g., Ps. 99:5; 132:7), the place where he presides as king on the cherub throne (e.g., I Sam. 4:4; II Sam. 6:2). The entry of Yahweh into his temple was celebrated as a cultic reenactment of the proclamation of his kingship following victory over the forces of chaos:

211

> Yahweh sits enthroned over the flood;
> Yahweh sits enthroned as king for ever.
> Psalm 29:10

This climactic moment of the vision, therefore, gathers together many of the themes and archetypes reflected in Israelite worship and, at the same time, anticipates the historical moment when the returned exiles would celebrate, after many vicissitudes, the dedication of the rebuilt temple (Ezra 6:16–18).

The oracle from the temple also insists on absolute dissociation from the false cults ("harlotry") which had brought the First Temple into disrepute and in which the monarchy had played a leading role. There is also implied a rejection of the layout of the old temple which, being a dynastic shrine, was part of the palace complex. There also seems to be a suggestion that the temple was ritually polluted by proximity to royal burials. But most Judean kings were buried in a location, thus far unidentified, somewhere in the City of David which is some distance from the temple area. The exceptions were Manasseh and his son Amon, both reprobates according to the biblical historian, who were buried in a garden in the palace grounds (II Kings 21:18, 26; II Chron. 33:20). Whether their remains were too close to the temple for comfort, we do not know, but it has been suggested that the Hebrew word *peger,* here translated "corpse," may also refer to a monument or stele (as perhaps at Lev. 26:30) and that therefore the complaint is directed against the practice of setting up such memorial stelae in the temple precincts, a practice attested in temples excavated in Israel (Arad and perhaps Hazor). The main point, in any case, is clear and reinforces the message implicit in the architectural specifications revealed in the tour.

Ezekiel, finally, is directed to instruct his fellow exiles on the plan and layout of the temple with the help of a design or drawing. Exactly parallel to the vision at Sinai in which Moses received the blueprint of the tabernacle and its furnishings, this plan will be accompanied by detailed stipulations covering temple personnel, the conduct of temple services, and the like. The basic postulate is the status of the entire temple mound area as a most holy enclave. As the text stands, it is this postulate which appears to be identified as "the law of the temple." More probably, however, the phrase was meant to serve as the title for the detailed prescriptions that follow, beginning with the construction of the altar.

Ezekiel 43:13—44:3
The Altar and Closed Gate

The stipulations governing the temple, its cult, and its personnel begin with the altar of sacrifice in the inner court in front of the building. Its significance within the architectural layout of the complex is that it marks the point of contact between the Enthroned One in the recesses of the temple and the community for which the actual building is out of bounds. We must bear in mind that for Ezekiel and the priestly tradition which he represents there is no access to the deity and no way to remove sin and thus be acceptable other than the priesthood and the sacrificial system. It is not surprising, therefore, that the first act of the repatriates from the Babylonian diaspora was to set up the altar and resume the daily offering (the *tamid*) even before the temple was rebuilt (Ezra 3:1–3). In doing so, they acted in accordance with the Deuteronomic law which required the setting up of an altar immediately upon entering the land (Deut. 27:6–7), following the example of David, who built the first altar in Jerusalem to avert disaster from the land (I Chron. 21:18—22:1).

The dimensions of the altar are given in some detail (43:13–17), though uncertainties of interpretation inevitably remain. The units of measurement are the long cubit (cf. 40:5), based on the distance from the elbow to the fingertips plus a handbreadth, and the handspan, roughly half that length. The altar was built in three stages or levels, each two cubits shorter than the one below it, on a base set into the ground. The total height, exclusive of the horns of the altar, was 10 cubits (ca. 5.2 meters), the base was 18 cubits square (ca. 9.3 meters), and the altar surface 12 cubits (6.2 meters). The "rim" (RSV) or border surrounding the base may have contained a channel for draining off the blood into the ground. The base itself is described curiously as "the cavity [or bosom] of the earth," which may contain a faint echo of the old idea of holy foundations set in or over the underworld. Rather more obscure is the term, variously spelled "harel" or "ariel," for the surface of the altar (43:15–16). The

213

meaning "altar hearth" (RSV) finds support in the Moabite inscription and is referred in Isa. 29:1–2, by extension, to Jerusalem. But *harel* can also mean "mountain of God," and it may be that this alternate spelling contains an allusion to the Mesopotamian ziggurat, a stepped temple mound sometimes represented with horns around the summit. It would not be surprising if the author of this material, writing in the Babylonian diaspora, took over something of the rich cosmic symbolism of Mesopotamian religious architecture.

The horns of the altar were projections at each corner of the surface on which the sacrificial blood was smeared (Exod. 29:12; Lev. 4:7). Grasping the horns of the altar was also supposed to assure immunity from death for a fugitive from justice, though it did not always work out that way (I Kings 1:50–51; 2:28–34). The original significance of this feature, illustrated also by altars discovered at Megiddo, Shechem, and Beersheba, has not been successfully explained. The steps necessitated by the great height of the altar (in spite of an ancient prohibition, Exod. 20:24–26) were on the east side, requiring the officiating priest to face the temple and the Presence during the sacrificial liturgy.

The liturgy for the dedication of the altar is communicated in the form of a prophetic oracle delivered by Yahweh himself (43:18–27), suggesting that the original vision context has been left behind for the time being. Like the dedication of the First Temple, and presumably also the Second Temple (I Kings 8; Ezra 6:16–18), this ceremony of consecration lasted seven days. The curious language of freeing the altar from sin and making atonement for it by a succession of animal sacrifices may be understood as withdrawing it completely from the world of profane reality into the sphere of the sacred. Only then could it be put to use as the place where the worshiper is unburdened of sin, finds acceptance, and experiences communion with God.

Like all religious institutions, sacrifice can get detached from its original purposes, degenerating into the routine performance of socially sanctioned acts devoid of inner meaning. The prophetic polemic against this practice, which was the central expression of the religious life of their contemporaries, focused on this disjunction between external act and internal disposition. (It did not, however, amount to advocacy of a *purely spiritual* religion, whatever that might be.) Stated in our terms, they condemned not religion but religiosity, the cultiva-

214

tion of religious appearances for their own sake, and their diatribe was directed against an attitude that managed to combine
a high level of religious observance with a notable disregard for
the norms of social justice. As the final sentence of the present
chapter clearly states, acceptance by God was the goal of the
sacrificial liturgy. As far as we can tell, the prophets would not
have denied this, but they would have wanted to say that it does
not come about automatically, by virtue of the act itself. Amos
leaves us in no doubt:

> I hate, I despise your feasts,
>   and I take no delight in your solemn assemblies.
> Even though you offer me your burnt offerings and cereal
>   offerings,
>   I will not accept them,
> and the peace offerings of your fatted beasts
>   I will not look upon. . . .
> But let justice roll down like waters,
>   and righteousness like an ever-flowing stream.
>   Amos 5:21–24, RSV

Isaiah too speaks of vain offerings made by those who do not
seek justice or espouse the cause of the weak and powerless in
society (Isa. 1:12–17). Micah, a contemporary of Isaiah, sums it
up in a much-quoted statement by contrasting the offering of
thousands of rams and rivers of oil with the basic requirements
of the religious life, individual and social: justice, fidelity, and a
humble and receptive attitude toward God (Micah 6:6–8). In
the same spirit, one of the psalmists, in what may be described
as a prayer for spiritual renewal, anticipates much later developments by a complete internalization of the idea of sacrifice:

> For thou hast no delight in sacrifice;
>   were I to give a burnt offering, thou wouldst not be pleased.
> The sacrifice acceptable to God is a broken spirit;
>   a broken and contrite heart, O God, thou wilt not despise.
>   Psalm 51:16–17, RSV

So strongly does he put it that a later, probably exilic editor, felt
obliged to add a "clarification" before the psalm could be put
to public use:

> Do good to Zion in thy good pleasure;
>   rebuild the walls of Jerusalem,
> then wilt thou delight in right sacrifices,
>   in burnt offerings and whole burnt offerings;
> then bulls will be offered on thy altar.
>   Psalm 51:18–19, RSV

215

While there is some evidence of more direct opposition to the resumption of animal sacrifice after the return from exile (Isa. 66:1–4), the practice was resumed and continued as a primary focus of religious life throughout the Second Temple period. The emphasis on internal disposition was, for obvious reasons, intensified after the sacrificial cult was brought to an end with the destruction of the temple in A.D. 70. But even earlier it was widely understood that corporal and spiritual works of mercy and prayer (described curiously as "the bullocks of our lips" in the Prayer Book) substituted for animal sacrifice. There were also those like Philo who searched for a deeper level of significance by means of allegory. "The true offering," says Philo, "what can it be but the devotion of a soul which is dear to God?" (*Life of Moses* 2.108). Early Christianity did not, therefore, originate this process of spirtualization; it simply extended it to the circumstances of its own forms of life and mission. Paul speaks of Christians offering their bodies—that is, the entire range of their bodily activities—as a spiritual worship to God (Rom. 12:1), and the author of I Peter urges his readers to offer spiritual sacrifices acceptable to God through Christ (I Peter 2:5). The institution continues its life cycle as metaphor.

After the vision of the divine effulgence seen from the inner court, the guide returns with his charge to the east gate of the outer perimeter, where he observes that it is now closed (44:1–3). The idea of a special processional entrance reserved for passage of the deity was probably familiar in ancient Israel (cf. Ps. 24), and the exiles would have known of the great gate of the Esagila sanctuary in Babylon opened only for the procession of the god Marduk during the *akitu,* or new year festival. The same feature is attested residually in Byzantine liturgy, and perhaps also in the *porta santa* of St. Peter's basilica in Rome opened only for the jubilee every twenty-fifth year. Use of the inner plaza of the gate for sacrificial liturgy involving the civic ruler, who may enter this area only from the outer court, anticipates the more detailed description to be given later (46:1–8).

Ezekiel 44:4–31
Liturgical Personnel and Their Functions

Return to the inner court in front of the temple was necessary in order to receive "the ordinances of the temple and all its laws." The situation now is exactly parallel to the priestly version of the Sinai revelation in which Moses in a vision receives detailed regulations concerning the sanctuary, its personnel, and the cult to be carried out in it. It seems that the typological relationship between Sinai and the "very high mountain" of Ezekiel's vision was already familiar by the time these evidently controversial prescriptions about cult personnel were interpolated into the vision narrative. A passage that occurs in both Isaiah (Isa. 2:3) and Micah (Micah 4:2) points clearly in this direction:

> Out of Zion shall go forth the law,
>   and the word of Yahweh from Jerusalem. (RSV)

The parallelism between the law (i.e., instruction) and the word of Yahweh (i.e., the prophetic word) is also consonant with the representation of the Mosaic cultic law, communicated in a vision, as a form of prophecy. All of this conspires to confer the highest authority on these regulations concerning who may and who may not officiate in the sanctuary.

The contentious nature of the stipulations, presented in the form of a prophetic oracle ("Thus says the Lord Yahweh"), is apparent in the allusion to "the rebellious house," reminiscent of Ezekiel's earlier diatribe. They deal successively with three categories: foreigners (vs. 6–9), Levites (vs. 10–14), and Zadokite priests (vs. 15–31). The first problem awaiting a solution is the identity of these foreigners, "uncircumcised in heart and flesh," who not only have been admitted to the sanctuary but have been carrying out liturgical functions in it.

A fairly obvious clue may be found at once in the order in which these three classes of cultic personnel are dealt with here: foreign liturgical assistants, Levites, and Zadokite priests. For these correspond, in inverse order, to the enumeration of cultic personnel in postexilic lists, namely: priests, Levites, and temple servants (I Chron. 9:2; Ezra 2:36–58 = Neh. 7:39–60; Ezra 7:7). To this last category is sometimes appended descendants of Solomon's slaves and liturgical musicians; the former seem to have merged with the temple servants, while the latter were eventually absorbed into the Levitical ranks. In later Jewish tradition the temple servants, or *netinim* (given over to the service of the temple), were thought to be descended from the Gibeonites, non-Israelites who entered into a treaty with Joshua by sleight of hand and were subsequently assigned the task of "hewers of wood and drawers of water for the congregation and for the altar of Yahweh" (Josh. 9:27, RSV; cf. Deut. 29:11). Whatever may be thought of this tradition, the high percentage of non-Israelite personal names in the lists of temple servants in Ezra-Nehemiah suggests that they counted many foreigners in their ranks. And since their function was to assist the Levites in the performance of their tasks, the blame for bringing them into the temple could be plausibly laid at the Levites' door.

Given the ever-present danger of assimilation during and after the exile, a more intense concern for ethnic-religious purity in general and for the purity of the cult in particular is understandable. We see it at work in Ezra's campaign against foreign marriages (Ezra 9—10)—which was almost certainly unsuccessful—and at the conclusion of his personal memoir Nehemiah boasts of having cleansed the temple clergy from everything foreign (Neh. 13:30). A legal paragraph in Deuteronomy (23:1–8), probably one of the latest additions to the book, excludes the sexually mutilated and certain ethnic categories from membership in the Israelite assembly and therefore from participation in its worship. The prohibition in Ezekiel has a more limited scope but is informed by the same anxious concern to resist the pull toward assimilation.

Christian scholars in the modern period have often found in these and similar injunctions the beginnings of the self-absorption and xenophobia which were to become routine charges leveled against Judaism from the Roman period onward. It is therefore all the more important to appreciate the difficulty for this kind of community, in situations that were generally unfavorable and often hostile, to retain its own ethos, characteristic way of life, and identity. It is arguable that many Christian communities today are not even aware of the extent to which they have already assimilated to their environment. It

218

is also important to note that these measures did not go unchallenged. A remarkable passage in Isaiah (Isa. 56:1–8), from the early postexilic period, assures the sexually mutilated and foreigners of their good standing in the community in defiance of the Deuteronomic law; and another passage toward the end of the book (Isa. 66:21) even foresees the possibility of foreigners serving as priests and Levites. By virtue of its own dynamic, as well as by pressure of circumstances, early Christianity took over this open admissions policy, and we may be happy that it did so. But for both Judaism and Christianity, as is evident in the open world of today, there is always a delicate balance between integration and assimilation.

Attention is now focused on those responsible for introducing foreigners into temple service, the Levites (vs. 10–14). Originally all those who claimed descent from Levi had priestly status. At an earlier point in the book (40:45–46) a distinction was made between altar priests and others responsible for the temple maintenance, but there is no suggestion of essentially different status. It seems reasonable therefore to follow the majority of commentators who identify a later editorial strand according to which altar priests are recruited exclusively from that branch of the priesthood claiming descent from Zadok, priest of David and Solomon (II Sam. 8:17; 15:24–29; I Kings 4:4; etc.). All other branches of the priesthood were either eliminated or had to accept a subordinate position in the temple hierarchy, and it is these who are referred to here as Levites. The distinction is not unambiguously attested in the preexilic period and is absent from Deuteronomy (with the sole exception of a late strand in Deut. 27:14). The history of the Israelite priesthood is notoriously obscure, but it looks as if, as a result of internecine strife among priestly clans, one group claiming descent from Zadok emerged victorious and fortified their claim by providing Zadok with a fictitious pedigree as descending from Levi through his third son, Eleazar (I Chron. 6:1–15). Given the importance of control of the temple with its spiritual and material resources, such strife is not surprising. It is reflected very clearly in the present passage and more obliquely in certain narratives in the Pentateuch, especially the account of Korah's rebellion against the authority of Moses and Aaron and its predictable outcome (Num. 16).

219

The reason given for the demotion of these Levites is lapse into apostasy. Since the Pentateuchal narratives just mentioned do not specify this as the bone of contention, the allegation, assuming it to be true, must be based on more recent history. While Ezekiel himself has surprisingly little to say in condemnation of the priesthood, there are passages denouncing false worship in the Jerusalem temple and elsewhere which necessarily implicate large numbers of priests (5:11; ch. 8). The priests who, like Ezekiel, were deported would also not have looked with favor on the ones who survived to stay in the land where syncretic cults were much more likely to flourish. Thus the distinction between first and second order clergy is likely to have developed between the time of Ezekiel's activity and the Zadokite insertions into the temple vision narrative, and it most likely took place in the Babylonian diaspora. This will help to explain the relatively low percentage of Levites in the census of the first return (Ezra 2:40)—the precise date of which is uncertain—and the difficulty encountered by Ezra himself in recruiting Levites for his mission (Ezra 8:15–20). And even among the priests who did return, the claims of several to sacerdotal status was put on hold subject to later authoritative confirmation (Ezra 2:59–63).

The final section of the clergy law deals with the duties and prerogatives of the Zadokite altar priests (vs. 15–31). Zadok was an undoubtedly historical figure who served David and Solomon and whose position as chief priest was unchallenged after the expulsion of Abiathar (I Kings 2:26–27). His successors, as we have seen, succeeded in either ousting rival priestly factions or reducing them to ancillary status in the temple service, and it is their point of view which is presented in the so-called Zadokite strand in these chapters (40:46b; 43:19; 44:6–31; 48:11). The Zadokites maintained control of the temple until the year 171 B.C., when Jason the high priest was deposed. The illegitimacy of later holders of the office was an important factor in the emergence of the Qumran community which included Zadokite priests among its members.

Most of the responsibilities and prerogatives of the Zadokite clergy here listed are spelled out at greater length in the cultic legislation in Leviticus, though for obvious reasons the name Zadok does not occur there. They, and they alone understood, may serve as altar priests and offer sacrifice (vs. 15–16). Their vestments are to be made of linen, and wool is to be avoided either because it makes the wearer perspire and thus risk ritual contamination or on account of a taboo against bringing an animal product into the holy enclave (Lev. 6:10; 16:4; cf. Exod. 39:27–29). They are to wear a linen turban and trousers, the latter to avoid the risk of accidental exposure (Lev. 6:10; 16:4; cf. Exod. 28:42). After the priest ministers at the altar, he is to leave the sacred vestments in the sacristy (42:13–14) to avoid transmitting holiness to the laity in the outer court or, in other words, violating the distinction between the holy and the profane (vs. 17–19). The hair is to be trimmed, not shaven or allowed to grow long (Lev. 21:1–10; cf. Deut. 14:1–2), and drinking wine in the inner court is forbidden (vs. 20–21). The choice of marriage partner is restricted to an Israelite virgin or another priest's widow (v. 22). This may be one of the points that exercised Hananiah, burner of the midnight oil, for the corresponding stipulations in Leviticus are not quite identical. There only the high priest is forbidden to marry a widow; to all other priests, only marriage with a prostitute, a victim of rape, or divorcee is disallowed (Lev. 21:7, 13–15).

Apart from serving at the altar, the principal duty of the priest is not–as now–preaching but instruction. Priesthood is therefore a learned ministry; "the lips of a priest should guard knowledge, and people should seek instruction from his mouth" (Mal. 2:7). The area of their special competence is ritual law, the ordering of life according to the categories of the holy and the profane, the clean and the unclean, as set out in the priestly law in Leviticus. Their learning is also put to work in the tribunals, a situation that still obtains residually in the State of Israel (cf. Deut. 17:9; 21:1–5). They are to observe and of course also inculcate observance of the religious calendar, including Sabbath (vs. 23–24).

Regulations governing corpse contamination are given in greater detail in the ritual legislation in the Pentateuch (Lev. 21:1–3, 11; Num. 19:11–22). Contact with the dead communicates ritual uncleanness, as does contact with any type of corruption viewed as a violation of the natural order. The only exceptions for the priest are near relatives, excluding a married sister. According to Lev. 21:11, however, these exceptions do not apply in the case of the high priest. The purification ritual involved sprinkling with water on the third and the seventh day and a waiting period of another seven days, after which the priest made the requisite sin offering and resumed his functions (vs. 25–27).

221

In Israel as elsewhere in the ancient Near East the clan

holding *(nahalah)* was viewed as a fief granted by the deity which was therefore in principle inalienable. The history of the settlement and allotment of land is obscure, but it seems that the tribe of Levi, like the Magi of ancient Iran, lost out in the struggle for territory and became religious specialists instead. It was therefore the duty of the laity to support the priest by the kinds of offerings listed here. To the theological statement "Yahweh is their inheritance" (cf. Deut. 10:9; 18:2; Josh. 13:14, 33) correspond the economic realities of the cultic system as a whole, including the considerable wealth of the temple. These realities also governed the institution of sacrifice: the fat and the blood offered to the deity have theological priority but are gastronomically unserviceable; the prime cuts are reserved for the clergy (Deut. 18:1–5), and the rest is for the layperson or family on whose behalf the sacrifice is being offered (vs. 28–30).

The final stipulation prohibits eating meat from an animal that has either died from natural causes or been killed by another animal, a practice that Ezekiel himself passionately disavowed (4:14). Eating meat of any kind not ritually slaughtered was prohibited not only to priests (Lev. 22:8) but to any Israelite (Lev. 7:24; 17:14–16). The law, dictated already to Noah after the flood (Gen. 9:4), is intended to give concrete expression in the circumstances of everyday life to the role of God, for "the blood is the life" and life is bestowed only by God (v. 31).

Ezekiel 45:1–8
The Land, an Extension of the Sanctuary

This passage anticipates the full account of the allotment of land (47:13—48:29) and is excerpted from it, perhaps because it leads into the regulations concerning the civic leader. It is obviously a learned, schematic construct, comparable to the priestly description of the sanctuary in the wilderness, which extends the holiness of the sanctuary outward, in diminishing degrees, to the land adjacent to it. Together with the liturgical calendar which follows (45:18–25), it illustrates how the concept of holiness must bear decisively on all aspects of human life along both the spatial and the temporal axis.

The quadratic form of the temple, measuring 500 by 500

222

cubits (42:15–20), is extended outward, using the same units of five and twenty-five, to a large square measuring 25,000 cubits on each side (almost 13 kilometers). The main section of this square, 25,000 by 20,000, is the sacred area reserved for the temple clergy. It is divided into two equal parts 25,000 by 10,000, the one to the north, contiguous with the tribal territory of Benjamin, for the Levites, the other in the center for the priests. The temple is situated in the center of the priests' area and is surrounded by an open space, a kind of holy no-man's-land, 50 cubits wide. The extension of the theological principles governing the architecture of the temple is apparent in the terminology: the entire temple is now the holy of holies (v. 3), which results in it being a kind of temple within the greater temple of the sacred enclosure. The narrowest of the three bands, 25,000 by 5,000 cubits, lying to the south contiguous with the territory of Judah, is for the city and its agricultural hinterland. The city itself is 4,500 cubits square surrounded by a kind of green belt 250 cubits across, the remainder of the space being occupied by agricultural land to the east and the west. The schematic arrangement is filled out with the territory allotted to the prince which extends east and west of the great square to the borders of the land, the Jordan and the Mediterranean respectively.

The idealistic and theoretical nature of this construct is obvious. Levitical cities are concentrated in their own area of second-order holiness and not located in different parts of the land (Num. 35:2–8). The priests are assigned an area of some 67 square kilometers, though we have just heard that they are to have no landholdings (44:28). The intent is clearly to make a symbolic statement about the principles governing the ideal theocracy which is to be "a kingdom of priests and a holy nation" (Exod. 19:6, RSV). The need for secular governance is acknowledged, but the territory—and therefore, by implication, the authority—of the civic ruler, the "prince," is carefully circumscribed. We should note, finally, that in this political-religious schema landownership is intimately associated with temple and cult. Henceforth Israel is to be not a nation-state in the usual sense of that term but a temple-community. Civic status, and with it title to land, is to be tied in with participation in and support of the temple cult (see commentary on 11:14–25), a situation that to some extent was actually realized in the period following return from exile.   223

Ezekiel 45:9–17
Duties and Perquisites of the Secular Ruler

The next long section of the laws appended to the temple vision (45:9—46:18) deals primarily with the responsibilities of the civic ruler, not excluding the regulation of the festivals (45:18–25) for which he shared responsibility with the temple clergy. We saw earlier that Ezekiel for the most part avoided the term "king," preferring instead the term "prince" *(nasi')*, which is less suggestive of political domination. Though he used "prince" for contemporary Judean kings (12:10; 21:25) and for the Davidic ruler of the future age (34:24; 37:25), the present context strongly suggests allusion to the provincial governors in Judah during the two centuries of Persian rule (539–334 B.C.). According to our principal source, the first of these, Sheshbazzar, is called *nasi'* (Ezra 1:8), and several of the regulations that follow are reminiscent of what Nehemiah, governor of the province in the second half of the fifth century, has to say about his own activities and those of his predecessors in that office. Some of these correspondences will be noted briefly in the commentary.

Description of the civic ruler's territorial allotment leads naturally into a fairly detailed survey of his obligations and perquisites. The prophetic oracle with which the survey opens emphasizes the primacy of justice and righteousness as attributes of governance. There is to be no more violence and oppression of the kind that, according to Nehemiah, characterized the tenure of office of his predecessors (Neh. 5:15). Enclosure of peasant land and forced expropriation of holdings by Israelite kings and their retinue must have been of frequent occurrence under the monarchy. Isaiah denounces the joining of field to field (Isa. 5:8), and the expropriation of Naboth's vineyard (I Kings 21:1–16) was certainly not an isolated occurrence. The harsh economic conditions that obtained in Judah after the return often led to the mortgaging of holdings and distraining of the property of the subsistence farmer, a situation that Nehemiah had to confront during his tenure of office (Neh. 5). It was also the ruler's responsibility, in Israel as elsewhere, to enforce just weights and measures. Amos denounced those who, in defiance of the law (Lev. 19:35–36; Deut. 25:13–16), made the ephah small and the shekel large (Amos 8:5; cf. Hos. 12:8; Micah 6:10–12). Thus, the statutory equivalencies are carefully specified. The standard measure is to be the homer (literally, a donkey load; actually about six bushels). The ephah, a dry measure for grain and other commodities, and the bath, a liquid measure, are set at one tenth of a homer. The standard weight is the shekel (rather more than eleven grams) divided into twenty gerahs, and there are to be true weights of five, ten, and fifty shekels, the fifty shekel weight being the mina. Note that the shekel is a weight, not a denomination as in contemporary Israel. Coinage—in the form of darics and drachmas—was introduced only at the beginning of the fifth century, and its use was probably restricted for some time thereafter to paying the imperial tax.

The statutory contributions to the upkeep of the civic ruler and his entourage are now listed (vs. 13–16). They are fairly distributed in measure proportionate to the individual's possessions: a sixtieth of cereal, a hundredth of oil, and one sheep out of two hundred. We may note, again, how Nehemiah claimed to have forgone this food allowance, whereas his predecessors in office went far beyond it (Neh. 5:14–15). He also takes pride in having provided such necessities for the sacrificial cult as are now listed (v. 17). Perhaps, then, the situation envisaged by these regulations appended to the vision narrative is that of the province of Judah under governance which is meant to prefigure, even in the uncongenial situation of foreign domination, the future kingdom of justice and peace foretold by Ezekiel (cf. 37:24–28).

Ezekiel 45:18—46:8
Cultic Responsibilities of the Secular Ruler

The next logical step is to specify the contributions that the secular ruler is to make for the festivals, the Sabbath, and the new moon (see 45:17). But first the purification ritual for the temple, comparable to the ritual for the dedication of the altar

225

(43:18–27), has to be described. This ceremony has to be per-formed on the first and the seventh day of the first month following the new or Babylonian usage according to which the year begins in the month Nisan (March–April). Several of the commentators have found it odd that such a ritual should be repeated within the space of a week; they have therefore fol-lowed LXX in dating the second ceremony to the first day of the seventh month which, according to the old calendar, marked the beginning of the year in the fall—as it still does in the Jewish liturgical year. But it would be strange to find two calendars being followed in respect of the same practice, and they may in addition have overlooked the possibility that this second purifi-cation ritual was intended to prepare for Passover, which fol-lowed a week later. It is worth noting that the first Passover celebrated after the return from exile was preceded by such a ritual (Ezra 6:20).

The details of the ceremony follow rather closely the altar ritual already described (43:18–27). The blood of the sacrificed bull is smeared on the doorposts of the temple, on the corners of the upper ledge of the altar, and on the jambs of the east gate leading to the inner court, this last being the position assigned to the ruler in the liturgy (46:1–2). It is clear that the blood symbolizes what the ritual was thought to achieve, namely, the removal of sin and the restoration of the divinely ordained order which is disturbed by even inadvertent sin. In concluding that "without the shedding of blood there is no forgiveness," the author of the Epistle to the Hebrews preserves the symbol-ism by transferring it to Jesus and the sacrificial offering of his life (Heb. 9:22, RSV).

The description of Passover (Pesach) and Tabernacles (Sukkoth)—the former in the first month (Nisan) and the latter in the seventh (Tishri)—is limited to an account of the contri-butions encumbent upon the secular ruler (45:21–25). Why the other great pilgrim festival of Pentecost (Shavuoth) is omitted is a matter of speculation. While it is possible that no contribution in kind was demanded of the *naśi'* on this occa-sion, it seems more likely that this festival, of such great im-portance at the time of the Qumran community and early Christianity, was of lesser significance at the time of writing. It is at least of interest to note that the history of the restored community in Ezra-Nehemiah speaks only of Passover and Tabernacles, without mentioning Pentecost (Ezra 3:1–6; 6:19–

22; Neh. 8:13–18). As in the Pentateuchal legislation (Exod. 12:6; Lev. 23:5; Num. 9:3, 5), Passover begins on the fourteenth day of the first month and unleavened bread *(maṣṣoth)* is to be eaten for seven days from the fourteenth inclusive (cf. Exod. 12:15, 18–20; 23:15; 34:18; Lev. 23:6; Num. 28:17; Deut. 16:3–4). The rich symbolism of this festival of freedom, which has been mined anew by the Jewish people in every phase of its historical existence, has also passed over into Christianity as a rich source of theological reflection. The quantities of livestock, grain, and oil to be supplied by the civic ruler are considerably in excess of those demanded for the same festival in the Pentateuch (Num. 28:16–25), a discrepancy that helps to explain why these chapters were deemed problematic in the early rabbinic period. There are similar problems with the provisions for Tabernacles (45:25), except that in this instance Num. 29:12–38 calls for a much greater investment of livestock. The festival also lasts longer, ending as it does with a solemn assembly on the eighth day.

It remains only to stipulate what offerings are to be made by the *naśi'* for Sabbaths and new moon festivals (46:1–8), and here too we find similar discrepancies (cf. Num. 28:9–15). On these occasions the secular ruler assists at the sacrificial liturgy at a distance, his appointed place being at the inside entrance of the east gate leading into the inner court. The rest of the laity ("the people of the land") are even farther away, outside the same gate in the outer court. That the gate was opened only on these days and specifically for these liturgical occasions would have permitted them some degree of participation, but they could hardly have seen what was going on at the altar of sacrifice from the other side of a gate area 50 cubits (almost 26 meters) long (cf. 40:15). In this instance we see clearly how sacred architecture and the liturgical act itself embody a strong sense of holy order and hierarchy. The diffusion and, to some extent, the loss of that strong sense of the holy and awesome have permitted a more participatory idea of worship to prevail in most sectors of Christianity and Judaism, which in itself is not a bad thing, but there is loss as well as gain. Here, however, as we would expect, the lines are clearly drawn between the priest in the inner court and the laity in the outer court, with the secular leader in the gate acting as a link and go-between: both the bearer of the gift to the altar and the transmitter of blessing back to the people whom he represents.

Ezekiel 46:9–18
Various Appendixes

The first appendix (vs. 9–10), which appears to deal with crowd control in the outer court, was probably suggested by the previous statement about the route to be taken by the leader before and after a liturgy. Since the main east gate was permanently closed (44:1–2), the only approaches were from north and south. A question arises, however, with the requirement of the civic leader's presence. Since this entire section has to do with his cultic function, the allusion may be to processional liturgies of the kind reflected in certain psalms (Ps. 24:7–10; 48:12–14; 68:24–27). The procession celebrating the dedication of the rebuilt wall of Jerusalem recorded in Neh. 12:27–43 was, of course, a special case, but it is worth noting that Nehemiah himself took a leading part in it. (Its two groups also processed north and south but not in the outer court.)

Another footnote (v. 11) specifies once again (see 45:24 and 46:5) the quantity of grain and oil that is to accompany animal sacrifices. There follows a codicil to the regulations about the east gate (46:1–8) permitting it to be opened for the ruler's voluntary offerings (v. 12). These were offerings not mandated by temple law and distinct from those made in fulfillment of vows (Lev. 7:16; 22:18; Num. 15:3; etc.); and offerings on special occasions, or for favors received, or as a contribution to the temple's endowment (e.g., Exod. 35:29; Ezra 1:4; 8:28). In these cases, the rules governing the condition of the animal or goods offered were less strict (Lev. 22:23). It is also stipulated that the ruler must provide for the daily burnt offering (the *tamid*) a yearling lamb with the appropriate quantities of grain (a sixth of an ephah) and oil (about two pints) to mix with the flour (vs. 13–15). Pentateuchal legislation gives rather different quantities; more important, it prescribes a lamb sacrifice for the morning and the evening (Exod. 29:38–41; Num. 28:3–8). The difference cannot be explained by reading these formulations as reflecting a later development, for the morning and the evening sacrifice seem to have been well established in the preex-

228

ilic period (I Kings 18:29, 36; II Kings 16:15). Perhaps the ruler was responsible only for the morning offering, which would be a heavy enough drain on his resources. In the course of time the *tamid* came to represent the sacrificial system as a whole, *pars pro toto.* The historian of the restoration records that the first thing the repatriates did was to resume this practice (Ezra 3:2–3), and its cessation during the persecution of Antiochus IV in 167 B.C. was seen as a decisive turning point in the history (Dan. 11:31; 12:11). The salutary practice of morning and evening prayer also seems to have developed out of this central act of the liturgical day (see, e.g., Dan. 9:21).

The last of these appendixes legislates on the disposition of the ruler's estates (vs. 16–18). In general, the disposition of land in Israel was never left to the vagaries of the market; it was governed by the theological conviction of divine ownership, a conviction intensified in the present context by the close link forged between temple and land (45:1–8). The ruler may therefore hand on part of his landholdings to a son, but if he grants land as a fief to a retainer, it must be as leasehold, reverting to its original owner at the jubilee in the fiftieth year. Most important, the ruler may not alienate any of the ancestral holdings of the people. This point has already been made, also in the compelling form of a prophetic oracle, Yahweh speaking out on behalf of *his* people (45:9). During the Persian period we hear of the confiscation and enclosure of small holdings, generally due to insolvency, and we can see the emergence of the great estates that flourished in the Hellenistic period. However this section is dated, it would therefore have been seen as particularly relevant in the province of Judah at that time.

Ezekiel 46:19–24
The Temple Kitchens

After a long interval we encounter once again the supernatural tour guide whom we had left in front of the temple (44:1–4). The long intervening section (44:5—46:18) may therefore be seen as a distinct collection of laws in which Yahweh (not the guide) speaks and which is punctuated by the traditional prophetic oracle formula (44:6, 9; 45:9, 18; 46:1, 16). Like the

Priestly version of the Sinai event, therefore, it illustrates the increasing dovetailing of law and prophecy. What follows now is a side excursion to view the sacrificial cooking installations, after which the observer and his guide return to their point of departure (47:1). While their movements are not entirely clear, it seems that they passed either through or between the two rows of vestries or sacristies on the north side of the temple (42:1–14), which enabled them to see the priests' kitchen attached to the large western building (41:12) on its north side. Given the concern for symmetry throughout the temple complex, there was probably a similar installation on the south side too, though it would not have been visible from where they stood. After leaving the inner court, the guide then pointed out the Levitical cooking areas, each 40 by 30 cubits, in the four corners of the outer court behind low stone barriers. These were for the sacrificial offerings of the laity which it was the responsibility of the Levites to prepare.

The point of this diversion, which serves as a kind of supplement to the description of the priests' quarters (42:1–14), is to reassure the reader that the regulations governing the purity of the temple are observed in the preparation of the sacrificial food. The Levites are restricted to the outer court, and the danger of contact between the laity and the sacrificial material reserved to the priests, a contact fraught with danger, is avoided. Every detail of the blueprint, therefore, reflects the concern for order and holiness which, according to the priestly theology, must permeate the whole of life.

Ezekiel 47:1–12
"Everything Lives Where the River Goes"

The extensive series of injunctions dealing with different cultic functions and actions (43:6—46:24) tends to obscure the logic of the narrative according to which the water flowing from inside the temple is the direct consequence of the return of the *kabod* to the inner sanctuary (43:1–5). So, after a detour to inspect the temple kitchens, the seer and his guide returned to the east front and saw water trickling under the threshold of the main entrance and flowing into the inner court to the right of the altar of sacrifice. After it disappeared under the east gate, they left the inner court by way of the northern gate and went outside the perimeter wall to the east, where the water was by then pouring out under the main eastern gate. Following its course, the guide with his companion took soundings four times at intervals of one thousand cubits. At first ankle deep, the water reached to their knees, then to their thighs, finally taking them completely out of their depth—a mighty river which, as the guide explained, continued its course down through the Judean wilderness, into the Jordan Rift Valley, debouching into the Dead Sea, which, as we know but they did not, is the lowest point on the surface of the planet. And, as if by magic, fruit-bearing trees suddenly appeared on both of its banks.

The guide explained further that this great flood of water would desalinate the appropriately named Dead Sea, leaving only the salt flats unaltered, salt being essential for preserving and seasoning food, including sacrificial food. Fish of every variety would flourish in its waters, and the Dead Sea would be transformed into a fisherman's paradise from the oasis of En-gedi on the western shore to En-eglaim on the eastern shore. (The latter is sometimes identified with Ain Feshka near the Qumran foundation, but without adequate support.) Trees would flourish the year round along the banks of the river, bearing fruit that could be harvested every month, and its leaves had medicinal properties. In short, the entire barren area of the country would undergo a profound and utterly beneficial ecological transformation once the sanctuary was readied to receive the long-absent divine presence.

No amount of exegetical finesse or insistence on "what the Bible plainly says" can transform the poetry of this passage into a topographically and ecologically realistic account of an event in time. The richly symbolic language of water healing and bringing life and fertility to the wounded earth recalls, as we saw earlier, the great water source that fertilized Eden, flowing out in four branches around the inhabited world (Gen. 2:10–14). The logic of the symbolism requires that the headwaters arise on high land, the "very high mountain" to which Ezekiel was transported (40:2), the "holy mountain of God" on which, according to the poem on the king of Tyre (28:14), Eden was located. We find the same symbolic language in some of the Zion hymns which speak of life-bestowing water flowing from city and temple (Ps. 46:4; 65:9). It is the divine presence in the

231

sanctuary which brings life to a world threatened with infertility and death.

The Ezekiel version of this archetypal image keeps on recurring throughout Jewish and Christian history. In somewhat later prophetic texts we hear of a fountain springing from the temple and flowing down into the Jordan Valley, or in both directions, to the Mediterranean and the Dead Sea (Joel 3:18; Zech. 14:8). In early Christianity the growth of the stream from a trickle to a mighty river was seen as symbolic of the increase in the number of believers, and the four stages marked by the guide were taken to represent the four Gospels, the fourth being the most profound. This same Gospel uses the occasion of the water-pouring ceremony at Tabernacles to speak of Jesus as the water of life and the believer as the source of rivers of living water—this with reference to the Spirit (John 7:37–39). It was inevitable that early Christian writers should associate this great life-giving river with the water of baptism. They even found a convenient point of departure in the Old Greek version of v. 3 where the translator, unfamiliar perhaps with the Hebrew word for "ankle-deep water" *(me 'apsayim),* rendered it as "water of remission" *(hudor aphēseos).* And, finally, the seer of Patmos incorporated his own version in his apocalyptic vision of the transformed world which lay beyond the suffering and evil of the present age:

> Then he showed me the river of the water of life, bright as crystal, flowing from the throne of God and of the Lamb through the middle of the street of the city; also, on either side of the river, the tree of life with its twelve kinds of fruit, yielding its fruit each month; and the leaves of the tree were for the healing of the nations.
>
> Revelation 22:1–2, RSV

Ezekiel 47:13—48:29
The Ideal Boundaries and Divisions of the Promised Land

This next section appears to mark a completely new departure in speaking almost exclusively of the land, its boundaries and tribal territories. We shall see, however, that the entire construct has its focal point and epicenter in the sacred area reserved for the sanctuary (48:8; cf. 45:1–2). The intimate association between sanctuary and land has, in any case, been established by the river which brings life and fertility to the most barren regions of the land. In this respect the theological point of view is no different from that of the Priestly narrative in which the setting up of the sanctuary after the settlement is followed at once by the distribution of the land among the tribes (Josh. 18—19).

At the time of writing, the province of Judah was much reduced in size from what it had been before the fall of Jerusalem and subsequent deportations. It covered an area no more than about twenty-five by thirty-five miles and was also, of course, under foreign domination. This description of the boundaries (47:13–21), therefore, which corresponds roughly to the Greater Israel of the Davidic-Solomonic era (I Kings 8:65), could be read as a political statement, in some respects comparable to the kind of language used occasionally in the State of Israel today (e.g., "Judea and Samaria"). There were many in Judah who never acquiesced in foreign rule, whether Babylonian or Persian. Their aspirations found expression in prayers for deliverance (e.g., Neh. 9) and, occasionally, in messianic and nationalistic movements, the best known of which focused on the person of Zerubbabel, scion of the Davidic line (Hag. 2:20–23; Zech. 6:9–14). But the boundary description is meant to prepare for the equitable distribution of the land among the tribes (47:14) and therefore recalls a situation before the rise of the monarchy, the situation contemplated by the indefectible promise of land made to the ancestors (e.g., Gen. 15:18; Deut. 11:24). We are therefore invited to read it more as a utopian statement—certainly with political implications—than as a program for national emancipation.

The description itself should be read in conjunction with the very similar delineation of boundaries in Num. 34:1–12, generally attributed to a later strand of the Priestly source. Both move in a clockwise direction, though one begins from the north and the other from the south. The northern border is the most problematic, since none of the place-names either here or in Num. 34:7–9 can be identified with certainty. If we accept the explanatory notes in the text itself (47:16, 17), it runs from the Mediterranean to a point somewhere between Damascus and Hamath (modern Hama) about 115 miles farther north,

233

which would correspond to the greatest extent of Solomon's empire (I Kings 8:65). The alternative is to identify Hazar-enon, the hinge of the northern and eastern boundaries, with a location in the Golan (Banias—Caesarea Philippi?), which of course would leave out Damascus. We cannot exclude the possibility that the author himself was not too clear about the topographical details. The eastern boundary presents fewer difficulties, since it follows the course of the Jordan to the Dead Sea. Numbers 34:10–12 includes the eastern shore of the Sea of Galilee, but both exclude the region east of the Jordan where Reuben, Gad, and the half-tribe of Manasseh settled (Num. 34:13–15; Josh. 18:7). Tamar (= palm tree), the hinge with the southern boundary, is sometimes identified with En-gedi on the western shore of the Dead Sea, but a location farther south seems to be called for. Numbers 34:3–5 gives a much fuller description of the southern extremity of the land which passes through the oasis of Kadesh-barnea in the northern Sinai and ends where the "Brook of Egypt" (wadi el-Arish) empties into the Mediterranean. On the west the land is, of course, bounded by the Mediterranean as far north as the Entrance of Hamath (Lebo-hamath) mentioned earlier.

The logical sequence to the boundary description is the allotment of land to the tribes, but first an important point must be made: in the future settlement, resident aliens and their descendants are to enjoy the same property rights as the native-born (47:22–23). The social phenomenon of individuals relocating to another country and settling there under the protection of a civic or clan dignitary was not confined to ancient Israel—witness the presence of metics as a distinct class in Athens, for example. The legislation governing this class of resident aliens *(gerim)* in Israel is remarkable for its liberality and interesting for the light it throws on the ethos informing the laws in general. Together with other disadvantaged classes such as widows and orphans, they are accorded the full protection of law and judicial process (e.g., Exod. 22:21; 23:9; Deut. 1:16; 24:14), and it is possible to trace the process by which they became fully integrated into the religious and liturgical life of the community (e.g., Deut. 16:11, 14; 26:11; Lev. 17:8–9, 10–13). The Israelite is to love the alien, even to love him as himself, "for you were aliens in the land of Egypt" (Deut. 10:19; Lev. 19:34): an interesting illustration of the impact of shared historical memory on the formation of a community ethos and the laws that embody it.

234

The Babylonian conquest and ensuing exile brought about a change from nation-state to confessional community, which in its turn raised the possibility of accepting adherents from the Gentile world. While we have little to go on, there can be no doubt that this was happening in Babylon and elsewhere during the period in question, and it is this new situation which is being addressed here. Proselytes and their offspring are not to be regarded as second-class citizens, and as far as land rights are concerned, they are to be on the same footing as the native-born. We had occasion to note earlier—in discussing 44:6–9—how controversial this issue of incorporation into the community was then and remained throughout the period of the Second Commonwealth. The liberality of this land law is not inconsistent with the exclusion of foreigners from temple service (44:6–9), though the tone of that passage is quite different. Isaiah 56:1–8 also states a point of view at odds with the laws of exclusion from the community in Deut. 23:1–8, as also from the policies pursued by Ezra and Nehemiah. Early Christianity did not adopt an open admissions policy (reflected in the parable of the great banquet, Luke 14:15–24) in defiance of contemporary Jewish practice but rather in continuity with attitudes and practices affirmed from the very beginning of Second Temple Judaism.

The allotment of tribal territories (48:1–7, 23–29) follows the same order as the boundary description, beginning in the north and ending in the south, the description of both boundaries being taken over from the previous section. The sacred enclave around the temple, described separately (48:8–22; cf. 45:1–8), divides seven tribes to the north from the remaining five to the south. Since Levi is no longer counted among the secular tribes, and therefore has no land patrimony (cf. Num. 2:33; Josh. 13:14; 18:7), the number twelve is made up (as in Josh. 14:3–4) by counting the Joseph tribes, Ephraim and Manasseh, separately, following the etiological narrative in Gen. 48:8–20.

It will be obvious that this division of the land completely ignores geographical and historical realities. All of the twelve strips of land are of equal size, whereas in the Priestly account of land distribution in the Pentateuch the area is to be proportionate to the size of the tribe, and its location is to be decided by a holy lottery (Num. 26:52–56). A quite different logic dictates the arrangement here. Farthest from the sacred center

235

are the tribes that, according to the tradition, derive from the concubines Bilhah and Zilpah—namely, Dan, Naphtali, Asher, and Gad (see Gen. 30:5–13). Closest are Judah and Benjamin, which together designate the inhabitants of the province of Judah in the postexilic period (Ezra 1:5; 4:1; etc.). In defiance of historical geography, however, Benjamin is to the south and Judah to the north of the sacred area, perhaps because of the original location of Jerusalem in the tribal territory of Benjamin. As the firstborn, Reuben is next to Judah, and the three Leah tribes of Simeon, Issachar, and Zebulun are kept together. In keeping with the territorial limits of the land established in the previous section, the Transjordanian settlements of Reuben, Gad, and the half-tribe of Manasseh are left out of account.

The very obviously schematic and idealistic distribution of land presented here communicates, by the very fact of ignoring the realities of political geography, the need to revive the ideal of a united people in the form of the egalitarian tribal structure of the archaic period. We find this ideal twelve-tribal Israel continually being pitted against contemporary realities throughout the period of the Second Commonwealth. The author of Chronicles begins his work by tracing this twelve-tribal entity back to creation, meaning that this and this alone is the Israel willed by God from the beginning (I Chron. 1—9). Even in Ezra-Nehemiah, which seems to concentrate exclusively on the province of Judah, we are continually reminded of the same theme: the twelve leaders of the first return (Ezra 2:2 = Neh. 7:7), the twelve priests who traveled in Ezra's own caravan (Ezra 8:24), and the offering of twelve sacrificial animals on behalf of all-Israel (Ezra 6:17; 8:35). At a much later date, the Qumran community, which thought of itself as the true Israel, embodied this conviction in its structures and organization. While convinced that God had initiated a decisively new venture in the person and mission of Jesus, early Christianity saw itself as the contemporary embodiment of the old Israel and the heir of the promises addressed to it. Not surprisingly, therefore, the first action recorded of the new community is the recomposition of the Twelve by electing a successor to Judas (Acts 1:15–26).

236   The description of the central reserve not assigned to individual tribes (the analogy limps, but one might think of the

District of Columbia) has already been anticipated in 45:1–8, and little more need be said about it. Its total area is 25,000 square cubits of which two bands, each 25,000 by 10,000 cubits, are assigned to the priests and the Levites respectively. These together form the sacred area, the part set aside for Yahweh (*terumah* in Hebrew), with the sanctuary in the middle of the priests' section. The topographical arrangement provides another occasion for Zadokite polemic directed against the Levites (see 40:46; 43:19; 44:10–15), and it is emphasized that this sacred area may not be sold or alienated. The nonsacred area reserved for the city and its hinterland forms a band 25,000 by 5,000 cubits south of the sanctuary, with the city itself and its "green belt" taking up 5,000 cubits in the middle. As the focal point for the secular activity of the people, the city is to be populated by representatives of all the tribes. During his tenure as governor of the province, Nehemiah came close to implementing this requirement by obliging one in ten of the provincial population to settle in the then depopulated city, though these settlers included priests and other temple personnel (Neh. 11). The territory of the civic ruler is located east and west of the sacred and city areas (vs. 21–22; cf. 45:7–8).

It would be tempting to dismiss this entire construct as a product of fantasy and wishful thinking, or at least to set it alongside other idealistic projections—Plato's Republic, More's Utopia, or even Swift's Houyhnhnm Country. It might, on the other hand, be argued that the capacity to project a reality different from the reality in which we are immersed and which we take for granted is the only safeguard against acquiescence in and assimilation to an imperfect and often corrupt status quo. The construct presented in this section is indeed utopian, but it incorporates values that, as Thomas More pointed out of his own creation, can be realized if we desire them enough. It is of the essence of Judaism and, following it, Christianity, to aspire toward and strive for the perfect commonwealth, God's kingdom of love and justice, and therefore to reject the kind of realism that simply accepts the status quo as given. The situation of those who returned from exile to rebuild the commonwealth on their own land was far from ideal, and it is doubtful whether they would even have attempted the task of rebuilding without the motivation provided by this and similar projections of a possible future.

237

Ezekiel 48:30–35
The New Jerusalem

The vision ends with a return to the "structure like a city" seen by the prophet at the beginning (40:2, RSV). The principal concern is with the city gates named for the twelve tribes, three on each of the four sides. The dimensions of the city are taken from the blueprint already described: 4,500 cubits on each side giving a total circumference of 18,000. From now on, it will bear the symbolic name *Yahweh shammah,* Yahweh is there.

This extremely terse description of the Jerusalem of the future is different in some important respects from the preceding account. In the latter, Jerusalem is not part of the sacred enclave, and therefore Yahweh is *not* there. Levi no longer stands for a class of clerical assistants but is one of the twelve tribes, and, to preserve the number twelve, Ephraim and Manasseh are telescoped into the one tribe of Joseph. The arrangement of the gates does not correspond to what we know of the topography of the city at any time in its history. The fairly detailed account of the rebuilding of the city wall by Nehemiah (in Neh. 3) mentions several gates, but none is named for a tribe. In the preexilic period, there was a Benjamin gate and an Ephraim gate (Jer. 37:13; II Kings 14:13), but they were on the north side, not the east side, of the city. Perhaps the naming of the gates in this way was intended to reinforce the collective responsibility of the entire community for the defense and well-being of the city (cf. 48:18–19).

While the order in which the tribes are located is unattested elsewhere, it seems to have its own logic. Judah and Levi are on the north side and therefore closest to the sacred area together with Reuben, the firstborn. All three are Leah tribes. Opposite them, on the south side, are Simeon, Issachar, and Zebulun, the other three Leah tribes. Three concubine tribes—Gad, Asher, and Naphtali—are grouped together on the west, while the Rachel tribes, Joseph and Benjamin, with the son of Rachel's concubine Bilhah, are opposite them on the east. The entire arrangement is reminiscent of the sanctuary in the wilderness

238

surrounded by the tribal camps, three on each of the four sides (Num. 2). The point is clear: a diverse but united people organized around a sacred point of reference, drawing its identity and substance from the divine presence in its midst.

Whatever the intention of the author of this final paragraph, we may agree that it was a happy thought to bring together city and temple, the sacred and the secular, in a new symbolic statement. That this was no innovation is clear from the exalted language in which prophet and psalmist (e.g., Isa. 60; Ps. 46) spoke of Zion as the place of the divine presence. After the second destruction of the temple in A.D. 70, Jerusalem alone remained to carry the symbolism of the sacred center. The author of Revelation, who, like Ezekiel, saw a vision on a very high mountain but saw no temple in the city, ends his narrative with what might be called a Christian targum on this final passage. Of the city he says:

> It had a great, high wall, with twelve gates, and at the gates twelve angels, and on the gates the names of the twelve tribes of the sons of Israel were inscribed; on the east three gates, on the north three gates, on the south three gates, and on the west three gates. And the wall of the city had twelve foundations, and on them the twelve names of the twelve apostles of the Lamb.
>
> Revelation 21:12–14, RSV

READING LIST

The following list is highly selective and, for the most part, confined to more recent works written in or translated into English.

1. Commentaries

CARLEY, KEITH W. *The Book of the Prophet Ezekiel.* CAMBRIDGE BIBLE COMMENTARY ON THE NEW ENGLISH BIBLE. Cambridge: Cambridge University Press, 1974).

CODY, AELRED. *Ezekiel: With Excursus on Old Testament Priesthood.* OLD TESTAMENT MESSAGE 11. Wilmington: Michael Glazier, 1984.

COOKE, G. A. *A Critical and Exegetical Commentary on the Book of Ezekiel.* INTERNATIONAL CRITICAL COMMENTARY. Edinburgh: T. & T. Clark, 1936.

EICHRODT, WALTHER. *Ezekiel, A Commentary.* OLD TESTAMENT LIBRARY. Philadelphia: Westminster Press, 1970.

GREENBERG, MOSHE. *Ezekiel 1–20.* ANCHOR BIBLE 22. Garden City, N.Y.: Doubleday & Co., 1983.

MAY, HERBERT G. "The Book of Ezekiel." In *The Interpreter's Bible,* vol. 6. Nashville: Abingdon Press, 1956, 41–338.

TAYLOR, JOHN B. *Ezekiel: An Introduction and Commentary.* TYNDALE OLD TESTAMENT COMMENTARIES. Downers Grove, Ill.: Inter-Varsity Press, 1969.

WEVERS, JOHN W. *Ezekiel.* NEW CENTURY BIBLE. Greenwood, N.C.: Attic Press, 1976.

WILSON, ROBERT R. "Ezekiel." In *Harper's Bible Commentary,* ed. by James L. Mays. San Francisco: Harper & Row, 1988, 652–694.

ZIMMERLI, WALTHER. *Ezekiel.* 2 vols. HERMENEIA. Philadelphia: Fortress Press, 1979, 1983.

2. Other Studies   1

ACKROYD, PETER R. *Exile and Restoration.* OLD TESTAMENT LIBRARY. Philadelphia: Westminster Press, 1968, 103–117.

BERRY, GEORGE R. "The Composition of the Book of Ezekiel." *Journal of Biblical Literature* 58:163–175 (1939).

———. "The Glory of YHWH and the Temple." *Journal of Biblical Literature* 56:115–117 (1937).

BLENKINSOPP, JOSEPH. *A History of Prophecy in Israel.* Philadelphia: Westminster Press, 1983.

———. "Introduction to the Prophetic Books." In *Harper's Bible Commentary,* ed. by James L. Mays. San Francisco: Harper & Row, 1988, 530–541.

BRIGHT, JOHN. *A History of Israel,* 3rd ed. Philadelphia: Westminster Press, 1981.

BUBER, MARTIN. *The Prophetic Faith.* New York: Macmillan Co., 1949.

CARLEY, KEITH W. *Ezekiel Among the Prophets.* London: SCM Press, 1975.

CLEMENTS, RONALD E. "The Ezekiel Tradition: Prophecy in a Time of Crisis." In *Israel's Prophetic Heritage: Essays in Honour of Peter Ackroyd,* ed. by R. Coggins, A. Phillips, and M. Knibb. Cambridge: Cambridge University Press, 1982, 119–136.

CODY, AELRED. *A History of the Old Testament Priesthood.* ANALECTA BIBLICA 35. Rome: Pontifical Biblical Institute, 1967.

EISSFELDT, OTTO. *The Old Testament: An Introduction.* New York: Harper & Row, 1966.

FOHRER, GEORG. *Die Hauptprobleme des Buches Ezechiel.* BEIHEFTE ZUR ZEITSCHRIFT FÜR DIE ALTTESTAMENTLICHE WISSENSCHAFT 72. Berlin: Töpelmann, 1952.

FREEDMAN, DAVID NOEL. "The Book of Ezekiel." *Interpretation* 8:446–471 (1954).

GESE, HARTMUT. *Das Verfassungsentwurf des Ezekiel.* Tübingen: J. C. B. Mohr, 1957.

HARFORD, JOHN B. *Studies in the Book of Ezekiel.* Cambridge: Cambridge University Press, 1935.

HÖLSCHER, GUSTAV. *Hesekiel, der Dichter und das Buch.* BEIHEFTE ZUR ZEITSCHRIFT FÜR DIE ALTTESTAMENTLICHE WISSENSCHAFT 39. Giessen: Töpelmann, 1924.

HOWIE, CARL GORDON. *The Date and Composition of Ezekiel.* JOURNAL OF BIBLICAL LITERATURE MONOGRAPH SERIES 4. Philadelphia: Society of Biblical Literature, 1950.

———. "Ezekiel." In *The Interpreter's Dictionary of the Bible,* vol. 2. Nashville: Abingdon Press, 1962, 203–213.

IRWIN, WILLIAM A. *The Problem of Ezekiel.* Chicago: University of Chicago Press, 1943.

KRAUS, HANS-JOACHIM. *Worship in Israel: A Cultic History of the Old Testament.* Richmond: John Knox Press, 1966.

LEVENSON, JON D. *Theology of the Program of Restoration of Ezekiel 40–48.* Missoula, Mont.: Scholars Press, 1976.

LUST, J., ed. *Ezekiel and His Book: Textual and Literary Criticism and Their Interrelation.* Louvain: University Press and Uitgeverij Peeters, 1986.

MAY, HERBERT G. "The Departure of the Glory of Yahweh." *Journal of Biblical Literature* 56:309–321 (1937).

NOTH, MARTIN. "The Jerusalem Catastrophe of 587 B.C. and Its Significance for Israel." In *The Laws in the Pentateuch and Other Essays.* Philadelphia: Fortress Press, 1967, 260–280.

RAD, GERHARD VON. *Old Testament Theology,* vol. 2. New York: Harper & Row, 1965 = *The Message of the Prophets.* New York: Harper & Row, 1967.

———. "The City on the Hill." In *The Problem of the Hexateuch and Other Essays.* New York: McGraw-Hill Book Co., 1966, 231–242.

ROWLEY, HAROLD H. "The Book of Ezekiel in Modern Study." *Bulletin of the John Rylands Library* 36:146–173 (1953) = *Men of God: Studies in Old Testament History and Prophecy.* London: Thomas Nelson & Sons, 1963, 169–210.

241

SAWYER, JOHN F.A. *Prophecy and the Prophets of the Old Testament.* OXFORD BIBLE SERIES. Oxford: Oxford University Press, 1987.

TORREY, CHARLES CUTLER. *Pseudo-Ezekiel and the Original Prophecy.* New Haven: Yale University Press, 1930; reprint, New York: KTAV Publishing House, 1970.

de VAUX, ROLAND. *Ancient Israel: Its Life and Institutions.* 2 vols. New York: McGraw-Hill Book Co., 1965.

ZIMMERLI, WALTHER. "The Message of the Prophet Ezekiel." *Interpretation* 23:134–136 (1969).

———. "The Word of God in the Book of Ezekiel." *Journal for Theology and the Church* 4:1–13 (1967).